COOKING Fish

COOKING Fish

CHANCELLOR PRESS

CONTENTS

INTRODUCTION 5

SOUPS 7

STARTERS 17

LIGHT LUNCHES 37

SALADS 53

FAMILY MEALS 65

ENTERTAINING 105

STOCKS, SAUCES, DRESSINGS AND BUTTERS 145

INDEX 156

CONTRIBUTORS

Compiled and edited by: Anne Johnson

Main authors: Anne Johnson, Clare Gordon-Smith, Caroline Ellwood

Contributing authors: Rhona Newman, Wendy Godfrey, Jeni Wright, Mary Morris, Clare Ferguson, Carole Handslip, Julia Roles, Norma MacMillan, Gwyneth Loveday, Michelle Berriedale Johnson, Rosamond Man, Sue Probert, Rita Greer, Naomi Good

Special photography: Clive Streeter

NOTES

Standard spoon measurements are used in all recipes
1 tablespoon = one 15 ml spoon
1 teaspoon = one 5 ml spoon
All spoon measures are level.

Size 3 eggs should be used unless otherwise stated.

Ovens should be preheated to the specified temperature.

Use freshly ground black pepper where pepper is specified.

For all the recipes, quantities are given in both metric and imperial measures. Follow either set but not a mixture of both, because they are not interchangeable.

Fresh herbs are used unless otherwise stated. If unobtainable substitute a bouquet garni of the equivalent dried herbs or use dried herbs instead but halve the quantities stated.

First published in Great Britain in 1992

This 1998 edition published by Chancellor Press
an imprint of Reed Consumer Books Limited
Michelin House 81 Fulham Road London SW3 6RB
ISBN 0 7537 0029 8

Produced by Toppan Printing Co., (H.K.) Ltd.

Printed and bound in China

INTRODUCTION

Why eat fish? The answer is manifold.

It is delicious and also excellent value for money, particularly when you compare it with other protein-rich foods, and there is very little wastage.

It is easy to prepare. If you're pushed for time and you want to make something simple, quick and tasty in a matter of minutes, you just can't beat fish. Take a small white fish fillet, such as cod or plaice, wash it, put a small knob of butter on it, pop it under the grill – and hey presto: a ready-portioned meal with the minimum of fuss or preparation.

Fish comes in many different varieties, it's available all year round and it lends itself to many ways of cooking. These include poaching, steaming, baking, grilling and barbecuing, shallow- and deep-frying, and braising. It can be served with an infinite variety of delicious sauces and savoury butters to complement both flavour and texture.

Perhaps the most important reason is that it's good for you. It is very nutritious and a good source of protein, vitamins and minerals, particularly iodine. Canned fish with edible bones, such as sardines and mackerel are also a source of calcium. Oily fish such as herring, mackerel and sardine, so called because the oil is distributed throughout the flesh rather than being concentrated in the liver as it is in white fish, is particularly rich in vitamins A and D. Vitamin A, known reverently as the beauty vitamin, keeps the skin moist and healthy, as well as encouraging good eye-sight. Vitamin D helps build strong bones.

Fish is also extremely low in carbohydrates and saturated fat. Even the fat in the oiliest fish, such as herring and mackerel, is mainly polyunsaturated. Research now suggests, that a couple of meals containing white fish each week may help to lower the level of cholesterol in the blood and thus aid in warding off heart disease.

An added bonus for weight watchers is that it's also very low in calories, particularly when you compare it with other protein foods. Some fish are lower in calories than others: 125 g (4 oz) of sole, for example, contains only 90 calories, while herring has 190 calories. But when you compare these levels with the same amount of lamb, at 350 calories, there's just no contest!

And then there's shellfish, which falls into two groups: jointed shells such as crab, lobster, shrimps and prawns and hinged shells such as mussels, scallops, oysters and clams. Many of these can also be bought in jars, cans or frozen, and these are all very useful, especially if they are to be mixed with other ingredients. Shellfish is a gastronomic treat of the most delicate kind. The British shopper has an unrivalled opportunity to buy and enjoy it at its best.

SOUPS

A soup can mean a quick appetiser to a light lunchtime meal; a hearty starter to a wholesome family supper; a rich velvety concoction to stimulate the appetites and impress the guests at a formal dinner party; or a nourishing meal in itself. It can take minutes or hours to prepare; it can be hot or cold; its flavour can be fiercely spicy or subtly delicate; its ingredients can be basic and inexpensive or hugely extravagant; and it can be comfortingly traditional or enticingly unusual – the choice is yours.

There are recipes in this section from all over the world: Salmon Soup from Scandinavia; Sardine Soup from Portugal; Fish Soup from Spain; or Ratatouille Soup from the Mediterranean. And then, of course, there are the old favourites from these shores, such as Whiting and Apple Soup, and Cream of Crab Soup. Whether it's compliments you're after or just a regular favourite to add to your repertoire, something here is sure to fit the bill.

The garnish is a very important element of soups and you'll score points on both flavour and appearance by adding a sprinkling of freshly chopped herbs, a swirl of natural or Greek yogurt, a little grated cheese, a few crispy croûtons or a slice of lemon. An electric blender or food processor is invaluable for making soups, especially if you want a smooth velvety texture.

If time is crucial, you can often gain time by preparing the soup well ahead. Many of these soups can be prepared up to 48 hours in advance, reheated to perfection and then given a fresh garnish.

CREAM OF CRAB SOUP

50 g (2 oz) butter
250 g (8 oz) onions, sliced
750 g ($1\frac{1}{2}$ lb) tomatoes, chopped
1 bouquet garni
150 ml ($\frac{1}{4}$ pint) dry white wine
750 ml ($1\frac{1}{4}$ pints) Fish stock (see page 146)
300 g (10 oz) cooked fresh, or canned, crabmeat
1 clove garlic, crushed
strip of lemon rind
salt and pepper
150 ml ($\frac{1}{4}$ pint) double cream
chopped parsley to garnish

Melt the butter in a pan, add the onions and fry for 5 minutes, without browning. Add the tomatoes, bouquet garni, wine, fish stock, half the crabmeat, the garlic and lemon rind. Season with salt and pepper to taste. Bring to the boil, cover and simmer for 30 minutes. Remove the bouquet garni and lemon rind.

Sieve or work in an electric blender until smooth. Return to the pan and stir in the remaining crabmeat. Heat gently and stir in the cream.

Serve immediately, garnished with parsley.

Serves 4 to 6

Cream of Crab Soup

SMOKED HADDOCK SOUP

350 g (12 oz) smoked haddock
450 ml ($\frac{3}{4}$ pint) water
50 g (2 oz) butter
1 onion, chopped
50 g (2 oz) mushrooms, chopped
1 teaspoon curry powder
50 g (2 oz) plain flour
600 ml (1 pint) milk
pepper
2 tablespoons dry sherry

Poach the haddock in the water for 10 minutes; set aside. Reserve 300 ml ($\frac{1}{2}$ pint) of the cooking liquor.

Melt the butter in a large pan, add the onion, mushrooms and curry powder and fry for 5 minutes. Stir in the flour and gradually add the milk and reserved liquor.

Remove the skin from the cooked haddock and flake the fish. Add to the soup and heat through gently. Season with pepper to taste.

Pour into a serving bowl and stir in the sherry to serve.

Serves 6

FISH SOUP WITH ROUILLE

2 tablespoons olive oil
1 large onion, chopped
2 cloves garlic, chopped
250 g (8 oz) tomatoes, skinned and roughly chopped
1 litre ($1\frac{3}{4}$ pints) water
2 whiting fillets, skinned and chopped
250 g (8 oz) monkfish, cubed
bouquet garni
salt and pepper
French bread slices to serve

ROUILLE:
1 thick slice French bread, crust removed
2 cloves garlic
2 red peppers, cored and seeded
2 tablespoons olive oil

Heat the oil in a large pan, add the onion and garlic and fry until browned.

Add the tomatoes to the pan with the water. Add the whiting, monkfish, bouquet garni, and salt and pepper to taste. Bring to the boil and simmer for 20 minutes.

Meanwhile, make the rouille. Soak the bread in water to cover until soft.

Process the garlic and peppers in a food processor until smooth. Squeeze the bread, add to the processor bowl with the oil and process, adding enough liquor from the soup to make a thick sauce. Pour into a serving bowl.

Toast the French bread and put a slice in the bottom of individual soup bowls. Ladle the soup over the toast and top with a spoonful of rouille.

Serves 6 to 8

PORTUGUESE SARDINE SOUP

2 tablespoons olive oil
2 onions, finely chopped
1 clove garlic, finely chopped
1 × 396 g (14 oz) can tomatoes
juice of 1 lemon
2 tablespoons chopped parsley
pinch of dried basil
50 g (2 oz) vermicelli
600 ml (1 pint) Fish stock (see page 146)
black pepper
4 fresh sardines, cleaned and roughly chopped
4 slices French bread

Heat the olive oil over a low heat, and fry the onions and garlic gently until soft. Add the tomatoes, lemon juice, parsley, basil, vermicelli, fish stock and pepper. Bring to the boil and simmer for 15 minutes.

Add the sardines and continue to simmer gently for 8 to 10 minutes further, or until the fish is cooked through.

Meanwhile, toast the French bread until well browned. Stir the soup well to break up the pieces of sardine.

Place a slice of toast in each soup bowl and pour the soup over the top. Serve immediately.

Serves 4

SPANISH FISH SOUP

3 tablespoons olive oil
1 large onion, finely chopped
2 cloves garlic, finely chopped
1 kg (2 lb) assorted fish, including bass, halibut and hake, cleaned and cut into pieces
1 litre ($1\frac{3}{4}$ pints) water
salt and pepper
900 ml ($1\frac{1}{2}$ pints) mussels, scrubbed and beards removed
juice of 1 lemon
6 tablespoons sherry
5 tablespoons croûtons to garnish

Heat the oil in a heavy flameproof casserole and gently fry the onion and garlic over a low heat for 8 to 10 minutes until soft. Add the pieces of fish and cover with water. Season well with salt and pepper, bring to the boil, cover and simmer over a low heat for 15 to 20 minutes. Strain the soup, discarding any bones and skin.

Return the soup to the casserole and add the mussels, lemon juice and sherry. Return to the boil and simmer, covered, for another 5 minutes. Discard any mussels that remain closed. Serve immediately with a few croûtons sprinkled into each bowl.

Serves 4 to 6

Portuguese Sardine Soup; Spanish Fish Soup

BOURRIDE

1.5–1.75 kg (3–4 lb) mixed firm white fish, such as John Dory, monkfish, turbot, brill and cod
2 large onions, finely sliced
2 leeks, finely sliced
4–5 cloves garlic, crushed
2 tomatoes, roughly chopped
2 large strips of orange rind
bouquet garni
salt and pepper
1.2 litres (2 pints) Fish stock (see page 146)
150 ml ($\frac{1}{4}$ pint) Aïoli (see page 149)
2 tablespoons chopped parsley to garnish

Clean the fish and cut into generous slices. Put the onions, leeks, garlic and tomatoes in a large saucepan. Place the fish on top and add the orange rind, bouquet garni, salt and pepper, and fish stock or water to cover the fish.

Bring to the boil and simmer gently for about 10 minutes, being careful not to overcook the fish. As soon as it is cooked, lift it out and place on a heated serving dish to keep warm.

Reduce the cooking stock by half and check the seasoning. Then slowly strain the juices into the aioli in a large bowl, beating all the time. Return to a clean pan and stir over low heat until the mixture begins to thicken, but do not allow to boil.

Pour the soup over the fish, sprinkle with parsley and serve with boiled new potatoes and thick slices of French bread fried in olive oil.

Serves 6

TUNA AND SWEETCORN BISQUE

50 g (2 oz) butter
50 g (2 oz) plain flour
1 tablespoon curry powder
1 litre ($1\frac{3}{4}$ pints) milk
1 tablespoon dry sherry
1 chicken stock cube
2 × 350 g (12 oz) cans sweetcorn
1 × 198 g (7 oz) can tuna fish
black pepper

Melt the butter gently in a pan, then stir in the flour and curry powder. Cook gently over a low heat for a few minutes, stirring well. Add the milk and sherry and crumble in the chicken stock cube. Bring to the boil and simmer gently, stirring from time to time, until the liquid has thickened.

Meanwhile, drain the sweetcorn and tuna. Add the sweetcorn and return to the boil, stirring well. Add the tuna, stir well and heat through.

Season with black pepper to taste and serve immediately.

Serves 6 to 8

RUSSIAN SALMON BUBBLY SOUP

1 litre ($1\frac{3}{4}$ pints) Fish stock (see page 146)
2 egg whites
1 tablespoon chopped tarragon
salt and pepper
4 small salmon steaks
2 tablespoons chopped spring onion tops
$\frac{1}{2}$ bottle champagne or sparkling white wine
lemon slices to garnish

First clarify the stock. Warm gently over a low heat until just warm. Place the egg whites and tarragon in another pan, and whisk to mix. Pour on the warm stock and bring to the boil, whisking continuously. Simmer gently over a low heat for 30 minutes. Season with salt and pepper and strain through a fine strainer. The stock should now be clear.

Return the stock to the boil and add the salmon steaks. Poach over a low heat for 15 minutes.

Gently lift out the fish and arrange in a warmed soup tureen. Sprinkle with the spring onion and keep warm.

Meanwhile, heat the champagne in a separate pan until almost boiling, then add to the soup. Pour over the salmon steaks and garnish with slices of lemon. Serve immediately.

Serves 4

WHITING AND APPLE SOUP

15 g ($\frac{1}{2}$ oz) butter
2 small onions, sliced
1 large cooking apple, peeled, cored and chopped
500 g (1 lb) whiting, filleted, skinned and cut into chunks
300 ml ($\frac{1}{2}$ pint) dry cider
450 ml ($\frac{3}{4}$ pint) water
1 bay leaf
pinch of dried dill
white pepper
1 egg yolk
4 tablespoons double cream
dill sprigs to garnish

Melt the butter and fry the sliced onions gently over low heat. Add the apple and fish, then pour on the cider and water and add the herbs and pepper to taste. Bring to the boil and simmer for about 30 minutes.

Blend in an electric blender or food processor until smooth, or pass through a sieve. Reheat gently, then remove from the heat. Combine the egg yolk and cream and add this *liaison* to the soup. Stir gently, garnish with small sprigs of dill and serve immediately.

Serves 4

Tuna and Sweetcorn Bisque; Whiting and Apple Soup

MEDITERRANEAN RATATOUILLE SOUP WITH SHRIMPS

4 tablespoons olive oil
2 medium onions, sliced
2 cloves garlic, finely chopped
1 medium aubergine, peeled and finely diced
2 courgettes, finely diced
1 × 750 g (1½ lb) can tomatoes
250 ml (8 fl oz) dry white wine
1 large pinch of dried oregano
1 × 198 g (7 oz) can shrimps
2 tablespoons chopped parsley
black pepper
125 g (4 oz) Parmesan cheese, grated, to garnish

Heat half the oil in a large pan over a low heat, then add the onions and garlic and fry gently, covered, for 5 to 6 minutes. Add the aubergine and the remaining oil and continue to fry, uncovered and stirring occasionally, for about 5 minutes or until the aubergine begins to soften. Then add the courgettes and cook for another 3 minutes. Add the tomatoes, wine and oregano, and simmer over a moderate heat for 10 to 15 minutes or until all the vegetables are tender. Blend in an electric blender or food processor until smooth.

Return to a clean pan and reheat. Add the shrimps and parsley and season well with black pepper. Serve the soup in individual bowls sprinkled with a little grated Parmesan.

Serves 6

GARNISHES

Soups can be transformed into something special with an attractive garnish. A simple but effective garnish is a swirl of cream or natural yogurt sprinkled with freshly chopped herbs, like parsley or chives. Croûtons provide a crunchy contrast in texture to most soups. To make them, cut white bread into 1 cm (½ inch) cubes, or use small pastry cutters to make interesting shapes, then fry in equal quantities of hot oil and butter until crisp and golden; drain on kitchen paper. Garlic croûtons can be made by adding a crushed clove of garlic to the oil and butter before frying. Grated cheese – Parmesan, Gruyère or Cheddar – can be sprinkled over individual servings.

MUSSEL SOUP

Always use very fresh mussels and not frozen or canned ones for this tasty soup.

1 kg (2 lb) mussels, scrubbed, with beards removed
300 ml (½ pint) dry white wine
6 shallots or small onions, chopped
4 cloves garlic, finely sliced
1 tablespoon olive oil
3 leeks (white part only), thinly sliced
about 600 ml (1 pint) water
2 tablespoons Patna rice
4 tomatoes, skinned, seeded and chopped
1 bouquet garni
salt and pepper
3 tablespoons chopped parsley to serve

Put the mussels (discarding any that are open), into a wide-based pan with the wine, shallots or onions and half the garlic. Cover and cook until the shells open, discarding any that do not open. Remove the mussels with a slotted spoon and shell them. Strain the liquid through a muslin-lined sieve set over a measuring jug.

Heat the olive oil in a pan, add the leeks and remaining garlic, and fry gently for 5 minutes without browning. Make up the strained mussel liquid to 1 litre (1¾ pints) with water. Add to the leeks in the pan and bring to the boil, then add the rice and boil rapidly for 9 to 11 minutes, until the rice is tender.

Leave the soup to cool slightly, then work half to a purée in an electric blender or food processor. Stir the purée into the soup remaining in the pan, then add the tomatoes, bouquet garni and plenty of salt and pepper. Bring to the boil and simmer for 5 to 7 minutes, then discard the bouquet garni and stir in the shelled mussels. Simmer for a further 5 minutes, then stir in the parsley. Serve immediately, with French bread.

Serves 6 to 8

LEFT: *Mediterranean Ratatouille Soup with Shrimps*
RIGHT: *Mussel Soup*

OYSTER SOUP WITH PEANUT BUTTER

2 × 105 g (3·7 oz) cans oysters
25 g (1 oz) butter
6 spring onions, chopped
150 g (5 oz) smooth peanut butter
2 tablespoons plain flour
750 ml (1¼ pints) chicken stock
200 ml (⅓ pint) single cream
pinch of chilli powder
1 tablespoon chopped thyme
4 tablespoons sherry

Drain the oysters, reserving the liquid.

Melt the butter in a large pan and fry the spring onions over a moderate heat for 2 to 3 minutes. Stir in the peanut butter and flour, mixing well. Remove from the heat and add the stock, stirring continuously until smooth.

Return to the heat and simmer gently over a low heat until the soup thickens. Then add the cream and reserved oyster liquid. Season with chilli powder and add the thyme, oysters and sherry.

Heat through gently, and then serve.

Serves 6

Scandinavian Salmon Soup

SCANDINAVIAN SALMON SOUP

50 g (2 oz) long-grain rice
the head of a large salmon, washed
1.2 litres (2 pints) Fish stock (see page 146)
1 onion, sliced
2 carrots, sliced
1 celery stick, sliced
½ teaspoon dill seeds
salt and pepper
2 tablespoons double cream (optional)
TO GARNISH:
few peeled shrimps
chopped fresh dill or parsley

Put the rice in a strainer, rinse well, then leave to drain.

Place the salmon head in a large pan and pour in the fish stock. Bring to the boil, reduce the heat, then simmer gently for 20 minutes. Transfer the head to a dish.

Strain the liquid into a clean pan, then add the rice, onion, carrots, celery, dill seeds, and salt and pepper to taste. Bring to the boil, reduce the heat, and simmer for about 20 minutes, or until the rice and vegetables are tender.

Meanwhile, pick the flesh from the fish head and add to the soup with the cream, if using. Reheat gently and check the seasoning. Pour into a heated tureen or individual soup dishes and garnish with shrimps and dill.

Serve with crusty rye bread.
Serves 4

CREAM OF WHITING

2 medium whiting, filleted and skinned
1 small glass white wine
40 g (1½ oz) butter
20 g (¾ oz) plain flour
600 ml (1 pint) Fish stock, strained (see page 146)
salt and pepper
grated nutmeg
2 tablespoons chopped parsley
150 ml (¼ pint) double cream, lightly whipped
croûtons to garnish

Using a very shallow pan, poach the fillets gently in white wine for about 10 minutes, allowing the wine to reduce. Then pound the cooked fish with half the butter until smooth.

Melt the remaining butter in a pan, then remove from the heat. Stir in the flour and gradually add the fish stock, stirring continuously. Return to the heat and bring to the boil, stirring all the time, then stir in the puréed fish. Season with salt, pepper and a pinch of nutmeg to taste.

Just before serving, stir in the chopped parsley and fold in the cream. Serve with a few croûtons.
Serves 4

PRAWN AND NOODLE SOUP

600 ml (1 pint) water
125 g (4 oz) pork fillet or chicken breast
salt and pepper
175 g (6 oz) thin rice noodles
1½ tablespoons oil
5 shallots, sliced
4 spring onions, cut into small pieces
2 cloves garlic, crushed
1 teaspoon ground ginger
1 teaspoon ground coriander
½ teaspoon ground turmeric
175 g (6 oz) peeled prawns
300 ml (½ pint) thick coconut milk
2 blocks bean curd (tofu), cut into strips
75 g (3 oz) bean sprouts

Bring the water to the boil in a large pan. Add the pork or chicken, and salt and pepper to taste. Cover and simmer for 40 minutes.

Strain and reserve the liquid. Cut the meat into small cubes.

Put the rice noodles into a pan and cover with boiling water. Cover and leave to stand for 5 minutes. Drain thoroughly.

Heat the oil in a wok or deep frying pan, add the shallots and fry for 1 minute, then add the spring onions, garlic and spices. Fry for 30 seconds, stirring constantly, then add the reserved cooking liquid and simmer for 25 minutes.

Add the rice noodles, prawns and coconut milk and bring very slowly to the boil, stirring gently to prevent the coconut milk from curdling. Add the bean curd and bean sprouts and simmer for 5 to 8 minutes, stirring occasionally. Pour into a warmed soup tureen and serve hot.
Serves 4

CHILLED HADDOCK AND AVOCADO SOUP

500 g (1 lb) smoked haddock
300 ml ($\frac{1}{2}$ pint) milk
300 ml ($\frac{1}{2}$ pint) water
2–3 lemons, peeled and sliced
bouquet garni
2 ripe avocados
300 ml ($\frac{1}{2}$ pint) Fish stock (see page 146)
1 tablespoon natural yogurt
salt and pepper
pinch of nutmeg
1 tablespoon chopped chives to garnish

Cover the fish with milk and water. Flavour with lemon slices and the bouquet garni, and poach for about 5 to 6 minutes.

Lift the fish out of the poaching liquid and allow to cool. Strain the liquid and reserve.

Remove the skin from the fish and roughly flake the flesh. Peel the avocados, discard the stones and roughly chop the flesh. Place the flaked fish and chopped avocado in an electric blender or food processor, add the strained poaching liquid and blend until smooth. Transfer to a large tureen.

Stir in enough fish stock to dilute the soup to the desired consistency of a creamy soup. Stir in the yogurt and season with salt, pepper and nutmeg. Chill well, garnish with chopped chives and serve immediately.

Serves 4

FISH CHOWDER

This soup makes a substantial meal in itself, served with fresh French bread and butter.

2 tablespoons olive oil
1 medium onion, finely chopped
1 × 396 g (14 oz) can tomatoes, sieved
1 carrot, chopped
1 celery stick, chopped
500 g (1 lb) white fish (cod, haddock, whiting), filleted and skinned
250 g (8 oz) potatoes, peeled and diced
600 ml (1 pint) water
black pepper
300 ml ($\frac{1}{2}$ pint) milk
chopped parsley to finish

Heat the olive oil in a large fish kettle or saucepan. Add the vegetables (except the potatoes), and cook gently, stirring occasionally, for 5 minutes, or until the oil is absorbed into the vegetables. Meanwhile, cut the fish into bite-sized pieces. Add these, the potatoes and water to the pan and bring slowly to the boil, skimming off any scum with a slotted spoon. Lower the heat, add pepper to taste, cover the kettle or pan and simmer gently for 20 to 30 minutes or until the fish and vegetables are quite tender. Be careful not to overcook or they will disintegrate. Add the milk and reheat gently. Adjust the seasoning, stir in plenty of chopped parsley and serve.

Serves 4 to 6

Cream of Whiting; Prawn and Noodle Soup

STARTERS

Choosing the main course of a meal is rarely a problem, depending on the season and who you're catering for. But how to lead up to that main dish in style? Here are over 50 mouth-watering suggestions for both everyday meals and special occasion dinner parties.

Many of these recipes are classics – tried and tested favourites such as Moules à la Marinière, Gravad Lax and Fried Whitebait; others are more adventurous delights, such as Mussels in Curry Sauce, Insalata di Mare and Tapenade.

Whether you opt for a delicate opening line or a hearty first course depends largely on what you've chosen to follow. Meal planning is an art. The key word is balance: balancing hot against cold, weighty against light, rich against delicate, spicy against subtle. A meal should always provide a variety of flavours, textures and colours.

The other thing you need to balance is your time. Many of these starters can be prepared in advance, allowing you to devote time to a more elaborate main course that demands last-minute attention. Pâtés and terrines, for example, can be made up to 48 hours in advance, stored in the refrigerator, and will actually benefit from this time to allow their flavours to intermingle. Many other dishes, such as Cockles in Cream, can be prepared several hours in advance and given a fresh garnish just before serving. While others still, such as Fried Whitebait, which need to be cooked at the last moment, are actually very quick and simple to prepare.

Whatever your choice, it is important to remember that the first course is merely a prelude to the dishes that follow. Bearing this in mind, portions should be modest. The idea is to stimulate – not to spoil – the appetite; to awaken – not to overwhelm – it.

EGGS MIMOSA

4 hard-boiled eggs
1 × 42 g (1½ oz) can lumpfish caviar
6–8 tablespoons Mayonnaise (see page 152)
1 small lettuce to garnish

Halve the eggs lengthways, remove the yolks and arrange the whites in a serving dish. Fill the hollows with caviar.

Rub the yolks through a sieve and spoon over the caviar, reserving 1 tablespoon for garnish.

Spoon the mayonnaise over the eggs, covering them completely.

Garnish with the reserved sieved egg yolk and lettuce. Serve with thin slices of brown bread.

Serves 4

VARIATION: Replace the caviar with 125 g (4 oz) lumpfish cod's roe, 150 g (5 oz) natural yogurt and the juice of 1 lemon. Mash these ingredients together, adding salt and pepper to taste, and use to fill the egg whites.

Eggs Mimosa

HADDOCK AND EGG MOUSSE

175 g (6 oz) smoked haddock
1 hard-boiled egg, chopped
200 ml (⅓ pint) natural yogurt
1 teaspoon gelatine
1 tablespoon water
1 teaspoon lemon juice
salt and pepper
TO GARNISH:
watercress sprigs
hard-boiled egg slices

Poach the haddock in a little water for 6 minutes. Drain, skin and flake the fish. Mix with the egg and yogurt.

Place the gelatine in a small bowl with the water and lemon juice and heat over a pan of hot water until dissolved. Cool and fold into the fish mixture with salt and pepper to taste.

Spoon into 4 ramekin dishes and chill until set. Garnish with watercress and egg.

Serves 4

QUICK SARDINE PÂTÉ

1 × 120 g (4¼ oz) can sardines in oil, drained
grated rind and juice of ½ lemon
5 tablespoons natural yogurt
50 g (2 oz) cottage cheese, sieved
2.5 cm (1 inch) piece cucumber, finely chopped
garlic salt
black pepper
TO GARNISH:
4 cucumber twists
4 parsley sprigs

Place the sardines in a bowl with the lemon rind and juice and mash with a fork until smooth. Beat in the yogurt, cottage cheese and cucumber. Season to taste with garlic salt and black pepper. Place in 4 ramekin dishes and chill.

Garnish with the cucumber and parsley and serve with toast.

Serves 4

CANNED FISH

Convenience foods are just what their name suggests and no sensible cook should be without some. A well-stocked cupboard is a must, both for family meals in moments and for impromptu entertaining. Canned fish and shellfish are a particularly useful standby, including tuna, sardines, prawns, crab, lumpfish caviar and anchovies.

SESAME PRAWN TOASTS

175 g (6 oz) shelled prawns
125 g (4 oz) haddock fillet, skinned
2 eggs
salt and pepper
4 slices white bread, crusts removed, toasted
4 tablespoons sesame seeds
oil for deep-frying
watercress sprigs to garnish

Place the prawns, haddock, 1 egg, and salt and pepper to taste in a food processor or electric blender and purée until smooth. Spread evenly over the toast.

Beat the other egg and brush over the fish mixture, then coat evenly with sesame seeds and press firmly into place.

Deep-fry each slice separately in hot oil for 2 minutes. Drain and cut into 8 to 12 fingers.

Serve warm, garnished with watercress.

Serves 4

SEAFOOD RAVIOLI

250 g (8 oz) pasta dough (see page 132)
1 × 198 g (7 oz) can tuna fish, drained
1 × 50 g (1¾ oz) can anchovies, drained
2–3 basil or parsley sprigs, chopped
2 teaspoons grated lemon rind
salt and pepper
Tomato and orange sauce (see page 150) or 50 g (2 oz) butter
freshly grated Parmesan cheese

Chill the pasta dough while preparing the filling.

Place the tuna fish and anchovies in the processor bowl and process until smooth. Transfer to a basin. Stir in the basil or parsley, lemon rind and plenty of salt and pepper.

Divide the pasta dough in half and roll out each piece to a rectangle 45 × 15 cm (18 × 6 inches). Put a rounded teaspoon of filling at 5 cm (2 inch) intervals on one piece. Brush the edges and between the filling with water.

Carefully place the second piece of pasta dough over the top and press down between the filling and along the edges to seal. Cut between each round with a knife or pastry wheel.

Bring a large pan of salted water to the boil and drop in the ravioli, stirring to avoid sticking. Cook for 8 to 10 minutes, until *al dente*. Drain.

Serve topped with tomato and orange sauce or butter, and sprinkled with grated Parmesan.

Serves 4 to 6

Sesame Prawn Toasts; Seafood Ravioli

MUSSELS IN CURRY SAUCE

1.75 kg (4 lb) mussels in shells
300 ml water (½ pint)
25 g (1 oz) butter
1 onion, chopped
1 teaspoon curry powder
1 teaspoon tomato purée
4 tablespoons dry white wine
2 tablespoons apricot jam, sieved
salt and pepper
150 ml (¼ pint) double cream
150 ml (¼ pint) Mayonnaise (see page 152)
juice of ½ lemon
350 g (12 oz) cooked long-grain rice, cooled
parsley sprigs

Scrub the mussels clean. Cook for about 5 minutes in a pan of boiling water, until the shells open, discarding any that do not; drain. Reserve a few for garnish and remove the rest from their shells.

Melt the butter in a pan, add the onion and sauté for 2 to 3 minutes. Stir in the curry powder and fry for a few minutes, then stir in the tomato purée, wine, apricot jam, and salt and pepper to taste.

Allow the sauce to cool. Lightly whip the cream, then fold into the sauce with the mayonnaise and lemon juice. Cover and chill for 2 to 3 hours, then fold in the shelled mussels.

Arrange the rice on individual serving dishes and spoon the mussel mixture into the centre. Garnish with the reserved mussels and parsley.

Serves 4 to 6

THREE-FISH TERRINE

500 g (1 lb) plaice fillets, skinned
350 g (12 oz) smoked haddock, skinned
150 g (5 oz) natural yogurt
2 eggs
grated rind and juice of 1 lemon
250 g (8 oz) smoked cod's roe
1 tablespoon tomato purée
white pepper
TO GARNISH:
lemon slices
parsley sprigs

Line a 1 kg (2 lb) loaf tin or terrine with most of the plaice fillets, skinned side inwards.

Place the haddock, 7 tablespoons of yogurt, 1 egg and the lemon rind and juice in a food processor or electric blender, and purée until smooth, then place half the mixture in the terrine.

Process the cod's roe with the remaining yogurt, tomato purée and the yolk of the remaining egg. Whisk the egg white until stiff and fold in. Spoon into the terrine and season with pepper. Spoon the remaining haddock mixture over, and cover with the remaining plaice fillets.

Cover with a lid or foil and place in a roasting pan half-filled with water. Cook in a preheated moderate oven, 180°C (350°F), Gas Mark 4, for 1 hour. Leave to cool.

Pour off any juices and turn onto a serving plate. Garnish with lemon slices and parsley sprigs to serve.

Serves 6 to 8

PRAWN-STUFFED CUCUMBERS

1 large cucumber, cut into 8 pieces
75 g (3 oz) cream cheese
2 tablespoons lemon juice
125 g (4 oz) prawns
1 × 99 g (3½ oz) can pimentos, drained and chopped
8 mint leaves, chopped
salt and pepper
paprika

Hollow out the centre of each cucumber section to form cup shapes and stand upright on a serving dish.

Mix the cream cheese and lemon juice together. Set aside 8 prawns for garnish. Add the remainder to the cheese mixture, along with the pimentos and mint. Season with salt, pepper and paprika to taste. Mix well.

Pile the filling into the cucumber cups and garnish with the reserved prawns. Serve with brown bread and butter.

Serves 4

INDIVIDUAL FISH FLANS

PASTRY:
250 g (8 oz) plain flour
125 g (4 oz) butter or margarine
2–3 tablespoons iced water

FILLING:
6 small plaice fillets, skinned
300 ml (½ pint) milk
salt and pepper
125 g (4 oz) peeled prawns
25 g (1 oz) butter
25 g (1 oz) plain flour
2 tablespoons chopped parsley
1 egg yolk

Sift the flour into a bowl. Rub in the butter or margarine until the mixture resembles breadcrumbs. Add the water gradually and mix to a firm dough.

Turn out onto a floured surface and knead lightly. Roll out and use to line six 7.5 cm (3 inch) flan rings. Line with greaseproof paper and dried beans and bake in a preheated moderately hot oven, 200°C (400°F), Gas Mark 6, for 10 minutes. Remove the paper and beans and return to the oven for 5 minutes. Remove the flan rings and cool on a wire rack.

Roll up the plaice fillets and place in a buttered ovenproof dish with 4 tablespoons of the milk. Season with salt and pepper to taste and cover with buttered paper. Cook in a preheated hot oven, 220°C (425°F), Gas Mark 7, for 10 minutes.

Divide the prawns between the flan cases. Transfer the cooked plaice with a slotted spoon to the flan cases; reserve the cooking juices.

Melt the butter in a small pan, stir in the flour then gradually add the remaining milk and reserved cooking juices. Bring to the boil, then add the parsley and salt and pepper to taste. Cool slightly and beat in the egg yolk.

Spoon the hot sauce over the fish in the flan cases and place under a preheated moderate grill until golden brown. Serve immediately.

Serves 6

INSALATA DI MARE

4 squid
4–6 shelled scallops, quartered
12 mussels in shells, scrubbed clean
250 g (8 oz) peeled prawns
1 × 177 g (6 oz) can crabmeat, drained
4 tablespoons olive oil
2 tablespoons lemon juice
1 clove garlic, crushed
2 tablespoons chopped parsley
salt and pepper
lemon slices to garnish

Discard the ink sacs from the squid and cut the flesh into small pieces.

Cook the scallops in a pan containing 300 ml (½ pint) boiling water for 2 to 3 minutes. Remove with a slotted spoon and set aside.

Add the squid to the pan and cook for 15 minutes, until tender. Remove with a slotted spoon and set aside.

Add the mussels to the pan and cook for about 5 minutes until the shells have opened; discard any that do not. Drain and remove the top shell from each mussel.

Put all the shellfish into a bowl. Mix the oil, lemon juice, garlic and parsley together, adding salt and pepper to taste. Pour over the fish and toss well. Cover and chill for 30 minutes.

Garnish with lemon slices and serve with brown bread.

Serves 4 to 6

LEFT: *Mussels in Curry Sauce*
RIGHT: *Insalata Di Mare*

SMOKED HADDOCK MOUSSE

175 g (6 oz) smoked haddock
120 ml (4 fl oz) milk
1 bay leaf
15 g (½ oz) butter
1 tablespoon plain flour
1 tablespoon lemon juice
4 tablespoons double cream
salt and pepper
few cucumber slices to garnish

Put the haddock, milk and bay leaf in a saucepan. Bring to the boil, cover and simmer for 10 minutes. Strain and reserve the milk; flake the fish.

Melt the butter in a saucepan and blend in the flour. Gradually add the reserved milk and bring to the boil, stirring, until thickened.

Remove from the heat and stir in the lemon juice, then fold in the flaked fish. Whisk the cream until thick and fold into the mixture. Season with salt and pepper to taste.

Transfer to 2 ramekin dishes and chill until required. Garnish with cucumber slices to serve.

Serves 2

Smoked Haddock Pancakes

SMOKED HADDOCK PANCAKES

500 g (1 lb) smoked haddock fillets
50 g (2 oz) butter
1 small onion, finely chopped
40 g (1½ oz) plain flour
300 ml (½ pint) milk
6 tablespoons double cream
1 tablespoon lemon juice
1 tablespoon chopped chives
1 tablespoon chopped parsley
125 g (4 oz) Cheddar cheese, grated
salt and pepper
2 tablespoons grated Parmesan cheese

PANCAKES:
125 g (4 oz) plain flour
pinch of salt
1 egg
scant 300 ml (½ pint) milk
2 tablespoons cold water
oil for shallow-frying

TO GARNISH:
lemon wedges
rosemary sprigs (optional)

First, make the pancakes. Sift the flour and salt into a bowl, make a well in the centre and add the egg and half the milk. Mix until smooth. Gradually add the remaining milk and the water and beat until smooth.

Heat a little oil in a 15 to 18 cm (6 to 7 inch) frying pan. Pour in about 2 tablespoons batter and quickly tilt the pan to coat the bottom evenly. Cook until the underside is brown, then turn over and cook the other side. Repeat with the remaining batter, to make 12 pancakes. Stack them on a plate, with a sheet of greaseproof paper between each, as they are cooked.

Place the haddock in a pan and add just enough water to cover. Bring to the boil, cover and poach gently for 10 minutes. Drain, then remove the skin and any bones. Flake the fish.

Melt the butter in a pan, add the onion and cook for 5 minutes, without browning. Stir in the flour and cook for 1 minute. Gradually add the milk, stirring constantly, bring to the boil and cook for 2 minutes. Stir in the cream, lemon juice, herbs, Cheddar cheese, and pepper to taste and stir until the cheese has melted. Fold in the flaked fish and season with salt to taste.

Divide the haddock mixture between the pancakes and roll up. Arrange in an ovenproof dish and sprinkle with the Parmesan cheese. Cover with a lid or foil and bake in a preheated moderate oven, 180°C (350°F), Gas Mark 4, for 20 to 25 minutes, until hot.

Uncover and return to the oven for 5 minutes, until lightly browned. Serve immediately, garnished with lemon wedges and rosemary if using.

Serves 6

GRILLED CRAB

4 small cooked crabs
juice of ½ lemon
25 g (1 oz) butter
1 small onion, finely chopped
120 ml (4 fl oz) dry sherry
1 teaspoon Worcestershire sauce
1 teaspoon French mustard
1 teaspoon crumbled thyme
2 teaspoons chopped parsley
284 ml (10 fl oz) double cream
salt and pepper
2 tablespoons fresh breadcrumbs
1 tablespoon grated Parmesan cheese
4 prawns to garnish

Twist off the claws and legs from the crabs, crack open and extract all the meat. Remove the white and brown meat from the body shells. Discard the grey sac and feathered gills.

Flake the crabmeat into a basin and add the lemon juice. Scrub the crab and shells and set aside.

Melt the butter in a pan, add the onion and cook until golden. Pour in the sherry and cook rapidly until the liquid is reduced by two-thirds.

Stir in the Worcestershire sauce, mustard and herbs. Pour in the cream and cook until thickened, then stir in the crabmeat. Season with salt and pepper to taste.

Spoon into the crab shells and sprinkle with the breadcrumbs and Parmesan cheese. Cook under a preheated moderate grill until bubbling and golden brown. Serve hot, garnished with prawns.

Serves 4

FRITTO MISTO DI MARE

4 squid
6 king-size prawns, peeled
2 fillets plaice or sole, cut into 5 cm (2 inch) strips
oil for deep-frying

BATTER:
125 g (4 oz) plain flour
pinch of salt
2 tablespoons olive oil
150 ml (¼ pint) water
1 large egg white (size 1), stiffly whisked

TO GARNISH:
lemon slices
fried parsley

Remove the ink sacs from the squid and cut the flesh into small pieces. Place in a pan of boiling water and cook for 2 minutes. Drain and dry on kitchen paper. Set aside with the prawns and the plaice or sole.

To make the batter, sift the flour and salt into a bowl, gradually add the oil and water, then fold in the egg white.

Heat the oil in a deep-fryer to 190°C (375°F). Dip each type of fish in turn into the batter, drain off any excess, then fry in the hot oil until golden brown. Drain on kitchen paper and keep hot while frying the remaining fish.

Arrange the fritto misto on a warmed serving dish. Garnish with lemon slices and fried parsley.

Serves 6

Grilled Crab; Fritto Misto Di Mare

MOULES À LA MARINIÈRE

50 g (2 oz) butter, softened
6 shallots or small onions, finely chopped
1 bouquet garni
450 ml ($\frac{3}{4}$ pint) dry white wine
salt and pepper
3.5 litres (6 pints) mussels, scrubbed clean
25 g (1 oz) plain flour
chopped parsley to garnish

Melt half the butter in a pan, add the shallots or small onions and fry gently until golden. Add the bouquet garni, wine, and salt and pepper to taste.

Bring to the boil, add the mussels, cover and simmer for about 5 minutes until the shells open; discard any that do not. Remove the mussels from the pan with a draining spoon and pile into a warmed serving dish. Keep hot.

Bring the sauce to the boil and boil until reduced by half. Remove the bouquet garni.

Blend the remaining butter with the flour, divide into small pieces and gradually add to the stock, stirring until dissolved. Bring to the boil, stirring, then simmer for 2 minutes. Pour over the mussels and sprinkle with parsley.

Serves 6

SEAFOOD RISOTTO

50 g (2 oz) butter
1 large onion, finely chopped
2 cloves garlic, crushed
350 g (12 oz) Italian rice
300 ml ($\frac{1}{2}$ pint) dry white wine
1 bouquet garni
salt and pepper
1 litre ($1\frac{3}{4}$ pints) Fish stock (see page 146)
6 shelled scallops, chopped
12 mussels in shells, scrubbed clean
12 cooked unshelled prawns
4 tablespoons grated Parmesan cheese
2 tablespoons chopped parsley

Melt the butter in a pan, add the onion and garlic and cook until lightly browned. Stir in the rice and wine. Add the bouquet garni and salt and pepper to taste. Pour in two-thirds of the stock, bring to the boil and cook rapidly for 10 minutes.

Meanwhile, cook the scallops and mussels in boiling salted water for about 5 minutes until the mussel shells have opened; discard any that do not. Drain thoroughly.

Add the scallops and mussels to the rice with the prawns. Add more stock if necessary: do not allow the risotto to become dry. Heat through gently for 3 to 5 minutes, until the rice is cooked and the liquid is absorbed. Discard the bouquet garni.

Stir in the Parmesan and parsley and serve hot.

Serves 6 to 8

CEVICHE

500 g (1 lb) monkfish
juice of 2 lemons
4 tomatoes, skinned, seeded and diced
1 green pepper, cored, seeded and diced
4 tablespoons olive oil
1 tablespoon white wine vinegar
2 tablespoons chopped parsley
salt and pepper
TO GARNISH:
1 small lettuce
1 avocado, peeled and sliced
6 black olives, stoned and sliced

Remove the skin and bones from the fish and cut the flesh into dice. Put into a basin and pour over the lemon juice. Leave to marinate for at least 3 hours, preferably overnight.

Add the tomatoes and green pepper to the fish with the remaining ingredients, seasoning with salt and pepper to taste. Stir well to mix.

Line 6 individual plates with lettuce leaves. Divide the mixture into 6 portions and pile on top of the lettuce. Garnish with avocado and olive slices.

Serves 6

SPAGHETTI WITH MUSSELS

1 kg (2 lb) mussels in shells, scrubbed clean
2 tablespoons olive oil
1 small onion, finely chopped
2–3 cloves garlic, crushed
1 × 397 g (14 oz) can tomatoes
3 tablespoons tomato purée
2 tablespoons dry white wine
2 tablespoons chopped parsley
1 bouquet garni
salt and pepper
350 g (12 oz) spaghetti
Parmesan cheese to serve

Put the mussels in a pan of boiling water and cook for about 5 minutes, until the shells have opened; discard any that do not. Shell the mussels and set aside.

Heat the oil in a pan, add the onion and garlic and cook gently for 5 to 7 minutes. Stir in the tomatoes with their juice, tomato purée and wine and bring to the boil. Stir in the parsley, bouquet garni, and salt and pepper to taste. Cook, uncovered, for 25 to 30 minutes, until thickened.

Meanwhile, cook the spaghetti in boiling salted water for 10 to 12 minutes until just tender; drain thoroughly.

Discard the bouquet garni and add the mussels to the sauce; heat through gently. Add the sauce to the spaghetti and toss well. Serve immediately, and sprinkle with Parmesan.

Serves 4 to 6

SMOKED EEL MOUSSE

350 g (12 oz) smoked eel
125 g (4 oz) cottage cheese
142 ml (5 fl oz) soured cream
2 teaspoons grated lemon rind
1 tablespoon lemon juice
2 tablespoons chopped parsley
salt and pepper
TO GARNISH:
frisé leaves
radish slices

Remove the skin and bones from the eel and flake the fish.

Place in an electric blender or food processor, add the remaining ingredients, with salt and pepper to taste, and work until smooth. Transfer to a bowl and chill until required.

Spoon the mousse onto individual serving plates. Garnish with frisé and radishes to serve.

Serves 4

LEFT: *Seafood Risotto*
RIGHT: *Mackerel and Peppercorn Pâté*

MACKEREL AND PEPPERCORN PÂTÉS

350 g (12 oz) smoked mackerel, skinned, boned and flaked
50 g (2 oz) butter, softened
150 ml (¼ pint) double cream
1 tablespoon lemon juice
dash of Worcestershire sauce
dash of Tabasco sauce
salt (optional)
1 tablespoon finely chopped parsley
1 tablespoon green peppercorns, drained and lightly crushed
fresh dill leaves
3 tablespoons clarified butter, melted

Place the mackerel flesh in a bowl and gradually beat in the butter. Transfer to an electric blender or food processor and work until smooth. Return to the bowl.

Whip the cream until it will just hold its shape, then fold into the fish with the lemon juice, Worcestershire and Tabasco sauces. Taste and add a little salt, if necessary. Stir in the parsley and peppercorns. Spoon into 6 ramekins and level the surface.

Arrange the dill attractively on top of the pâtés, then slowly pour over the clarified butter. Chill in the refrigerator for at least 30 minutes until the butter has solidified. Serve chilled with thinly sliced hot buttered toast.

Serves 6

TARAMASALATA

175 g (6 oz) smoked cod's roe, chopped
113 g (4 oz) curd cheese
50 g (2 oz) fresh white breadcrumbs
2 tablespoons lemon juice
8–10 tablespoons olive oil
pepper
1 teaspoon lumpfish caviar to garnish

Place the cod's roe, curd cheese, breadcrumbs and lemon juice in a food processor or electric blender and work until smooth.

Gradually add the olive oil with the machine running, and blend until smooth and creamy. Season with pepper to taste. Chill for 2 hours.

Garnish with lumpfish caviar and serve with toast.

Serves 4

SCALLOPS WITH DILL

juice of 2 limes
350 g (12 oz) scallops
salt and pepper
2 tablespoons chopped dill
1 tablespoon chopped mint
$\frac{1}{4}$ cucumber, diced
2 teaspoons oil
TO GARNISH:
lime slices
mint sprigs

Pour the lime juice into a saucepan, add the scallops, and salt and pepper to taste. Bring to the boil, then simmer for 2 to 3 minutes, until white in appearance.

Remove from the heat and allow to cool. Add the dill, mint, cucumber and oil and place in a serving dish. Chill for 2 hours.

Garnish with lime slices and mint sprigs and serve with hot toast.

Serves 4

SALMON AND MONKFISH MOUSSELINES

25 g (1 oz) butter
125 g (4 oz) asparagus spears, trimmed and blanched
50 g (2 oz) peeled prawns
MONKFISH FILLING:
300 g (10 oz) monkfish, off the bone and trimmed of membrane
2 tablespoons dry white wine
2 tablespoons crème fraîche
2 tablespoons chopped tarragon
1 tablespoon chopped chervil
salt and pepper
1 egg, beaten
SALMON FILLING:
300 g (10 oz) salmon fillet
2 tablespoons crème fraîche
dash of Tabasco

Grease 4 individual loaf tins $10 \times 6 \times 4$ cm ($4 \times 2\frac{1}{2} \times 1\frac{1}{2}$ inches) with butter. Arrange the asparagus and prawns attractively in the tins.

Roughly chop the monkfish and place in a food processor or electric blender with the remaining monkfish filling ingredients, adding salt and pepper to taste and half the beaten egg. Work until smooth and divide between the 4 tins.

Place the salmon filling ingredients and remaining beaten egg in the food processor or electric blender and work until smooth. Divide between the 4 tins, placing on top of the monkfish filling.

Cover each tin with foil and place in a roasting pan. Pour in enough boiling water to come half-way up the tins. Cook in a preheated moderate oven, 180°C (350°F), Gas Mark 4, for 15 to 20 minutes or until firm when touched.

Unmould the mousselines onto individual serving plates and serve warm with Hollandaise sauce (see page 148).

Serves 4

ABOVE: *Scallops with Dill; Taramasalata; Salmon and Monkfish Mousselines*
RIGHT: *Mackerel and Spinach Cannelloni; Fried Whitebait; Haddock and Leeks*

MACKEREL AND SPINACH CANNELLONI

175 g (6 oz) smoked mackerel fillets, flaked
125 g (4 oz) cottage cheese
125 g (4 oz) frozen chopped spinach, thawed
salt and pepper
8 tubes cannelloni
300 ml ($\frac{1}{2}$ pint) Tomato sauce (see page 149)
2 tablespoons grated Parmesan cheese

Mix together the fish, cottage cheese, spinach, and salt and pepper to taste. Divide between the cannelloni and place in an ovenproof dish. Pour over the tomato sauce and sprinkle with the Parmesan cheese.

Cook in a preheated moderate oven, 180°C (350°F), Gas Mark 4, for 15 to 20 minutes. Serve hot with a green salad.

Serves 4

FRIED WHITEBAIT

3 tablespoons plain flour
$\frac{1}{2}$ teaspoon salt
$\frac{1}{4}$ teaspoon paprika
500 g (1 lb) whitebait
oil for deep-frying
TO GARNISH:
chopped parsley
lemon wedges

Mix the flour with the salt and paprika and use to coat the whitebait.

Deep-fry in batches in hot oil for 2 to 3 minutes, until lightly browned and crisp. Drain and place on a warmed plate.

Sprinkle with parsley and garnish with lemon. Serve immediately.

Serves 4

HADDOCK AND LEEKS

250 g (8 oz) smoked haddock
65 g ($2\frac{1}{2}$ oz) butter
2 leeks, sliced
500 g (1 lb) potatoes, boiled and diced
142 ml (5 fl oz) soured cream
salt and pepper
1 tablespoon chopped parsley to garnish

Place the fish on a plate over a saucepan of boiling water. Dot with 15 g ($\frac{1}{2}$ oz) of the butter, cover and steam for 10 minutes, until the fish flakes.

Melt the remaining butter in a large pan, add the leeks and cook for 5 minutes, until soft. Add the fish and potatoes, then stir in the soured cream, and salt and pepper to taste.

Serve garnished with parsley.

Serves 4

COCKLES IN CREAM

1½ kg (3 lb) cockles
25 g (1 oz) butter
few parsley stalks
1 onion, sliced
150 ml (¼ pint) dry white wine
142 ml (5 fl oz) double cream
salt and pepper
1 tablespoon chopped dill or fennel to garnish

Steep the cockles for 1 to 2 hours in fresh water, then wash them well in more fresh cold water. Put them in a pan with the butter, parsley stalks and onion, then add the wine.

Cover and cook for 4 minutes over a brisk heat. Strain the liquor into a small pan, and reserve.

Remove the cockles from their shells with a pin, then keep them warm. Reduce the liquor to half by boiling rapidly. Remove from the heat, stir in the cream and season to taste with salt and pepper. Reheat carefully, but do not allow to boil.

Put the cockles into a hot serving dish, pour over the sauce and sprinkle with the dill or fennel.

Serves 4

Crab and Herb Mousse

CRAB AND HERB MOUSSE

250 g (8 oz) crabmeat, fresh, frozen or canned
2 tablespoons grated Cheddar cheese
142 ml (5 fl oz) double cream
2 tablespoons chopped tarragon
1 tablespoon chopped chervil
1 tablespoon chopped basil
1 tablespoon lemon juice
1 tablespoon tomato ketchup
salt and pepper
15 g (½ oz) gelatine, soaked in 3 tablespoons cold water
2 egg whites
TO GARNISH:
cucumber slices
whole prawn in shell

Flake the crabmeat finely and place in a bowl. Stir in the cheese, cream, herbs, lemon juice, tomato ketchup, and salt and pepper to taste.

Heat the gelatine gently until dissolved, then carefully fold into the crab mixture.

Whisk the egg whites until soft peaks form, then fold into the crab mixture using a metal spoon.

Spoon the mixture into an 18–20 cm (7–8 inch) round cake tin or mould and chill for several hours, until set.

To serve, invert the mould onto a serving plate and garnish with cucumber slices and a whole prawn.

Serves 6

DEVILLED SARDINES

500 g (1 lb) sardines
1 tablespoon made mustard
1 tablespoon Worcestershire sauce
pinch of paprika
small bunch of watercress to garnish

There is no need to gut fresh sardines. Rinse quickly and dry, then lay them on a greased baking sheet.

Mix the mustard with the Worcestershire sauce and brush the fish with it. Cook under a hot grill for 3 minutes. Turn the fish over carefully and brush again with the mustard mixture. Grill for another 3 minutes to finish cooking.

Sprinkle the fish with paprika, then serve, garnished with watercress and accompanied with fingers of toast and Niçoise sauce (see page 152).

Serves 4

RIGHT: *Smoked Salmon Profiteroles; Smoked Trout Mousse*

SMOKED SALMON PROFITEROLES

50 g (2 oz) butter
150 ml ($\frac{1}{4}$ pint) water
125 g (4 oz) plain flour, sifted
pinch of chilli powder
2 eggs
FILLING:
2 tablespoons soured cream
1 teaspoon tomato purée
black pepper
50 g (2 oz) smoked salmon, finely sliced
TO GARNISH:
chilli powder
parsley sprigs
lemon wedges

Place the butter and water in a saucepan and bring to the boil. Remove from the heat and beat in the flour and a pinch of chilli powder until the resultant dough leaves the sides of the pan. Allow to cool, then gradually beat in 1 egg at a time.

Arrange 18 teaspoons of dough on a lightly greased baking tray and bake in a preheated moderately hot oven, 200°C (400°F), Gas Mark 6, for 20 minutes or until well risen and firm. Cool on a wire rack.

Meanwhile, prepare the filling. Stir together the soured cream and tomato purée. Season with pepper. Cut the salmon into small strips, add to the mixture and stir well.

Cut open each choux bun and fill.. Dust with chilli powder and garnish with parsley and lemon wedges.

Serves 6

SMOKED TROUT MOUSSE WITH PERNOD

325 g (11 oz) smoked trout, filleted and flaked
125 g (4 oz) cottage cheese
125 g (4 oz) fromage frais or cream cheese
juice of $\frac{1}{2}$ lemon
1 teaspoon Pernod
black pepper
lemon slices, quartered, to garnish

Combine all the ingredients, either by hand or, for a smoother finish, in a food processor. Spoon into individual ramekins and chill.

Garnish with quartered slices of lemon and serve with toasted triangles of brown bread.

Serves 6

SMOKED FISH

There are two methods of smoking – hot and cold. Cold smoked fish, such as kippers and haddock, have a smoky flavour but are still raw and need to be cooked before eating. Hot smoked fish, such as mackerel, salmon and trout, are smoked at much higher temperatures and are 'cooked' in the heat, so are ready to eat as they are.

SKATE WITH MAYONNAISE

1 kg (2 lb) skate
1.2 litres (2 pints) water
2 tablespoons white wine vinegar
1 carrot, sliced
1 onion, sliced
12 peppercorns, lightly crushed
salt
3 tablespoons Vinaigrette (see page 153)
300 ml (½ pint) Mayonnaise (see page 152)
TO GARNISH:
crisp lettuce leaves
capers
chopped parsley

Place the skate in the water, along with the wine vinegar, carrot, onion, peppercorns and salt. Slowly bring to the boil, then simmer very gently for 10 to 15 minutes or until just cooked.

Remove from the pan, drain well and transfer to a plate. Moisten with vinaigrette.

Arrange the lettuce leaves on a serving dish and arrange the skate on top. Pour on the mayonnaise and garnish with capers and chopped parsley. Serve well chilled.

Serves 4

GREY MULLET WITH SAGE AND BACON

2 × 500 g (1 lb) grey mullet, scaled and cleaned
8 sage leaves, finely chopped
4 rashers smoked back bacon, finely chopped
40 g (1½ oz) fresh breadcrumbs
salt and pepper
50 g (2 oz) butter
150 ml (¼ pint) dry vermouth
sage leaves to garnish

Slash the fish in 3 or 4 places on each side. Pound the chopped sage and bacon together and push a little of this mixture into the slashes. Mix the remaining bacon and sage with breadcrumbs and salt and pepper to taste, and fill the cavities of the fish.

Butter a baking dish generously and arrange the fish side by side. Bake in a preheated moderately hot oven, 200°C (400°F), Gas Mark 6, for 15 minutes. Then pour on the vermouth and bake for a further 10 to 15 minutes. Garnish with sage. Serve with green beans and new potatoes for a light lunch.

Serves 4

FRESH HADDOCK MOUSSE

750 g (1½ lb) haddock, filleted and skinned
3 tablespoons sunflower oil
125 g (4 oz) fromage frais
4 eggs
juice of ½ lemon
salt and pepper
125 g (4 oz) carrots, cut in julienne strips
2 parsley sprigs, finely chopped
2 fennel sprigs, finely chopped

Cut the fish into pieces and place in a food processor with the oil, fromage frais, eggs, lemon juice, salt and pepper. Purée until smooth.

Pour half the purée into a greased 1 kg (2 lb) loaf tin lined with greaseproof paper.

Blanch the strips of carrot and arrange evenly on top of the fish mixture. Work the remaining haddock purée with the chopped herbs and pour this mixture on top of the carrots.

Place the loaf tin in a *bain-marie* and bake in a preheated moderate oven, at 160°C (325°F), Gas Mark 3, for 40 to 45 minutes or until set.

Turn out the mousse, remove the greaseproof paper and cut into slices. Serve warm with a hot tomato sauce or cold with a tomato salad.

Serves 4

MÉLANGE OF FISH RILLETTES

250 g (8 oz) squid
250 g (8 oz) salmon
250 g (8 oz) cod
250 g (8 oz) monkfish
1 fennel bulb
1 carrot
1 courgette
2 shallots, sliced
1 tablespoon chopped tarragon
1 tablespoon chopped parsley
1 tablespoon chopped chives
1 tablespoon chopped chervil
1 teaspoon green peppercorns
2 teaspoons grated orange rind
450 ml (¾ pint) Hollandaise sauce (see page 148)

Cut the squid into rings and the fish into a mixture of matchbox- and matchstick-sized pieces. Cut the fennel bulb, carrot and courgette into julienne strips. Place the squid in a single layer in a steamer, then add a layer of vegetables and then a layer of fish. (It is better to do this in batches than to overload the steamer.) Finally, add the herbs, peppercorns and orange rind.

Steam, with a tightly fitting lid, for 3 to 5 minutes, being careful not to overcook the fish.

Pour the hollandaise sauce onto 4 warmed (not hot) plates, and place the contents of the steamer next to the sauce on each plate.

Serves 4 to 6

Grey Mullet with Sage and Bacon; Mélange of Fish Rillettes

BAKED AVOCADOS WITH BACON AND PRAWNS

1 medium onion, finely chopped
50 g (2 oz) butter, melted
250 g (8 oz) lean back bacon rashers, rinded and finely chopped
3 large ripe avocados
2 teaspoons lime juice
salt and pepper
175 g (6 oz) peeled prawns
TO GARNISH:
large unshelled prawns
lime wedges

Fry the onion gently in the melted butter until soft. Add the bacon and continue frying gently until it softens, stirring frequently. Drain and cool.

Halve the avocados, remove the stones and scoop out the flesh. Mash it thoroughly, then beat in the lime juice, salt and pepper to taste, and fold in the bacon, onion and prawns.

Wrap the avocado shells in foil to prevent them from blackening and stand in a shallow ovenproof dish. Spoon in the bacon and prawn mixture.

Cook in a preheated moderately hot oven, 200°C (400°F), Gas Mark 6, for 15 to 20 minutes, until well heated through.

Serve hot, garnished with a whole prawn and a wedge of lime.
Serves 6

TROUT AND LEMON MOUSSE

6 large lemons
2 smoked trout, skinned, boned and flaked
50 g (2 oz) unsalted butter, softened
4 tablespoons double cream
1 tablespoon chopped chives
1 tablespoon chopped parsley
pinch of chilli powder
salt and freshly ground white pepper
1 tablespoon finely chopped herbs (mint, lemon balm or parsley) to garnish

Cut the tops off the lemons. Squeeze and strain the juice from the lemons and reserve 2 tablespoons. Carefully scoop out the membranes from the lemon shells and cut away the excess pith, taking care not to cut through the skin. Cut the base of each lemon so that it stands upright.

Put the trout flesh in an electric blender or food processor with the butter. Work until smooth, then add 1 tablespoon lemon juice. Whip the cream until it will just stand in soft peaks, then fold into the trout mixture. Add the herbs, chilli powder, and salt and pepper to taste. Add more lemon juice to taste.

Spoon the mixture into the lemon shells and shape the tops into domes. Stand the lemons in individual dishes and top with chopped herbs. Surround with crushed ice and serve immediately with Melba toast.
Serves 6

STUFFED MUSSELS

48 fresh mussels, scrubbed clean
salt
2 lemon slices
2 teaspoons lemon juice
125 g (4 oz) butter, softened
3 cloves garlic, crushed
1 shallot, chopped
2 tablespoons chopped parsley
3 tablespoons fresh wholewheat breadcrumbs
TO GARNISH:
parsley sprigs
lemon wedges

Place the mussels in a pan of boiling salted water, add the lemon slices, cover and cook for about 7 minutes, until the mussels have opened. Remove with a slotted spoon, discarding any that have not opened. Remove the empty top shells.

Beat the remaining ingredients together and spread the mixture on top of the mussels.

Place on a baking sheet and cook in a preheated moderately hot oven, 200°C (400°F), Gas Mark 6, for 5 minutes, until golden.

Arrange on a warmed serving dish, garnish with parsley and lemon, and serve with crusty French bread.
Serves 4

SKEWERED MONKFISH

750 g (1½ lb) monkfish tails
about 12 bay leaves
2 tablespoons melted butter
salt and freshly ground white pepper

SAUCE:
4 teaspoons cornflour
250 ml (8 fl oz) cold water
grated rind of 1 lemon
25 g (1 oz) butter
3 tablespoons lemon juice
1 egg yolk
3 tablespoons medium sherry
2 tablespoons double cream
salt and freshly ground white pepper

Prepare the monkfish tails by removing the flesh, in 2 pieces, from the central bone and slice into bite-sized 'medallions'.

Thread the monkfish onto 4 short skewers, alternating with the bay leaves. Brush with the butter and sprinkle with salt and pepper to taste.

Place on a grill rack and cook under a preheated hot grill for 12 to 15 minutes until cooked, turning frequently.

Meanwhile, place the cornflour in a pan and stir in the cold water. Add the lemon rind and butter and bring to the boil, stirring constantly. Cook for 2 minutes, then remove from the heat.

Beat the lemon juice with the egg yolk. Add a little of the hot sauce, then return to the sauce in the pan, blending well. Heat gently until hot but not boiling. Stir in the sherry and cream with salt and pepper to taste.

Serve at once, spooning a little of the sauce over the monkfish kebabs and serving the rest separately.

Serves 4

CHOOSING FISH

Fish is classified into two main categories: white fish, where the oil is found only in the liver; and oily fish, where it is distributed throughout the flesh.

White fish can be round or flat. The large round species, such as coley and cod, are sold in steaks, cutlets or fillets; the small round species, such as whiting and haddock, are usually sold in fillets. The large flat varieties, such as halibut and turbot, are either sold whole or in fillets and steaks; the smaller flat fish, such as plaice and sole, are usually sold whole.

Oily fish, such as herring and mackerel, are usually smaller than other species, and are a particularly good source of vitamins A and D. Their fat content is mainly polyunsaturated, which has been found to have a beneficial effect on the heart.

LEFT: *Stuffed Mussels* RIGHT: *Skewered Monkfish*

SMOKED MACKEREL POTS

250 g (8 oz) smoked mackerel, skinned, boned and finely flaked
65 g (2½ oz) butter, melted
50 g (2 oz) cream cheese
1 teaspoon lemon juice
1 tablespoon chopped parsley
½–1 teaspoon creamed horseradish
black pepper
TO GARNISH:
lemon slices

Place the mackerel in a bowl. Add 25 g (1 oz) of the melted butter with the cheese and stir well to mix.

Stir in the lemon juice, parsley, creamed horseradish, and pepper to taste. Mix thoroughly.

Divide the mixture evenly between 4 small individual ramekins or serving pots and smooth the surfaces.

Pour the remaining melted butter over each ramekin and chill in the refrigerator for at least 2 hours before serving, garnished with lemon slices. Serve with brown bread or wholewheat crackers.

Serves 4

TAPENADE

150 g (5 oz) stuffed green olives
1 × 100 g (3½ oz) can tuna fish, drained
1 × 50 g (1¾ oz) can anchovies, drained
3 tablespoons capers
2 teaspoons lemon juice
150 ml (¼ pint) olive oil
1 tablespoon brandy
Dijon mustard
pepper

Reserve a few olives for garnish, slicing them finely. Put the rest of the olives and the remaining ingredients, with mustard and pepper to taste, in an electric blender and work until smooth.

Pour into a serving bowl and garnish with the sliced olives. Serve as a dip with crackers.

Makes about 450 ml (¾ pint)

ABOVE: *Fresh Salmon Pâté*
RIGHT: *Gravad Lax*

FRESH SALMON PÂTÉ

750 g ($1\frac{1}{2}$ lb) fresh salmon or sea trout
1 small onion, sliced
1 carrot, sliced
2 bay leaves
150 ml ($\frac{1}{4}$ pint) white wine
175 g (6 oz) unsalted butter, creamed
SAUCE:
75 g (3 oz) butter
75 g (3 oz) plain flour
600 ml (1 pint) milk
2 teaspoons lemon juice
salt and pepper
TO GARNISH:
$\frac{1}{2}$ cucumber, cut into thin rings
1 hard-boiled egg, yolk sieved, white chopped
1 tablespoon chopped parsley

Place the salmon in a large saucepan and add the onion, carrot, bay leaves and wine. Add just enough water to cover, then bring the fish slowly to the boil. Simmer gently for 15 to 20 minutes, then remove from the heat and allow the fish to cool in the liquid.

Meanwhile make the sauce. Melt the butter in a saucepan, remove from the heat and stir in the flour. Cook the roux for 2 to 3 minutes, then gradually add the milk, beating well between each addition until really smooth. Simmer gently for 3 to 4 minutes, add the lemon juice, salt and pepper, and allow to cool.

Skin and flake the cooked salmon, and pass it through a food processor or pound with a pestle and mortar.

When all the ingredients are cool, blend together the fish, sauce and creamed butter. Check the seasoning and place the pâté in a dish. Cover with clingfilm until ready to serve.

Garnish at the last minute. Arrange the cucumber round the outside, then the chopped egg white and finish with the egg yolk and parsley.

Serves 12

ANCHOÏDE

4 slices brown bread, crusts removed
unsalted butter
1 × 50 g (2 oz) can anchovies in olive oil, drained and soaked in milk for 30 minutes
1 clove garlic, crushed
freshly ground black pepper

Toast the bread on one side only and butter the untoasted side. Cut into fingers. Drain the anchovies and pound to a paste with the garlic in a mortar and pestle. Season with pepper to taste and spread onto the buttered toast fingers.

Place on a baking sheet and bake in a fairly hot oven, 200°C (400°F), Gas Mark 6, for 10 minutes or until hot and crisp. Serve immediately with a glass of chilled white wine.

Serves 4

GRAVAD LAX

750 g–1 kg ($1\frac{1}{2}$–2 lb) salmon tailpiece, scaled and filleted
PICKLE:
1 heaped tablespoon sea salt
1 tablespoon sugar
1 teaspoon black peppercorns, crushed
1 tablespoon brandy
1 tablespoon chopped dill
TO GARNISH:
dill leaves
lime slices

Mix together the pickle ingredients in a small bowl and transfer a quarter of the mixture to a flat dish.

Place one salmon fillet, skin side down, in the pickle mixture. Spread half of the remaining pickle over the cut side of the salmon. Place the other fillet, skin side up, on top.

Cover with the remaining pickle mixture, rubbing it into the skin. Cover with foil, lay a board on top and weight it down.

Chill for at least 12 hours before serving; it can be left for up to 5 days.

Drain well and slice the salmon either on the bias for smaller slices or parallel to the skin to obtain larger slices. Garnish with dill and lime slices and serve with Mustard sauce (see page 148).

Serves 4 to 6

LIGHT LUNCHES

All too often a light lunch means grabbing a sandwich or opening a can. But it needn't. Whether you're eating on your own, lunching with the children or entertaining a friend, you deserve better.

It doesn't have to be complicated: what could be simpler, for example, than Herring Roes on Toast, or an Omelette Arnold Bennett, both of which are low on effort and expense, but high on enjoyment? If you've got a little more time on your hands, what about Brioches with Smoked Trout Mousse, or Monkfish with Roquefort Dressing? And if you really feel like splashing out, there are few more enticing delicacies than Salmon Mayonnaise with Peaches, or Ceviche of Scallops with Herbs.

So whether you want to rustle up a short sharp treat for the tastebuds or you'd like to opt for something rather more elaborate, and whether you want to spend pennies or pounds, there's no shortage of choice.

Some of these dishes could equally well be served – in smaller quantities – as starters, or – perhaps in larger quantities – as hearty supper meals. Versatility and imagination are crucial to successful cooking and the chapter sections suggested here are flexible.

OMELETTE ARNOLD BENNETT

50 g (2 oz) butter
4 tablespoons single cream
125 g (4 oz) smoked haddock, cooked, skinned and flaked
salt and pepper
3 eggs, separated
15 g (½ oz) grated Parmesan cheese
chopped parsley to garnish

Melt half the butter in a small saucepan. Remove from the heat and stir in half the cream and the fish. Season with salt and pepper to taste.

Stir the egg yolks into the fish mixture. Whisk the egg whites until just stiff enough to form peaks. Fold in the fish mixture and half the grated cheese.

Melt the remaining butter in a preheated 20 cm (8 inch) omelette pan. Add the fish mixture and spread evenly in the pan. Cook fairly quickly until just beginning to set.

Sprinkle with the remaining cheese and place under a very hot grill until the cheese is lightly browned. Slide the unfolded omelette onto a warmed serving dish. Pour over the remaining cream, sprinkle with parsley and serve immediately.

Serves 1 to 2

NORMANDY OMELETTE

4 mussels, scrubbed clean and beards removed (optional)
50 g (2 oz) peeled prawns
3 tablespoons dry white wine
1 bay leaf
1 parsley sprig
3 tablespoons double cream
salt and pepper
25 g (1 oz) butter
3 eggs, lightly beaten
TO GARNISH:
3–4 cooked whole prawns
parsley sprig

Place the mussels, if using, in a small pan, cover with cold water and bring to the boil. Simmer for about 5 minutes, until the shells open; discard any that do not. Remove from the pan, cool slightly, remove from shells, then chop the flesh.

Place the mussels and prawns in a small pan. Add the wine, bay leaf and parsley and simmer, uncovered, until all the excess liquid has evaporated. Remove the bay leaf and parsley and stir in the cream. Season with salt and pepper to taste.

Melt the butter in a preheated 20 cm (8 inch) omelette pan until sizzling. Add the eggs and cook until just beginning to set. Spoon the prepared fish mixture over the omelette and fold in half.

Turn onto a warmed serving dish, garnish with the prawns and parsley. Serve immediately.

Serves 1 to 2

BORNHOLM KIPPER OMELETTE

4 eggs
4 tablespoons milk
salt and pepper
25 g (1 oz) butter
1 onion, chopped
4 tomatoes, sliced
2 kippers, filleted and flaked
1 tablespoon chopped chives

Whisk the eggs lightly with the milk and a little salt and pepper.

Melt the butter in a preheated 20 cm (8 inch) omelette pan until sizzling. Add the egg mixture and cook gently.

While the top is still soft, cover with the onion, tomatoes and kipper. When just set, sprinkle with chives.

Slide unfolded onto a warmed serving plate and serve.

Serves 2

LEFT: *Bornholm Kipper Omelette*
RIGHT: *Egg and Anchovy Pâté*

LAYERED FISH TERRINE

350 g (12 oz) fresh spinach
1·2 litres (2 pints) water
salt and pepper
2 carrots, thinly sliced
875 g (1¾ lb) frozen plaice fillets, thawed and skinned
lemon juice
1 × 439 g (15½ oz) can pink salmon, drained
2 egg whites
1 teaspoon tomato purée
1 tablespoon double cream
grated nutmeg
2 teaspoons chopped chives or spring onions

Remove the thick stems from the spinach. Wash well and place in a pan, with just the water clinging to it. Cook for 1 to 2 minutes until beginning to soften; remove from the heat.

Pour the water into a pan and season with salt, add the sliced carrots and boil for 1 minute; remove from the heat.

Line the base and sides of a greased 750–900 ml (1¼–1½ pint) loaf tin with some of the spinach leaves, placing a few carrot slices between the leaves at intervals. Lay 3 or 4 plaice fillets on top, adding salt, pepper and lemon juice to taste.

Remove the skin and bones from the salmon, chop finely and mix with 1 egg white, the tomato purée, cream and salt and pepper to taste; beat well.

Chop the remaining plaice fillets and mix with the remaining egg white, adding salt and pepper to taste. Squeeze the remaining spinach dry and season with salt, pepper and nutmeg to taste.

Put two-thirds of the salmon mixture in a layer in the tin, cover with the remaining spinach and carrots. Top with two-thirds of the remaining fish fillet mixture. Stir the remaining fish mixtures together with the chives or spring onions and completely cover the top.

Cover with buttered foil and place in a *bain-marie* (water bath). Cook in a preheated moderate oven, 180°C (350°F), Gas Mark 4, for 1 hour.

Turn out the terrine and serve sliced, hot or cold, with Mayonnaise (see page 152) and quartered fennel bulbs, green beans and carrot curls.

Serves 4 to 6

EGG AND ANCHOVY PÂTÉ

2 × 50 g (1¾ oz) cans anchovy fillets in oil
6–8 stuffed olives, halved
25 g (1 oz) butter
1 onion, chopped
1–2 cloves garlic, crushed
25 g (1 oz) plain flour
150 ml (¼ pint) milk
150 ml (¼ pint) Fish stock (see page 146)
3 eggs, beaten
75 g (3 oz) fresh white breadcrumbs
50 g (2 oz) capers
3 hard-boiled eggs, chopped
pepper

Grease a 1 kg (2 lb) loaf tin and line the base with greaseproof paper. Arrange 8 anchovy fillets and the olives on the base. Chop remaining anchovies and reserve, with the oil.

Melt the butter in a pan, add the onion and garlic and fry gently for 5 minutes. Stir in the flour, then the milk and stock a little at a time. Bring to the boil, stirring until thickened. Remove from the heat and stir in the anchovies and oil. Cool slightly then add the remaining ingredients, and season with pepper to taste. Leave for 15 minutes, then spoon into the tin.

Bake in a preheated moderate oven, 180°C (350°F), Gas Mark 4, for 1 hour or until set. Leave until cold. Turn out and serve with salad.

Serves 8 to 10

Asparagus and Smoked Salmon Quiche

ASPARAGUS AND SMOKED SALMON QUICHE

PASTRY:
175 g (6 oz) plain flour
pinch of salt
125 g (4 oz) butter
2 tablespoons grated Parmesan cheese
1 egg yolk
about 1 tablespoon iced water

FILLING:
175 g (6 oz) asparagus
125 g (4 oz) smoked salmon pieces
3 eggs
200 ml (⅓ pint) double cream
squeeze of lemon juice
1 teaspoon chopped thyme
1 teaspoon chopped parsley
freshly ground black pepper

TO GARNISH:
lime slices
parsley or chervil sprigs

Sift the flour and salt into a bowl. Rub in the butter until the mixture resembles fine breadcrumbs. Stir in the Parmesan and egg yolk, and enough water to mix to a fairly stiff dough. Turn onto a floured surface, knead lightly until smooth, then roll out and use to line a 23 cm (9 inch) flan tin. Chill in the refrigerator for 30 minutes.

Prick the base of the dough and line with foil and baking beans. Bake 'blind' in a preheated moderately hot oven, 200°C (400°F), Gas Mark 6, for 10 minutes, then remove the foil and beans and return to the oven for a further 5 minutes. Remove from the oven and set aside. Reduce the oven temperature to moderate, 180°C (350°F), Gas Mark 4.

To make the filling, steam the asparagus for 5 minutes and pat dry with kitchen paper. Place the smoked salmon pieces on the base of the pastry, then arrange the asparagus in a circle on top, with the spears radiating out towards the edge.

Beat the eggs with the cream, lemon juice, herbs and salt and pepper to taste. Pour gently into the flan, taking care not to disturb the position of the asparagus. Bake in the oven for 20 to 25 minutes, until the filling is golden brown and just set. Leave to cool and serve warm or cold, garnished with lime slices and parsley or chervil.

Serves 6

KIPPER TOAST

1 × 175 g (6 oz) packet kipper fillets with butter
grated rind and juice of 1 lemon
1 tablespoon chopped parsley
pepper
2 slices wholemeal bread, toasted
parsley sprigs to garnish

Cook the kipper fillets according to the packet instructions.

Place the fish in a bowl and mash with a fork. Add the lemon rind, juice, parsley and pepper to taste. Mix well, then divide the mixture between the toast slices.

Place under a preheated medium grill for 4 to 5 minutes. Garnish with parsley sprigs and serve immediately.

Serves 2

GOOD VALUE

Shellfish is very versatile. It has an unfortunate reputation of being expensive, but this is rarely a problem because such small quantities can be used to make a highly delectable dish. The same applies to smoked salmon, of which small quantities of less expensive offcuts can often be bought to create an impressive dish.

PRAWN AND CHEESE TOASTIES

For this recipe use a special toasted sandwich maker.

175 g (6 oz) frozen peeled prawns, thawed and chopped
2 eggs, hard-boiled and chopped
125 g (4 oz) double Gloucester cheese with chives, grated
salt and pepper
8 slices buttered bread
1–2 teaspoons sesame seeds

Mix the prawns, eggs and grated cheese, seasoning well with salt and pepper. Sprinkle the buttered side of the bread with sesame seeds, pressing them evenly over the surface; shake off any excess.

Place 4 slices, buttered side down, in the preheated sandwich toaster. Spread with the prawn mixture and cover with the remaining bread, butter side up. Lower the lid and toast for 2 to 3 minutes, or according to maker's instructions. Serve hot.

Serves 4

SMOKED SALMON WITH SPINACH AND EGG

750 g ($1\frac{1}{2}$ lb) spinach, trimmed
75 g (3 oz) butter
150 ml ($\frac{1}{4}$ pint) single cream
salt and pepper
6 eggs
2 tablespoons milk
4 large slices smoked salmon

Wash the spinach thoroughly. Drain and place in a pan. Cover and cook over a moderate heat, without adding any extra water, until tender.

Drain well and purée in an electric blender or food processor with 50 g (2 oz) of the butter and the cream. Season with salt and pepper. Transfer to a serving dish and keep warm.

Beat the eggs, add the milk and season with salt and pepper. Melt the remaining butter in a pan over a low heat. Pour in the eggs and stir gently for 8 to 10 minutes until they begin to thicken. Remove from the heat and continue stirring until creamy.

Place a spoonful of scrambled egg on each slice of smoked salmon and roll up. Arrange on a bed of puréed spinach and serve immediately.

Serves 4

Smoked Salmon with Spinach and Egg

SEAFOOD PASTA

This is made in a pressure cooker and takes little time to prepare. Follow manufacturer's instructions for your cooker.

175 g (6 oz) smoked haddock
175 g (6 oz) cod fillet
1 onion, quartered
salt and pepper
250 g (8 oz) macaroni
1.2 litres (2 pints) boiling water
1 tablespoon oil
3 tablespoons sherry
1 × 298 g (10½ oz) can condensed cream of mushroom soup
2 tablespoons chopped parsley

Put the macaroni, 1 teaspoon salt, the water and oil in the cooker and stir.

Butter the unperforated basket of the pressure cooker. Put in the fish and onion and season well. Stand the basket in the cooker.

Seal the cooker and heat to high pressure. Cook for 5 minutes. Reduce the pressure at room temperature.

Lift out the unperforated basket. Drain and rinse the macaroni, return to the cooker and add the sherry and soup. Mix well and bring to the boil.

Flake the fish and break up the onion. Add to the cooker with the parsley; stir well. Check the seasoning and transfer to a warmed dish.

Serves 4

Cheese and Shrimp Soufflés

CHEESE AND SHRIMP SOUFFLÉS

2 large eggs (size 1)
150 ml (¼ pint) single cream
1 teaspoon English mustard
pinch of chilli powder
salt
75 g (3 oz) peeled shrimps
125 g (4 oz) matured Cheddar cheese, finely grated
1 tablespoon grated Parmesan cheese
French bread to serve

ANCHOVY PASTE:
2 × 50 g (1¾ oz) cans anchovy fillets
4 tablespoons milk
1 tablespoon oil
2 cloves garlic, crushed
1 tablespoon chopped parsley

To make the anchovy paste, drain the anchovy fillets and soak them in milk for 30 minutes. Rinse thoroughly in cold water and drain.

Pound the anchovies with the oil, garlic and parsley to a smooth paste. Put to one side.

Beat together the eggs, cream, mustard, chilli powder, and salt to taste. Stir in the shrimps and cheeses.

Lightly grease four individual soufflé dishes and pour in the mixture. Bake in a preheated moderately hot oven, 200°C (400°F), Gas Mark 6, for 20 to 25 minutes, until well risen and golden brown.

Meanwhile toast the French bread on both sides. Spread with the prepared anchovy paste and heat through under a preheated moderate grill. Arrange on a warmed serving platter. Serve the soufflés as soon as they are cooked, with the anchovy toasts.

Serves 4

HERRING ROES ON TOAST

500 g (1 lb) soft herring roes
2 tablespoons plain flour
salt and pepper
50 g (2 oz) unsalted butter
1 tablespoon anchovy essence
1 teaspoon lemon juice
2 drops Tabasco sauce
½ teaspoon paprika
2 slices wholewheat buttered toast to serve

Place the roes in a colander and pour over boiling water. Dry with kitchen paper. Season the flour with salt and pepper and use to coat the roes.

Melt the butter in a pan until foaming, and add the roes, anchovy essence, lemon juice, Tabasco and paprika. Fry for about 3 to 5 minutes, until crisp and golden.

Cut the toast into triangles. Put the cooked roe on a warmed serving plate, surround with the toast and serve immediately.

Serves 2 to 4

EGGS BENEDICT WITH SMOKED MACKEREL PÂTÉ

250 g (8 oz) smoked mackerel
grated rind of 1 lemon
juice of 2 lemons
2 tablespoons olive oil
1 clove garlic, crushed
freshly ground black pepper
4 eggs
dash of vinegar
4 slices brown toast
150 ml (¼ pint) Hollandaise sauce (see page 148)
2 tablespoons chopped parsley to garnish

Remove all the skin and bones from the mackerel and flake well. Blend to a smooth purée in a food processor with the lemon rind, juice, oil, garlic and black pepper.

Poach the eggs for 2 to 3 minutes in boiling water, to which you have added a few drops of vinegar to help the eggs keep their shape.

Top each slice of toast with smoked mackerel pâté, then a hot poached egg, and coat with hollandaise sauce. Serve immediately, garnished with chopped parsley.

Serves 4

PRAWN AND ARTICHOKE VOL-AU-VENT

1 × 300 ml (½ pint) packet onion sauce mix
150 ml (¼ pint) milk
150 ml (¼ pint) dry white wine
125 g (4 oz) frozen petits pois
1 × 397 g (14 oz) can artichoke hearts, drained and quartered
350 g (12 oz) frozen peeled prawns, thawed
2 tablespoons single cream
celery salt
white pepper
8 frozen vol-au-vent cases
parsley sprigs to garnish

Make up the sauce mix, following the directions on the packet, using the milk and wine. Add the petits pois, artichoke hearts and prawns. Simmer gently for 4 minutes.

Add the cream and season with celery salt and pepper to taste.

Cook the vol-au-vent cases from frozen, according to packet directions. Spoon in the prawn mixture and garnish with parsley. Serve immediately

Serves 4

Haddock and Mushroom Omelette; Herring Roes on Toast

HADDOCK AND MUSHROOM OMELETTE

250 g (8 oz) smoked haddock
25 g (1 oz) butter
125 g (4 oz) mushrooms, sliced
4 eggs, beaten

Place the fish on a plate over a pan of boiling water, cover and steam for 10 to 15 minutes, until the fish flakes. Remove skin and bones; flake fish. Melt butter in a pan, add mushrooms and fry until tender.

Add the eggs and cook over a low heat for 3 to 4 minutes. When just beginning to set, add the fish and cook for 1 minute. Fold the omelette in half and serve immediately.

Serves 2

PEPPERED MACKEREL SOUFFLÉ

40 g (1½ oz) butter
40 g (1½ oz) plain flour
300 ml (½ pint) milk
3 large eggs (size 1), separated
142 ml (5 fl oz) soured cream
300–350 (10–12 oz) peppered smoked mackerel, flaked
1 tablespoon lemon juice
1 tablespoon chopped parsley

Melt the butter in a pan, add the flour and cook, stirring, for 1 minute. Remove from the heat and gradually stir in the milk, mixing well between each addition. Bring to the boil, stirring, until thickened.

Remove from the heat and beat in the egg yolks, one at a time, then the soured cream. Stir in the mackerel, lemon juice and parsley. Leave to cool.

Whisk the egg whites until stiff. Stir about 2 tablespoons into the fish mixture, to make it soft. Carefully fold the egg whites into the fish mixture, using a metal spoon.

Turn into a buttered 1.2 litre (2 pint) soufflé dish placed on a baking sheet. Bake immediately in a preheated moderately hot oven, 190°C (375°F), Gas Mark 5, for 45 to 50 minutes, until well risen and golden brown. Serve immediately.
Serves 4

SMOKED HADDOCK SOUFFLÉ OMELETTE

50 g (2 oz) butter
2 smoked haddock fillets, cooked, skinned, and flaked
5 tablespoons single cream
4 tablespoons grated Parmesan cheese
salt and pepper
6 eggs, separated
parsley sprigs to garnish

Melt half the butter in a saucepan. Add the haddock, cream and half the grated cheese, and heat gently until the cheese is melted.

Remove from the heat and season with salt and pepper to taste. Stir in the egg yolks. Whisk the egg whites until stiff and fold into the haddock mixture.

Melt the remaining butter in a large frying pan. When sizzling, pour in the omelette mixture. Cook gently for 2 to 3 minutes until set, drawing the cooked edges towards the centre with a fork.

Cut into quarters and turn out onto warmed plates. Sprinkle with the remaining cheese and garnish with parsley. Serve immediately.
Serves 4

HERRING ROE SOUFFLÉS

25 g (1 oz) butter
250 g (8 oz) soft herring roes
hot milk to cover
2 eggs
150 ml (¼ pint) Béchamel sauce (see page 150)
25 g (1 oz) Gruyère cheese, grated
salt and pepper

Butter an ovenproof dish and place the herring roes in it. Pour over just enough hot milk to cover and poach in a preheated moderately hot oven, 200°C (400°F), Gas Mark 6, for 5 minutes until just firm. Drain and arrange in 4 individual soufflé dishes.

Separate the eggs and beat the yolks, one at a time, into the Béchamel sauce. Stir in half the cheese and season with salt and pepper. Whisk the egg whites until stiff and fold into the soufflé mixture.

Pour on to the roes to fill the soufflé dishes and sprinkle with the remaining cheese. Return to the oven and bake for 7 to 10 minutes until well risen and golden. Serve immediately.
Serves 4

LEFT: *Peppered Mackerel Soufflé*
RIGHT: *Tuna and Oyster Omelette*

SMOKED MACKEREL GOUGÈRE

25 g (1 oz) butter
1 onion, chopped
25 g (1 oz) plain flour
150 ml (¼ pint) milk
3 tablespoons dry cider
2 tablespoons natural yogurt
350 g (12 oz) smoked mackerel, flaked
3 tablespoons chopped watercress
1 small dessert apple, peeled and chopped
salt and pepper
CHOUX PASTRY:
300 ml (½ pint) water
50 g (2 oz) butter
175 g (6 oz) plain flour
4 eggs, beaten
75 g (3 oz) Cheddar cheese, grated
1 teaspoon dry mustard
salt and pepper
TOPPING:
1 tablespoon fresh brown breadcrumbs
25 g (1 oz) flaked almonds, chopped
TO GARNISH:
apple slices tossed in lemon juice
mint leaves

First make the filling. Melt the butter in a pan, add the onion and fry until softened. Stir in the flour and milk, bring to the boil, stirring, then simmer for 3 minutes.

Remove from the heat and stir in the remaining ingredients, with salt and pepper to taste. Leave to cool. Cover the filling and chill.

To make the choux pastry, place the water and butter in a pan and heat gently until melted, then bring to the boil. Remove from the heat, add the flour and beat until smooth.

Return to the heat and beat for 40 seconds, until the mixture leaves the side of the pan and forms a ball.

Remove from the heat and allow to cool slightly, then beat in the eggs a little at a time, beating well after each addition to form a thick glossy dough. Stir in the cheese, mustard, and salt and pepper to taste.

Spoon the choux pastry around the edge of a shallow 1.75 litre (3 pint) ovenproof dish. Place the filling in the centre and sprinkle with the breadcrumbs and almonds.

Cook in a preheated moderately hot oven, 200°C (400°F), Gas Mark 6, for 40 to 45 minutes, until risen and golden. Garnish with apple and mint and serve immediately.

Serves 4 to 6

SOUFFLÉS

A soufflé is as light as a feather. Its lightness comes from the air trapped by whisking the egg whites and is held by 'setting' the egg white by heating it. A soufflé is usually cooked and served in a traditional straight-sided china soufflé dish, although any fairly deep ovenproof dish can be used provided it will look good when set on the table. A soufflé will collapse very quickly after removal from the heat and so must be served immediately after it has been taken out of the oven, and never turned out of its dish.

TUNA AND OYSTER OMELETTE

6 eggs, separated
salt and white pepper
1 tablespoon water
25 g (1 oz) butter
175 g (6 oz) bean sprouts
1 × 99 g (3½ oz) can tuna fish, drained and flaked
1 × 105 g (3.7 oz) can smoked oysters, drained
2 tablespoons chopped parsley to garnish
SAUCE:
150 g (5.2 oz) natural yogurt
1 teaspoon made mustard
1 tablespoon lemon juice

Whisk the egg whites with a pinch of salt until soft peaks form. Whisk the yolks with the water and pepper to taste until very frothy. Fold the yolks into the whites.

Melt the butter in a 28 cm (11 inch) omelette pan, turning the pan so the butter coats the base and sides. Add half the bean sprouts, then pour in half the egg mixture and smooth over. Add the remaining bean sprouts, then the remaining egg. Cook for about 5 minutes, lifting the edges occasionally with a palette knife, until firm.

Arrange the tuna around the edge of the omelette, with a ring of oysters inside. Put under a preheated moderate grill for 2 to 3 minutes, until the top is firm and golden.

Meanwhile, mix the sauce ingredients in a small basin.

Scatter the parsley in the centre of the fish. Serve the omelette with the sauce and a salad.

Serves 4

HAKE IN BEETROOT SAUCE

750 g ($1\frac{1}{2}$ lb) hake, filleted and skinned
25 g (1 oz) butter
salt and pepper
juice of 1 lemon
1 bay leaf
milk and water, mixed, to cover
SAUCE:
300 ml ($\frac{1}{2}$ pint) thick Béchamel sauce *(see page 150)*
1 egg yolk
1 medium cooked beetroot, finely chopped
parsley sprigs to garnish

Arrange the fish on a well-greased ovenproof dish. Season with salt and pepper, and pour on the lemon juice. Add the bay leaf and cover with the milk and water, bake in a preheated moderate oven, 180°C (350°F), Gas Mark 4, for 20 to 30 minutes. Drain the fish, reserving the poaching liquid, and keep warm while making the sauce.

Dilute the prepared béchamel sauce to taste with a little of the poaching liquid. Then add the egg yolk and beetroot and stir well.

Pour the sauce over the fish and serve immediately, garnished with parsley sprigs.

Serves 4

CEVICHE OF SCALLOPS WITH HERBS

10 large scallops
4 scallop shells
150 ml ($\frac{1}{4}$ pint) lemon juice
$1\frac{1}{2}$ tablespoons chopped shallot
$\frac{1}{2}$ tablespoon chopped tarragon
$\frac{1}{2}$ tablespoon chopped dill
$\frac{1}{2}$ tablespoon chopped chives
$\frac{1}{2}$ tablespoon chopped parsley
$1\frac{1}{2}$ tablespoons sunflower oil
parsley sprigs to garnish

Detach the scallops from their shells and scrape off the beard-like fringe and intestinal thread. Cut away the orange coral. Wash the white parts and pat dry. Cut in slices about 5 mm ($\frac{1}{4}$ inch) thick. Wash and prepare the coral in the same way.

Choose 4 medium shells, scrub well and leave to drain.

Put the sliced scallops in a bowl and pour over the lemon juice. (There should be enough almost to cover them.) Cover with clingfilm and put in the refrigerator for 24 hours, stirring occasionally.

When ready to serve, chop the shallots and the herbs very finely indeed. Drain off the lemon juice from the scallops and stir in the oil. Add the shallots and herbs and mix well. Spoon onto the shells and serve immediately, garnished with parsley, with brown bread and butter.

Serves 4

HUSS IN TOMATO SAUCE

Huss (roussette or dog fish) has firm tasty flesh thus making it an ideal choice for this recipe.

750 g ($1\frac{1}{2}$ lb) huss, cut into short lengths
50 g (2 oz) flour
salt and pepper
4 tablespoons olive oil
500 g (1 lb) ripe tomatoes, skinned, seeded and diced
3 cloves garlic, crushed
1 tablespoon chopped basil or marjoram
1 tablespoon chopped parsley
TO GARNISH:
12 black olives, stoned
croûtons

Rinse and dry the fish. Season the flour with salt and pepper and coat the fillets with it, shaking off the surplus. Heat half the olive oil in a frying pan and gently fry the fish, turning once, until golden.

In another pan, heat the remaining oil and add the tomatoes, garlic, herbs, and salt and pepper to taste. Cook gently for 5 minutes.

Arrange the fish on a hot serving dish and spread the sauce over. Garnish with the olives and croûtons.

Serves 4

STIR FRIED PRAWNS WITH BEAN SPROUTS

500 g (1 lb) prawns, shelled
6 tablespoons dry sherry
4–5 tablespoons sesame oil
salt and pepper
350 g (12 oz) bean sprouts
3 tablespoons soy sauce

Marinade the prawns in sherry for $1\frac{1}{2}$ to 2 hours. Then heat the oil in a wok or deep frying pan, add the drained prawns, season with salt and pepper and fry for 2 minutes.

Add the bean sprouts and fry for another 2 minutes. Add the soy sauce and stir well.

Serve with plain boiled rice.

Serves 4

Hake in Beetroot Sauce; Stir Fried Prawns with Bean Sprouts

HAM AND HADDIE

350 g (12 oz) smoked haddock
40 g ($1\frac{1}{2}$ oz) unsalted butter
4 small thin slices gammon
parsley sprig to garnish

Divide the haddock into 4 portions and poach in boiling water for 5 minutes. Drain well and remove any skin and bones.

Melt the butter in a large frying pan, add the gammon slices and fry gently for 3 minutes.

Put a piece of haddock on top of each slice of gammon in the pan, cover and cook for 5 minutes. Transfer to a warmed serving dish, garnish with parsley and serve hot.
Serves 4

VARIATION: For an extra special treat, pour 3 tablespoons double cream over the fish and gammon and place under a preheated hot grill for 2 minutes. Serve immediately.

SMOKED TROUT MOUSSE IN BRIOCHES

7 g ($\frac{1}{4}$ oz) fresh yeast
1 tablespoon warm water
125 g (4 oz) strong plain flour
pinch of salt
pinch of caster sugar
1 egg, lightly beaten
50 g (2 oz) butter
FILLING:
625 g ($1\frac{1}{4}$ lb) smoked trout
juice of $\frac{1}{2}$ lemon
pinch of chilli powder
pinch of dried mustard
freshly ground black pepper
20 g ($\frac{3}{4}$ oz) butter, melted
150 ml ($\frac{1}{4}$ pint) double cream
TO GARNISH:
parsley sprigs
lemon wedges

Blend the fresh yeast with the water. Sift together the flour, salt and sugar. Stir the diluted yeast into the flour, with the egg and butter. Work to a soft dough, turn out onto a floured surface and knead for about 5 minutes. Leave the dough to rise at room temperature for 1 to $1\frac{1}{2}$ hours until it has doubled in size and springs back when gently prodded with a floured finger.

Knead the dough well on a lightly floured surface. Divide the dough among 6 small brioche moulds, filling them about half full. Leave at room temperature for about 1 hour until the dough is light and puffy and nearly fills the moulds.

Bake in a preheated moderately hot oven, 200°C (400°F), Gas Mark 6, for 10 minutes, until well risen and golden.

Meanwhile, prepare the filling. Remove all the skin and bones from the smoked trout and place in a bowl. Flake well with a fork and stir in the lemon juice, chilli powder, mustard powder, black pepper, melted butter and double cream.

When the brioches are cooked, slice off the tops and fill with mousse. Replace the tops at an angle and garnish with parsley sprigs and lemon wedges.
Serves 6

LEFT: *Ham and Haddie*
RIGHT: *Plaice au Gratin; Coley Stroganoff*

PLAICE AU GRATIN

2 tablespoons sunflower oil
125 g (4 oz) mushrooms, sliced
2 small plaice, filleted and skinned
salt and pepper
juice of 1 lemon
25 g (1 oz) fresh breadcrumbs
50 g (2 oz) Cheddar cheese, grated
TO GARNISH:
lemon wedges
stuffed olives

Grease an ovenproof dish with a little oil and place half the mushrooms in it. Arrange the fillets of fish on top, folding them in half. Season with salt and pepper, and pour on the lemon juice. Add the remaining mushrooms and sprinkle with breadcrumbs, grated cheese and the remaining oil.

Cover with foil and bake in a preheated moderate oven, 180°C (350°F), Gas Mark 4, for 30 minutes.

Serve garnished with lemon wedges and stuffed olives.

Serves 4

COLEY STROGANOFF

750 g (1½ lb) coley, filleted and skinned
salt and pepper
1 lemon, sliced
200 ml (⅓ pint) soured cream
paprika
watercress sprigs to garnish

Arrange the fish in a baking dish and season with salt and pepper. Cover with lemon slices and bake in a preheated moderately hot oven, at 200°C (400°F), Gas Mark 6, for 20 to 30 minutes or until the fish flakes easily.

Uncover, pour on the soured cream and sprinkle generously with paprika. Grill until just beginning to brown and garnish with watercress. Serve with rice or noodles.

Serves 4

HERRING ROES PROVENCALE

40 g (1½ oz) butter
250 g (8 oz) soft herring roes
25 g (1 oz) plain flour
1 clove garlic, crushed
black pepper
TO GARNISH:
1 tablespoon chopped parsley
lemon wedges

Melt the butter in a small pan and dust the roes with flour. Place the roes in the melted butter and fry gently for 2 to 3 minutes. Add the garlic, turn the roes over and fry the other side for 2 to 3 minutes.

Season with pepper and garnish with parsley and lemon wedges.

Serves 4

COLD MONKFISH WITH ROQUEFORT YOGURT

juice of 1 lemon
750 g (1½ lb) monkfish, filleted and skinned
2 tablespoons chopped coriander to garnish
DRESSING:
50 g (2 oz) Roquefort cheese
250 g (8 oz) natural yogurt
COURT-BOUILLON:
1 carrot, sliced
1 onion, sliced
2 celery sticks, sliced
2 bay leaves
2 parsley stalks
8 peppercorns
1 teaspoon coriander seeds
juice of 1 lemon
1.5 litres (2½ pints) water

Prepare the dressing the day before you plan to eat, to allow the yogurt time to take on the flavour of the cheese. Crumble the Roquefort into the yogurt and stir. Cover and refrigerate.

On the day itself, prepare the court-bouillon. Place the vegetables, herbs, peppercorns, coriander seeds, lemon juice and water in a large pan, and bring to the boil.

Reduce the heat, cover and allow to simmer for 30 minutes. Strain and pour into a shallow roasting tin.

Add the lemon juice and place in a preheated moderate oven, 180°C (350°F), Gas Mark 4, for a few minutes until piping hot. Then add the monkfish. Poach for about 5 minutes or until the fish flakes easily.

Lift out the fish and transfer to a serving dish. Sprinkle with coriander and allow to cool. Serve well chilled, with the Roquefort yogurt.

Serves 4

SALMON MAYONNAISE WITH PEACHES

500 g (1 lb) cooked salmon
lettuce leaves
4 peaches, halved
150 ml (¼ pint) Mayonnaise (see page 152)
DRESSING:
2 tablespoons olive oil
1 tablespoon lemon juice
salt and pepper
1 tablespoon chopped chives

First make the dressing by combining all the ingredients and mixing together well.

Flake the fish and toss in the dressing. Arrange on a serving dish on a bed of lettuce leaves with the peach halves round the edges. Spoon the mayonnaise on top. Serve with brown bread and butter.

Serves 4

Cold Monkfish with Roquefort Yogurt; Kipper Vol-au-Vent

KIPPER VOL-AU-VENT

½ × 212 g (7½ oz) packet frozen puff pastry, thawed
beaten egg to glaze
75 g (3 oz) kipper fillets
15 g (½ oz) butter
2 tablespoons plain flour
150 ml (¼ pint) milk
40 g (1½ oz) Cheddar cheese, grated
2 teaspoons chopped parsley
salt and pepper

Roll out the pastry to a 15 cm (6 inch) circle. Using an 8.5 cm (3½ inch) cutter, mark a circle in the centre, cutting half-way through the pastry. Glaze with beaten egg.

Place on a baking sheet and cook in a preheated hot oven, 220°C (425°F), Gas Mark 7, for 20 minutes.

Cook the kipper fillets under a preheated medium grill for 2 to 3 minutes on each side, then flake.

Melt the butter in a saucepan and stir in the flour. Cook for 1 minute, then gradually blend in the milk. Heat, stirring, until the sauce thickens. Stir in the fish, cheese, parsley and salt and pepper to taste. Heat gently, stirring, until the cheese has melted.

When cooked, ease out the vol-au-vent lid and discard any soft pastry in the centre. Fill the case with the kipper mixture and replace the lid. Serve hot.

Serves 1 to 2

TROUT WITH MUSHROOMS, CREAM AND PERNOD

3 tablespoons plain flour
salt and pepper
4 × 300–350 g (10–12 oz) trout, cleaned
75 g (3 oz) butter
1 tablespoon vegetable oil
250 g (8 oz) mushrooms, sliced
2 cloves garlic, peeled and crushed
3 tablespoons Pernod
8 tablespoons double cream
watercress sprigs to garnish

Spread the flour out on a plate and season with salt and pepper. Dip the trout in the seasoned flour, turning to coat on all sides.

Heat the butter with the oil in a large frying pan. Add the trout and fry over a moderate heat for 5 minutes on each side, until cooked through and browned. Transfer the trout to a warmed serving dish and keep warm.

Add the mushrooms and garlic to the pan and fry over a moderate heat for 5 minutes or until softened, stirring from time to time. Add the Pernod and cream and allow to bubble for 1–2 minutes, stirring. Taste and adjust the seasoning.

Pour the sauce over the fish and serve, garnished with watercress.

Serves 4

Trout with Mushrooms, Cream and Pernod

SALADS

If the thought of salads makes you groan at visions of uninspiring rabbit food, think again! Salads nowadays mean a lot more than limp lettuce leaves interspersed with slices of cucumber and tomato. A great variety of flavours, colours and textures are readily available – try lamb's lettuce, chicory, radicchio, and cherry tomatoes to name a few. Salads are nutritious, refreshing, quick and easy to prepare. They provide valuable minerals, vitamins and fibre in the diet and are usually reassuringly low in calories.

These fish salads can be served, with crusty hunks of bread, as meals in themselves, or, with thin slices of brown bread, as scrumptious starters and promises of more to follow. They need not be eaten only in the summer months; indeed their health-giving properties are of even greater value in the winter and, with their imaginative combinations of root, leaf, pasta, pulse, fruit and nut ingredients, these salads are designed for year-round eating.

A careful selection of ingredients is essential for the appetising presentation of salads. It is better not to combine too many different ingredients, nor to chop them up too small, as both these approaches will appear – and taste – messy.

Fresh herbs greatly improve the flavour of most salads and should therefore be used liberally. Parsley, chives, mint, tarragon and coriander are particularly useful as they go well with most salad ingredients, while fennel and dill are the classic accompaniments to fish. Herbs can also be added to the salad dressings, which can lift a simple salad into the luxury class.

Sardine and Tomato Salad

SARDINE AND TOMATO SALAD

1 lettuce
500 g (1 lb) tomatoes, sliced
½ Spanish onion, cut into rings
2 × 120 g (4¼ oz) cans sardines in olive oil, drained
4 tablespoons French dressing (see page 154)
TO GARNISH:
parsley and marjoram sprigs
1 tablespoon capers, well drained

Arrange the lettuce on a shallow serving dish and cover with the tomato slices and onion rings. Arrange the sardines so that they are just overlapping the tomato slices and onion rings, with tails towards the edge of the plate. Spoon over the dressing to cover and sprinkle with parsley and marjoram sprigs and capers.

Serve with crusty bread.

Serves 4

TUNA AND BEAN SALAD

175g (6 oz) black-eye or haricot beans, soaked overnight and drained
salt
1 small onion, peeled and finely chopped
1 × 200 g (7 oz) can tuna fish, drained and flaked
DRESSING:
300 ml (½ pint) olive or salad oil
150 ml (¼ pint) lemon juice
4 tablespoons chopped parsley
black pepper

Cook the beans in boiling salted water for 40 minutes or until tender. Drain and refresh under cold running water. Put in a serving bowl with the onion and flaked tuna and stir carefully to combine.

To prepare the dressing, put the ingredients in a screw-top jar and shake well to mix.

Pour the dressing over the bean mixture and season to taste. Chill in the refrigerator for several hours. Stir well before serving with wholemeal bread and butter.

Serves 4

MEDITERRANEAN SALAD PLATTER

250 g (8 oz) cod fillet
150 ml (¼ pint) water
salt
3 tablespoons Mayonnaise (see page 152)
2 teaspoons lemon juice
1 × 198 g (7 oz) can tuna fish, drained and flaked
2 hard-boiled eggs, quartered
black pepper
1 lettuce, washed and drained
4 tomatoes, sliced
TO GARNISH:
1 green pepper, cored, seeded and cut into rings
6 black olives

Place the cod in a pan, add the water and salt to taste, then poach for about 8 minutes until the fish is tender. Drain, then skin and flake the fish.

Place the mayonnaise and lemon juice in a bowl and add the cod, tuna and eggs. Toss lightly and season to taste with salt and pepper.

Arrange the outside lettuce leaves on a large serving plate. Shred the inside lettuce leaves and place in the centre of the dish. Pile the fish and egg mixture on top and arrange the tomato slices around the sides.

Garnish the top of the fish with green pepper and black olives, and serve with crusty French bread.

Serves 4

DANISH SALAD

4 hard-boiled eggs
1 green dessert apple
1 red dessert apple
4 pickled Danish sweetened herring fillets
2 pickled dill cucumbers, sliced
4 small pickled beetroots, diced
4 small potatoes, boiled and diced
142 ml (5 fl oz) soured cream or natural yogurt
salt and pepper
apple slices to garnish

Slice the eggs, dice the apples and cut the herrings into small pieces.

Place the egg slices and dill cucumber slices around the edge of the serving plate. Arrange the beetroot next to the dill cucumber slices. Mix the remaining ingredients together, seasoning with salt and pepper to taste, and spoon onto the plate next to the beetroot.

Garnish with apple slices.

Serves 4 to 6

SALADE NIÇOISE

8 anchovy fillets
3–4 tablespoons milk
125 g (4 oz) small green beans
salt
pinch of ground nutmeg
½ small cucumber
250 g (8 oz) tomatoes
4 hard-boiled eggs
1 × 198 g (7 oz) can tuna in oil, drained
3–4 tablespoons French dressing (see page 154)
8–12 black olives, stoned, to garnish

Soak the anchovy fillets in the milk for 15 to 20 minutes. Drain and discard the milk.

Cook the beans in lightly salted boiling water, with the nutmeg added, until just tender but still firm. Drain, rinse under cold running water and drain again.

Cut the cucumber into sticks about half the size of the beans. Season very lightly with salt.

Cut the tomatoes and eggs into quarters and flake the tuna.

Arrange all the ingredients on 4 individual serving plates. Pour over the French dressing and garnish with the olives.

Serves 4

Danish Salad; Salade Niçoise

HOT KIPPER AND MUSHROOM SALAD

3 large kippers
250 g (8 oz) button mushrooms, wiped clean
5–7 tablespoons olive oil
3–4 tablespoons natural yogurt
2–3 tablespoons lemon juice
freshly ground allspice
freshly ground black pepper
3 tablespoons finely chopped parsley
6 large lettuce leaves, washed and drained
3 spring onions, green tops only, shredded diagonally, to garnish

Put the kippers, heads down, into a large jug. Fill with boiling water and press down on the fish tails to immerse them completely. Cover the jug and leave for 10 minutes.

Slice the mushrooms very thinly. Heat 5 tablespoons of oil in a large frying pan. Add the mushrooms to the pan and stir-fry for just 1 minute so that they are still quite crunchy. Quickly tip into a large, warmed bowl. If they seem a little dry, add a little extra oil.

Pour some boiling water into a saucepan over which the bowl will sit comfortably. Keep the water at a very gentle simmer.

Drain the kippers and, working as quickly as possible, cut off the heads and tails, then remove the large back bone and as many small bones as you can. Flake the fish and add to the mushrooms.

Mix well, then add the yogurt and a little lemon juice. Mix in a generous amount of allspice and some black pepper and stir in the parsley. Taste, adding more yogurt or lemon as you wish.

Arrange the lettuce leaves on individual plates. Spoon the fish mixture on top and sprinkle over the spring onion tops. Serve at once with brown bread and butter.

Serves 6

GARLIC BREAD

Many of these salads are delicious served with hot crusty garlic bread. Mash together 150 g (5 oz) butter, 1 teaspoon of salt and 3 crushed cloves of garlic. Cut 2 French sticks of bread into 5 cm (2 inch) slices, and spread on both sides with garlic butter. Reshape the loaves and wrap in foil. Store in the freezer for up to 2 months and use as required. Heat from frozen, still wrapped, for 30 minutes in a preheated moderately hot oven, 200°C (400°F), Gas Mark 6.

LEEK AND PRAWN SALAD

8 small leeks
300 ml (½ pint) Mayonnaise (see page 152)
2 tablespoons natural yogurt
500 g (1 lb) prawns, peeled
2 hard-boiled eggs, shelled and halved
salt and pepper
juice of ½ lemon
paprika

Boil the leeks for about 10 minutes, until just tender. Drain and allow to cool.

Lighten the mayonnaise to a good coating consistency with natural yogurt. Stir in the prawns.

Carefully separate the hard-boiled egg whites from the yolks. Cut the whites into shreds and pass the yolks through a fine strainer.

Arrange the leeks on a serving dish. Season well with salt and pepper and lemon juice. Coat well with mayonnaise.

Scatter the egg whites and sieved yolks over the top and dust with paprika.

Serve with crusty brown bread.

Serves 4

COD SALAD WITH MINT AND CUCUMBER

750 g (1½ lb) cod, filleted and skinned
juice of ½ lemon
salt
½ large cucumber, diced
2 tablespoons chopped mint
2 tablespoons chopped dill

DRESSING:
6 tablespoons olive oil
1½ tablespoons tarragon vinegar
salt and pepper
1 teaspoon made mustard

TO GARNISH:
125 g (4 oz) prawns, peeled
mint sprigs

Cut the cod fillet into 3 or 4 pieces. Sprinkle with lemon juice and salt. Steam for about 10 minutes until just cooked and leave, covered, until cold.

Flake the fish coarsely into a large bowl, discarding any bones or skin. Add the diced cucumber and chopped herbs.

Combine all the ingredients for the dressing and pour over the salad. Toss lightly, taking care not to break up the fish.

Pile onto individual plates and garnish with prawns and sprigs of mint. Serve with crusty French bread.

Serves 4

Leek and Prawn Salad; Cod Salad with Mint and Cucumber

SOUR CREAM HERRING SALAD

4 × 175 g (6 oz) herrings
1 medium onion, sliced
2 bay leaves
1 teaspoon pickling spice
salt and pepper
120 ml (4 fl oz) dry white wine
120 ml (4 fl oz) white wine vinegar
4 spring onions, finely chopped
142 ml (5 fl oz) soured cream
TO GARNISH:
1 red-skinned eating apple
lemon juice

Cut off the heads and tails of the herring, remove the fillets, and keep the soft roes. Rinse the fish and roes, clean them and place in a shallow ovenproof dish. Cover with the onion slices, bay leaves and pickling spice, and season with salt and pepper. Pour over the wine and vinegar. Poach in a preheated moderate oven, 160°C (325°F), Gas Mark 3, for 30 minutes. Remove from the oven and leave to cool.

Stir the spring onions into the soured cream and add salt and pepper to taste. Arrange the fish fillets and roes on a serving dish, strain a little of the fish liquor over them and smother with the cream.

Core and slice the unpeeled apple, dip in the lemon juice to prevent discoloration, then garnish the fish.

Serves 4

MEDITERRANEAN PRAWN AND BROCCOLI SALAD

500–750 g (1–1½ lb) young fresh broccoli, or 500 g (1 lb) frozen broccoli, thawed
sea salt
1 large avocado
18 peeled Mediterranean prawns
DRESSING:
1 small clove garlic, finely chopped
freshly ground black pepper
¼ teaspoon grated ginger root
6 tablespoons olive oil
2–3 tablespoons lemon juice
TO GARNISH:
3 spring onions, bulbs finely sliced, green tops cut into fine rings
2 tablespoons finely chopped parsley

Cut the broccoli into florets with about 5 cm (2 inches) of stem left on. Rinse in cold water.

Bring a large pan of lightly salted water to the boil, add the broccoli and cook for 3 to 5 minutes, until just tender but still with a bite. Drain, refresh under cold running water and leave to cool in the colander while making the dressing.

Mix the garlic, salt, a good grinding of black pepper and the grated ginger in a small bowl or jug. Briskly stir in the oil and lemon juice, mixing well. Taste, adding extra lemon juice if necessary – the dressing should be lemony but not sharp.

Pour 3 tablespoons of dressing into a bowl, add the broccoli florets (which should still be slightly warm) and toss until the dressing is completely absorbed.

Just before serving, quickly cut the avocado in half, remove the stone, then peel back the skin from each half. Cut the flesh into 18 slices. Arrange 3 slices on each plate, then lay 3 prawns on top and the broccoli around the outside edge.

Scatter over the spring onions and parsley. Pour a little dressing over the salad and serve at once, with a lightly chilled, crisp dry white wine.

Serves 6

NOTE: The prawns may be prepared up to 3 hours in advance, wrapped in clingfilm and kept in a cool place, preferably not the refrigerator. The 'dressed' broccoli can be prepared, covered and kept in a bowl for up to 3 hours. Do not chill.

LEFT: *Mediterranean Prawn and Broccoli Salad*
RIGHT: *Lobster and Chicken Salad*

SEAFOOD AND FENNEL SALAD

125 g (4 oz) long-grain rice
salt and pepper
2 × 175–250 g (6–8 oz) cod steaks
1 tablespoon lemon juice
350 g (12 oz) prawns
1 × 150 g (5 oz) jar mussels in brine, drained
4 spring onions, trimmed and sliced
1 fennel bulb
4 tablespoons French dressing (see page 154)
2 tablespoons single or soured cream

Cook the rice for 13 to 14 minutes in boiling salted water until it is just tender. Drain, rinse in boiling water, drain again thoroughly and turn into a bowl.

Poach the cod in the minimum of water seasoned with the lemon juice, salt and pepper, for 7 to 8 minutes until tender. Leave in the water until cold, then remove and flake the fish, discarding the skin and bones. Add the flaked cod to the rice.

Add the prawns to the rice with the drained mussels and the spring onions.

Remove any feathery fronds from the fennel and reserve for the garnish. Chop the fennel bulb, add it to the salad and mix well.

Combine the French dressing and the cream, season well with salt and pepper and add to the salad. Toss thoroughly and garnish with the reserved fronds of fennel. Chill until ready to eat.

Serves 8

LOBSTER AND CHICKEN SALAD

2 × 350 g (12 oz) cooked lobsters
250 g (8 oz) cooked chicken breast
150 ml (¼ pint) natural yogurt
150 ml (¼ pint) Mayonnaise (see page 152)
salt and pepper
2 tablespoons chopped tarragon to garnish

Remove the meat from the lobster and divide into neat bite-sized pieces. Crack the claws and remove the meat from these as well.

Cut the chicken into pieces about the same size as the lobster meat. Combine the lobster and chicken, and mix with the yogurt and mayonnaise. Season with salt and pepper and pile into serving dishes or into the lobster shells.

Garnish with chopped tarragon and serve with a green salad.

Serves 4

GRAPEFRUIT AND PRAWN SALAD

1 tablespoon sunflower oil
1 onion, chopped
250 g (8 oz) peeled prawns
2 tablespoons lemon juice
4 tablespoons dry white wine
salt and pepper
4 tablespoons Mayonnaise (see page 152)
1 teaspoon Tabasco
½ teaspoon chilli powder
2 ruby red grapefruit, peeled and segmented
1 red pepper, cored, seeded and diced
1 lettuce

Heat the oil in a pan, add the onion and sauté until transparent. Add the prawns, lemon juice, wine, and salt and pepper to taste and simmer for 5 minutes.

Leave to cool slightly, then remove the prawns and onion with a slotted spoon and place in a bowl. Add the mayonnaise, Tabasco and chilli powder and stir lightly to mix.

Cut each grapefruit segment in half and add to the prawn mixture with the red pepper.

To serve, divide between 4 serving plates, lined with lettuce leaves.

Serves 4

MARINATED HERRING AND NEW POTATO SALAD

1 tablespoon sea salt
2 tablespoons olive oil
1 tablespoon caster sugar
1 teaspoon white peppercorns, crushed
1 tablespoon finely chopped tarragon
½ teaspoon dill seeds, lightly crushed
2 large herrings, cleaned and boned, heads removed
500 g (1 lb) small new potatoes, scrubbed
175 ml (6 fl oz) Mayonnaise (see page 152)
1–2 teaspoons Dijon mustard

TO GARNISH:
tarragon sprigs
1 tablespoon fresh dill seed

Mix the salt, oil, sugar, peppercorns, tarragon and dill seeds together and spread a layer over the bottom of a shallow dish into which the herrings will fit snugly, lying flat.

Put one of the fish, skin side down, into the dish and spread more of the paste all over the flesh. Cover with the second fish, skin side up this time, then spread the remaining mixture over the skin. Cover the dish with foil and weight down (use a plate with a couple of cans on top). Chill for a minimum of 12 hours, up to 4 days if possible.

About 30 minutes before serving, boil the potatoes in lightly salted water for 8 to 10 minutes until done, checking after 5 to 6 minutes if they are really small. Drain thoroughly and cut in half if necessary. Set aside to cool slightly.

Cut the fish on the diagonal into thin slices, in the same way as slicing smoked salmon. Mix into the cooled potatoes.

Mix the mayonnaise with mustard to taste, then toss the fish and potatoes in the dressing.

Pile the fish and potato salad into a serving bowl and sprinkle with the tarragon and dill seeds. Serve at once.

Serves 6

SALADS

Fish salads make delicious light main dishes, especially suitable for hot summer days. Many of them can be packed into rigid polythene containers and taken on picnics. Most of these nutritious salads can also be served as starters, in which case the quantities should be adjusted accordingly. Most salads can be prepared a few hours in advance and left to chill in the refrigerator, but they should not be dressed until just before serving.

Grapefruit and Prawn Salad

SILVIA'S TUNA AND DATE SALAD

2 × 198 g (7 oz) can tuna fish, flaked
50 g (2 oz) dried dates, chopped
40 g ($1\frac{1}{2}$ oz) sunflower seeds
50 g (2 oz) mushrooms, sliced
1 Iceberg lettuce, cut into wedges
DRESSING:
4 tablespoons olive oil
1 tablespoon lemon juice
freshly ground black pepper

Combine all the salad ingredients in a large bowl and mix together.

Mix the dressing ingredients together well, pour over the salad and toss lightly.

Serve with jacket potatoes.

Serves 4 to 6

SMOKED TROUT RÉMOULADE

300 ml ($\frac{1}{2}$ pint) Mayonnaise (see page 152)
3 tablespoons natural yogurt
1–2 tablespoons Dijon mustard
juice of $\frac{1}{2}$ lemon
salt and pepper
1 small celeriac
4 smoked trout, filleted
TO GARNISH:
frisé
1 lemon, sliced
1 lime, sliced
black olives

Mix together the mayonnaise, yogurt, mustard, lemon juice, salt and pepper. Grate the celeriac and toss in the dressing.

Arrange the smoked trout on 4 individual serving plates and garnish with frisé, slices of lemon and lime and black olives. Place a heaped tablespoon of celeriac rémoulade on the sides of each plate and serve with crusty brown bread.

Serves 4

Silvia's Tuna and Date Salad; Smoked Trout Rémoulade

PRAWN, AVOCADO AND PASTA SALAD

500 g (1 lb) peeled prawns
300 g (10 oz) dried pasta twists
2 avocado pears, sliced
1 tablespoon each chopped thyme, marjoram, basil and parsley
DRESSING:
1 clove garlic, crushed
½ teaspoon French mustard
6 tablespoons olive oil
3 tablespoons lemon juice
1 teaspoon finely grated lemon rind
1 teaspoon honey
salt and pepper
TO GARNISH:
black olives
thyme and marjoram sprigs (optional)

Mix all the dressing ingredients together in a large bowl, adding salt and pepper to taste. Stir in the prawns, cover and chill for 30 minutes.

Cook the pasta until *al dente.*

Drain and cool quickly under cold running water. Drain thoroughly and add to the prawns. Carefully stir in the avocados and herbs.

Transfer the salad to a serving dish and garnish with black olives, and thyme and marjoram if using. Serve immediately.

Serves 4 to 8

TUNA PASTA SALAD

250 g (8 oz) pasta shells
salt and pepper
125 g (4 oz) button mushrooms, sliced
1 green pepper, cored, seeded and chopped
2 × 227 g (8 oz) cans tomatoes, drained and chopped
1 × 198 g (7 oz) can tuna, drained and flaked
2 tablespoons oil
1 tablespoon lemon juice
garlic salt
chopped parsley to garnish

Cook the pasta in plenty of boiling salted water until *al dente* (tender but still firm to the bite). Drain and rinse thoroughly under cold running water.

Place the pasta in a serving bowl and add the mushrooms, green pepper, tomatoes and tuna.

Blend the oil with the lemon juice, then add garlic salt and pepper to taste. Pour the dressing over the pasta and toss well.

Garnish with parsley before serving.

Serves 4

FISH SALAD

1 crisp lettuce
250 g (8 oz) cooked coley
125 g (4 oz) cooked unpeeled new potatoes, chopped
50 g (2 oz) cooked peas
½ small cooked cauliflower, divided into florets
50 g (2 oz) gherkins, chopped
2 spring onions, sliced
300 ml (½ pint) Mayonnaise (see page 152)

Arrange the lettuce leaves round the edge of a salad bowl. Combine all the other ingredients and place in the centre.

Serves 4

CORONATION FISH

500 g (1 lb) cod steaks, skinned
1 small mackerel, filleted and skinned
1 plaice, filleted and skinned
salt and pepper
1 bay leaf
few lettuce leaves
2–3 teaspoons curry powder
150 ml (¼ pint) Mayonnaise (see page 152)
watercress sprigs to garnish

Poach the cod, mackerel and plaice for 5 to 6 minutes in a little water, seasoned with salt, pepper and a bay leaf. When it is cooked, remove from the water and allow to cool. Discard the bones and any skin.

Divide the fish into bite-sized pieces and place in a serving dish lined with lettuce leaves. Stir the curry powder into the mayonnaise and spoon over the fish.

Garnish with sprigs of watercress.

Serves 4

HERRING AND APPLE SALAD

8 pickled herrings
4 red eating apples, quartered and cored
300 ml (½ pint) soured cream
1–2 teaspoons caraway seeds
1 large pickled gherkin, chopped
1 tablespoon chopped parsley
freshly ground black pepper
shredded lettuce to garnish

Cut the herrings into 2.5 cm (1 inch) chunks. Similarly, cut the apples into slightly smaller pieces.

Combine the cream, caraway seeds, gherkin, parsley and black pepper, and mix together.

Arrange some shredded lettuce on serving plates and pile the herring and apple mixture onto it. Spoon the cream mixture over the salad. Serve with jacket potatoes.

Serves 4

LEFT: *Prawn, Avocado and Pasta Salad*
RIGHT: *Coronation Fish; Herring and Apple Salad*

FAMILY MEALS

Have you run out of answers to that familiar hungry cry, "What's for dinner?" If you have, don't despair. Here is a wealth of suggestions to add to your repertoire.

Some of the dishes, like Potato Cod Bake, Cheesy Cod Steaks and Tuna Fish Cakes, are very simple and reassuringly familiar; others, like Crab and Spaghetti Bake, Pitta Parcels and Fish Goulash, are rather more exotic. But you probably know your family's tastes better than anyone; and they, in turn, will tell you better than any other guest exactly what they think of your cooking!

All these recipes are rewarding to prepare and, most important of all, they should make meal times at home enjoyable for everyone. So why not ask some old friends round too and spread the enjoyment a little further?

Whether your family's taste is for simple plaice or you're looking for a new way with canned tuna or for something a little more unusual, you'll find the answer here, with suggestions to suit every purse, every season and every family occasion. For a simple mid-week meal, try Smoked Mackerel Kedgeree; for a relaxed Sunday lunch, go for Cod and Pear Pie with Sultanas; and for a special birthday dinner, what about Red Snapper Creole?

CRISPY TUNA AND EGG

1 × 198 g (7 oz) can tuna, drained and flaked
4 tablespoons sweetcorn
4 hard-boiled eggs, chopped
25 g (1 oz) butter
3 tablespoons plain flour
300 ml (½ pint) milk
125 g (4 oz) Cheddar cheese, grated
1 tablespoon chopped chives
salt and pepper
1 × 25 g (1 oz) packet potato crisps, crushed
chopped chives to garnish

Place the fish in a 1.2 litre (2 pint) ovenproof dish. Spoon the sweetcorn and egg over the top.

Melt the butter in a saucepan, stir in the flour and cook for 1 minute. Gradually blend in the milk, then heat, stirring, until the sauce thickens. Add the cheese, chives, and salt and pepper to taste. Pour over the fish.

Sprinkle the crisps over the top and cook in a preheated moderate oven, 180°C (350°F), Gas Mark 4, for 30 minutes.

Serve hot, garnished with chives.
Serves 4

CHILLI SEAFOOD PIZZA

15 g (½ oz) fresh yeast
150 ml (¼ pint) tepid water
200 g (7 oz) plain flour
1 teaspoon salt
1 tablespoon olive oil
TOMATO SAUCE:
1–2 tablespoons oil
1 clove garlic, crushed
2–3 shallots, chopped
250 g (8 oz) tomatoes, skinned, seeded and chopped
150 ml (¼ pint) dry white wine
1 teaspoon dried mixed herbs
salt and pepper
TOPPING:
1 tablespoon dried oregano
2–3 green chilli peppers, seeded and thinly sliced
1 × 198 g (7 oz) can tuna fish, drained and flaked
125 g (4 oz) peeled prawns
125 g (4 oz) Bel Paese or Mozzarella cheese, grated
1 × 50 g (1¾ oz) can anchovies, drained
40 g (1½ oz) stuffed olives, halved

Cream the yeast with the water. Sift the flour and salt into a large bowl, make a well in the centre and pour in the oil and yeast mixture and knead to a soft, elastic dough; this will take 8 minutes by hand or 4 to 5 minutes in a food processor or electric blender. Cover and leave to rise in a warm place for 2½ to 3 hours, until doubled in size.

Meanwhile, make the tomato sauce. Heat the oil in a pan, add the garlic and shallots and cook for about 5 minutes, until golden. Add the tomatoes, wine and mixed herbs. Bring to the boil and cook rapidly for 20 minutes, until thickened. Season with salt and pepper to taste and leave to cool.

Place the dough on a floured surface and knead lightly. Roll out to fit a large baking sheet, measuring 25 × 30 cm (10 × 12 inches). Turn the dough during rolling to prevent shrinking.

Place on a large piece of floured cardboard. Using the fingertips, push the dough from the centre outwards to make the edges twice as thick as the rest.

Spread with the tomato sauce and sprinkle with the oregano. Spoon over the chillies, tuna and prawns, and sprinkle with the cheese. Arrange the anchovies in a lattice over the top and decorate with the olives.

Slide the pizza onto a hot baking sheet and bake in a preheated hot oven, 230°C (450°F), Gas Mark 8, for 15 to 20 minutes. Serve immediately.
Serves 6 to 8

LEFT: *Chilli Seafood Pizza*
RIGHT: *Red Snapper Creole; Marinated Mackerel*

RED SNAPPER CREOLE

4 × 175 g (6 oz) red snappers, cleaned
50 g (2 oz) plain flour
salt and pepper
1 lemon, sliced
SAUCE:
40 g (1½ oz) butter
2 small onions, chopped
2 celery sticks, chopped
1 green pepper, chopped
grated rind of 1 lemon
2 cloves
2 tablespoons chopped parsley
pinch thyme
pinch rosemary
1 bay leaf
2 cloves garlic, crushed
black pepper
2 × 539 g (1 lb 3 oz) cans tomatoes
1 tablespoon Worcestershire sauce
dash of Tabasco

First prepare the sauce. Heat the butter in a frying pan and gently fry the onion, celery and pepper until they begin to soften. Add the lemon rind, cloves, herbs, garlic and black pepper, and fry for 1 to 2 minutes longer.

Add the tomatoes and simmer over moderate heat, uncovered, for 20 minutes until well reduced and fairly thick. Then add the Worcestershire sauce and Tabasco. Sprinkle the fish with seasoned flour and arrange in an ovenproof dish with the lemon slices on top. Pour the sauce over them and bake in a preheated moderate oven, 180°C (350°F), Gas Mark 4, for 20 to 30 minutes, basting from time to time, until cooked. Discard the lemon slices and serve with plain boiled rice.

Serves 4

MARINATED MACKEREL

1 dessert apple, cored and cut into thin slices
625–750 g (1¼–1½ lb) smoked mackerel fillets
juice of 1 lemon
150 ml (¼ pint) dry cider
8 black peppercorns
6 juniper berries, lightly crushed
1 small onion, cut into rings
125 g (4 oz) seedless black grapes

Put the apple slices in a shallow ovenproof dish. Add the mackerel, flesh side down; make diagonal slashes on the skin side. Add the remaining ingredients, cover and leave to marinate for at least 2 hours.

Cook in a preheated moderately hot oven, 190°C (375°F), Gas Mark 5, for 30 minutes.

Serve hot with a potato and lettuce salad.

Serves 4

Mackerel Parcels

MACKEREL PARCELS

4 × 250 g (8 oz) mackerel, cleaned
salt and pepper
3–4 tablespoons olive oil
1 onion, finely chopped
2 celery sticks, finely chopped
1 tablespoon chopped parsley
1 clove garlic, crushed (optional)
½ teaspoon dried oregano or basil
juice of ½ lemon

Season the fish liberally with salt and pepper and brush with oil. Cut out heart-shaped pieces of foil 5 cm (2 inches) longer and wider than the fish; brush with oil.

Heat 2 tablespoons oil in a pan, add the onion and celery and fry gently for 10 minutes. Add the parsley, garlic if using, herbs, lemon juice, and a little salt and pepper.

Lay a fish on each foil shape and top with the vegetable mixture. Fold over the foil, sealing the edges well, to enclose the fish. Place on a baking sheet and cook in a preheated moderately hot oven, 200°C (400°F), Gas Mark 6, for 25 to 30 minutes. Serve in the partially opened foil cases.

Serves 4

HADDOCK AND SPINACH LAYER

500 g (1 lb) haddock fillet
150 ml (¼ pint) skimmed milk
1 bay leaf
salt and pepper
1 hard-boiled egg, chopped
500 g (1 lb) frozen leaf spinach
SAUCE:
150 ml (¼ pint) skimmed milk
25 g (1 oz) margarine
1 onion, chopped
25 g (1 oz) plain flour
grated nutmeg
TOPPING:
2 crispbreads, crushed
1 tomato, sliced, to garnish

Place the haddock in a pan. Add the milk, bay leaf, salt and pepper, then poach for about 10 minutes until the fish is tender. Drain, reserving the liquor. Flake the haddock and mix with the egg.

Cook the spinach as directed on the packet and drain well.

Make the fish liquor up to 300 ml (½ pint) with extra milk. Melt the margarine in a pan and fry the onion until soft. Stir in the flour and cook for 1 minute. Gradually blend in the milk then bring to the boil, stirring continuously. Cook, stirring, for a further 1 minute. Season to taste with salt, pepper and nutmeg. Stir in the fish and egg mixture; mix well.

Layer the spinach and fish mixture in a greased 1.2 litre (2 pint) ovenproof dish, finishing with a layer of spinach. Sprinkle with the crispbreads and cook in a preheated moderate oven, 180°C (350°F), Gas Mark 4, for 20 to 30 minutes.

Garnish with tomato slices.

Serves 4

MACKEREL WITH MUSTARD AND OATS

4 × 175 g (6 oz) mackerel fillets
2 teaspoons lemon juice
salt and pepper
25 g (1 oz) porridge oats
2 teaspoons mustard
TO GARNISH:
parsley sprigs
lemon twists

Place the mackerel on a grill rack lined with foil. Sprinkle with lemon juice and salt and pepper to taste.

Mix the oats and mustard together and spread lightly over the mackerel. Cook under a medium grill for 10 to 15 minutes. Transfer to a hot serving dish and garnish with parsley and lemon twists.

Serves 4

RIGHT: *Pitta Parcels; Tuna-Stuffed Potatoes*

PITTA PARCELS

500 g (1 lb) cod, coley or haddock, filleted and skinned
2 pitta breads
lemon wedges
MARINADE:
4 tablespoons olive oil
2 tablespoons white wine vinegar
1 teaspoon Worcestershire sauce
dash of Tabasco
salt and pepper
SALAD:
1 small onion, sliced
50 g (2 oz) white cabbage, shredded
½ green pepper, seeded and sliced
2 firm tomatoes, finely sliced
4 tablespoons Vinaigrette (see page 153)

Cut the fish into fairly thick strips and place in a bowl. Combine all the marinade ingredients and pour over the fish. Allow to marinate for at least 1 hour in the refrigerator.

Meanwhile, prepare the salad. Combine the onion, cabbage, pepper and tomato in a bowl, and pour over the dressing. Toss lightly.

Cut each of the pieces of pitta bread in half lengthways. Using a sharp knife, split them open and half-fill each one with salad.

Drain the fish, reserving the marinade. Grill the fish under a preheated hot grill for 10 minutes, turning once and brushing from time to time with marinade. Spoon the cooked fish into the pitta breads and squeeze over a little lemon juice.

Serves 4

TUNA-STUFFED POTATOES

4 × 175–250 g (6–8 oz) potatoes
1 tablespoon sunflower oil
FILLING:
1 tablespoon sunflower oil
1 small onion, finely chopped
50 g (2 oz) button mushrooms, finely sliced
1 × 175 g (6 oz) can tuna fish
2 tablespoons chopped parsley
pinch of sage
freshly ground black pepper
parsley sprigs to garnish

Scrub the potatoes, dry well and prick all over with a fork. Cut a thin slit all round the potato as if you were going to cut it in half lengthways. Rub a little oil over each potato and bake in a preheated moderately hot oven, 200°C (400°F), Gas Mark 6, for 1 hour until tender.

Meanwhile, prepare the filling. Heat the oil and fry the onion gently for 4 to 5 minutes. Add the mushrooms and fry for a further 3 to 4 minutes.

When the potatoes are cooked, cut in half where marked. Lower the oven temperature to 190°C (375°F), Gas Mark 5.

Scoop out the inside of the potato and mash. Add the onion and mushroom mixture, tuna fish, herbs and black pepper. Spoon the stuffing into the potato skins and bake for 15 minutes. Garnish with parsley sprigs and serve with a mixed salad.

Serves 4

FISH CURRY

25 g (1 oz) margarine
1 onion, chopped
½ green pepper, cored, seeded and chopped
1 carrot, thinly sliced
3 teaspoons curry powder
1 tablespoon plain flour
300 ml (½ pint) Fish stock (see page 146)
1 teaspoon lemon juice
1 small apple, peeled, cored and chopped
1 tablespoon sultanas
500 g (1 lb) haddock fillet or coley, cut into cubes
salt and pepper
chopped parsley to garnish

Melt the margarine in a pan and fry the onion, pepper, carrot and curry powder for 5 minutes. Stir in the flour and cook for 1 minute. Gradually blend in the stock and lemon juice. Heat, stirring until the sauce thickens.

Add the apple, sultanas and fish, then season to taste with salt and pepper. Cover and simmer for 20 to 25 minutes.

Transfer to a hot serving dish and garnish with chopped parsley. Serve with a selection of accompaniments, such as boiled rice, sliced tomato, diced cucumber and natural yogurt.

Serves 4

BAKED COD MEDLEY

4 cod cutlets
2 teaspoons lemon juice
freshly ground black pepper
15 g (½ oz) butter
1 onion, finely chopped
1 green pepper, cored, seeded and chopped
3 celery sticks, chopped
6 tomatoes, skinned and chopped
garlic salt
½ teaspoon oregano
parsley sprigs to garnish

Wash and dry the cutlets and place in a shallow, ovenproof dish. Sprinkle with the lemon juice and pepper to taste.

Melt the butter in a pan and lightly fry the onion, green pepper and celery. Add the tomatoes, garlic salt to taste, and oregano. Bring to the boil, cover and simmer for 10 to 15 minutes.

Spoon the vegetables over the fish, cover with foil and cook in a preheated moderate oven, 180°C (350°F), Gas Mark 4, for 30 minutes. Serve garnished with parsley.

Serves 4

SMOKED HADDOCK AU GRATIN

500 g (1 lb) smoked haddock fillets
milk for poaching
50 g (2 oz) butter
25 g (1 oz) plain flour
175 ml (6 fl oz) single cream
salt and pepper
50 g (2 oz) Cheddar cheese, grated
25 g (1 oz) fresh breadcrumbs
parsley sprigs to garnish

Put the haddock fillets in a saucepan, pour over enough milk to cover and poach gently for 15 minutes. Drain, reserving the milk, and flake the fish.

Melt the butter in a clean saucepan. Add the flour and cook, stirring, for 2 minutes. Gradually stir in the cream and 175 ml (6 fl oz) of the reserved poaching milk. Bring to the boil, stirring, and simmer until thickened. Season with salt and pepper to taste. Stir in all but 1 tablespoon of the cheese and, when it has melted, fold in the flaked fish. Turn into a greased casserole.

Mix together the breadcrumbs and remaining cheese and sprinkle over the top. Cook in a preheated moderately hot oven, 190°C (375°F), Gas Mark 5, for 20 minutes or until the top is golden brown. Garnish with parsley.

Serves 4

WHOLE FISH WITH TOMATO SAUCE

1 × 1.5 kg (3 lb) whole bass, bream or brill, cleaned
2 tablespoons plain flour
salt and pepper
65 g ($2\frac{1}{2}$ oz) butter
1 onion, chopped
1 green pepper, cored, seeded and chopped
1 red pepper, cored, seeded and chopped
2 celery sticks, chopped
2 × 397 g (14 oz) cans tomatoes
1 tablespoon tomato purée
1 tablespoon Worcestershire sauce
1 tablespoon lemon juice
few drops of Tabasco sauce
1 bay leaf
parsley sprigs to garnish

Rinse the fish and pat dry with kitchen paper. Season the flour and rub this all over the fish, inside and out. Place the fish in a casserole or baking dish into which it fits snugly.

Melt the butter in a saucepan. Add the onion, green and red peppers and celery and fry until the onion is softened. Stir in the tomatoes with their juice, tomato purée, Worcestershire sauce, lemon juice, Tabasco and the bay leaf. Bring to the boil and simmer for 15 minutes or until the vegetables are tender.

Remove the bay leaf, then purée the sauce by rubbing through a sieve or working in an electric blender. Adjust the seasoning, then pour the sauce around the fish. Cook in a preheated moderate oven, 180°C (350°F), Gas Mark 4, for 45 minutes or until the fish is tender. Baste the fish frequently with the sauce during cooking. Garnish with parsley.

Serves 4 to 6

BUYING FISH

You should always check that the fish you are buying – whatever the variety – is very fresh. Fresh fish can be recognised by its firm flesh; clear, full and shiny eyes; bright red gills; shiny moist skin; and clean appetising smell. When buying white fish fillets, look for neat, trim fillets and a white translucent flesh. Smoked fish should have a fresh smoky aroma and a glossy appearance. Frozen fish should be frozen solid with no sign of thawing, no matter how partial, and the packaging should not be damaged. Shellfish should have tightly closed undamaged shells.

LEFT: *Fish Curry*
RIGHT: *Cheddar Cod*

CHEDDAR COD

4 cod cutlets or steaks
2 teaspoons lemon juice
salt and pepper
SAUCE:
25 g (1 oz) margarine
25 g (1 oz) plain flour
300 ml ($\frac{1}{2}$ pint) skimmed milk
75 g (3 oz) Cheddar cheese, grated
$\frac{1}{2}$ teaspoon made mustard
TO GARNISH:
parsley sprigs
1 tomato, cut into quarters

Wash and dry the cod and place in a shallow ovenproof dish. Sprinkle with the lemon juice and salt and pepper to taste.

Place the margarine, flour and milk in a pan. Heat, whisking continuously until the sauce thickens. Continue cooking for 1 minute. Stir in the cheese, mustard and salt and pepper to taste.

Pour the sauce over the cod and cook in a preheated moderate oven, 180°C (350°F), Gas Mark 4, for 30 minutes. Garnish with parsley and tomato wedges.

Serves 4

FISH LASAGNE

75 g (3 oz) butter
1 kg (2 lb) smoked haddock
1.75 litres (3 pints) milk
1 onion, halved
1 celery stick
75 g (3 oz) plain flour
salt and freshly ground black pepper
grated nutmeg
50 g (2 oz) Parmesan cheese, grated
50 g (2 oz) Mozzarella cheese, coarsely grated
250 g (8 oz) lasagne

Butter a shallow ovenproof dish, using 15 g ($\frac{1}{2}$ oz) butter. Place the smoked haddock, milk, onion and celery in the saucepan, bring to the boil over a moderate heat and simmer gently for 5 minutes.

Remove from the heat and allow to cool. When nearly cold, strain the milk into a jug and flake the fish, discarding any skin and bones. Put to one side.

Melt the remaining butter in a pan over a low heat. Stir in the flour and cook for 1–2 minutes. Remove from the heat and gradually stir in the milk. Return to the heat and bring back to the boil, stirring continuously. Season to taste with black pepper and nutmeg. Remove from the heat and stir in three-quarters of the grated cheeses and the flaked fish.

Meanwhile, cook the lasagne in boiling salted water for 10 to 15 minutes (or according to package instructions) and drain well.

Cover the base of a fairly shallow ovenproof dish with the fishy sauce and place a layer of lasagne on top. Continue alternating layers of sauce and lasagne until both are used up, ending with a layer of sauce.

Finally, sprinkle with the remaining grated cheese.

Bake in a preheated moderate oven, 180°C (350°F), Gas Mark 4, for 45 minutes, until golden brown and bubbling on top. Serve at once accompanied by a green salad.

Serves 6

Kipper and Tomato Bake; Herring and Apple Pie

KIPPER AND TOMATO BAKE

4 kippers
150 ml ($\frac{1}{4}$ pint) milk
1 tablespoon fresh breadcrumbs
50 g (2 oz) butter
2 tablespoons chopped parsley
juice of $\frac{1}{2}$ lemon
freshly ground black pepper
200 g (7 oz) tomatoes, peeled and sliced

Just cover the kippers in milk and poach gently for about 5 minutes. Drain, reserving the poaching liquid, and allow to cool.

Skin and bone the kippers and flake the flesh. Moisten with a little of the poaching liquid. Add the breadcrumbs, butter, half the parsley, lemon juice, and season to taste with black pepper.

Spread in a lightly greased ovenproof dish and cover with the sliced tomatoes. Bake in a preheated moderate oven, 160°C (325°F), Gas Mark 3, for 20 minutes.

Sprinkle with the remaining chopped parsley before serving.

Serves 4

HERRING AND APPLE PIE

175 g (6 oz) plain flour
pinch of salt
90 g ($3\frac{1}{2}$ oz) butter
cold water to mix (about 6 teaspoons)

FILLING:

25 g (1 oz) butter
4 herrings, filleted and skinned
500 g (1 lb) potatoes, finely sliced
500 g (1 lb) cooking apples, peeled, cored and sliced
1 tablespoon chopped parsley
1 tablespoon chopped tarragon
1 tablespoon lemon juice
salt and pepper
1 egg, beaten

Sift the flour and salt into a mixing basin. Using both hands, rub the butter into the flour between finger and thumb until the mixture looks like fine breadcrumbs. Sprinkle evenly with water and stir with a palette knife until the dough begins to stick together in large lumps. Turn onto a floured surface and knead lightly. Allow to 'rest' for at least 15 minutes.

Meanwhile, lightly butter a deep pie dish. Cut the herring fillets into bite-sized slices.

Arrange the herring, potato and apple in alternate layers, seasoning with herbs, lemon juice, salt and pepper as you go. Dot with the remaining butter.

Roll out the pastry and cover the pie. Glaze with beaten egg and bake in a preheated moderate oven, 180°C (350°F), Gas Mark 4, for 45 minutes.

Serves 4

COD WITH MUSHROOMS

4 cod steaks
175 g (6 oz) mushrooms, sliced
4 tomatoes, skinned and sliced
1 clove garlic, crushed
2 tablespoons white wine
1 tablespoon lemon juice
salt and pepper
chopped parsley to garnish

Place the cod steaks in a well-greased ovenproof dish. Top with the mushrooms, tomatoes and garlic. Pour over the wine and lemon juice and season well with salt and pepper.

Cover with foil and cook in a preheated moderate oven, 180°C (350°F), Gas Mark 4, for 30 minutes. Garnish with chopped parsley.
Serves 4

PLAICE WITH SPINACH

750 g (1½ lb) spinach
3 tablespoons single cream
25 g (1 oz) butter, flaked
salt and pepper
grated nutmeg
8 small plaice fillets, skinned
2 tablespoons grated Parmesan cheese
tomato wedges to garnish

Cook the spinach, with just the water clinging to the leaves after washing, until tender. Drain thoroughly, then press through a sieve. Mix in the cream and butter. Season well with salt, pepper and nutmeg. Place in a greased casserole.

Roll up the plaice fillets and secure with cocktail sticks. Arrange them on the spinach and sprinkle with the cheese. Cover and cook in a preheated moderate oven, 180°C (350°F), Gas Mark 4, for 30 minutes. Garnish with tomato wedges.
Serves 4

HERRINGS IN OATMEAL

4 herrings
salt and pepper
125 g (4 oz) oatmeal
25 g (1 oz) butter
1 tablespoon oil
lemon wedges to serve

Cut the heads off the fish, gut them and remove the backbones. Rub the fish with a little salt. Rinse and dry, then sprinkle with salt and pepper.

Coat the fish with oatmeal, pressing it in well. Heat the butter and oil in a frying pan, add the fish and fry for about 8 minutes, turning once. Drain on kitchen paper and serve with lemon wedges.
Serves 4

FISHERMAN'S PIE

350 ml (12 fl oz) milk
1 bay leaf
1 onion, quartered
350 g (12 oz) smoked haddock or cod
350 g (12 oz) fresh haddock or whiting
25 g (1 oz) unsalted butter
25 g (1 oz) plain flour
125 g (4 oz) peeled prawns
125 g (4 oz) frozen peas
2 tablespoons chopped parsley
salt and pepper
2 × 370 g (13 oz) packets wholewheat puff pastry, thawed
beaten egg to glaze
TO GARNISH:
orange wedges
watercress sprigs

Place the milk, bay leaf and onion in a large saucepan and bring to the boil. Add the fish and cook gently for 10 minutes, until tender. Remove with a slotted spoon. Make up the cooking liquid to 350 ml (12 fl oz) with water and set aside.

Remove the skin and bones from the fish and flake the flesh.

Melt the butter in a large pan, stir in the flour and cook for 1 minute. Gradually stir in the reserved cooking liquid until smooth, then bring to the boil. Remove from the heat and stir in the fish, prawns, peas, parsley, and salt and pepper to taste. Leave to cool.

Roll out half the pastry on a floured surface to an oval about 23 × 30 cm (9 × 12 inches). Place on a dampened baking sheet and pour on the cooled fish mixture. Roll out the remaining pastry to the same size and shape, and place on top. Trim, reserving any left-over pastry for decoration. Dampen, seal and flute the edge. Make a small hole in the centre and decorate with pastry trimmings. Brush with beaten egg.

Bake in a preheated moderately hot oven, 200°C (400°F), Gas Mark 6, for 30 to 35 minutes. Lower the temperature to 180°C (350°F), Gas Mark 4, and bake for a further 20 minutes. Serve hot.

Serves 4 to 6

STUFFED MACKEREL WITH GOOSEBERRY SAUCE

1 onion, sliced
4 small mackerel, cleaned
salt and pepper
1 × 283 g (10 oz) can gooseberries
15 g (½ oz) fresh white breadcrumbs
pinch of allspice
5 cm (2 inch) strip orange rind, shredded
few tarragon leaves, chopped
4 tablespoons tarragon vinegar
1 × 539 g (19 oz) can new potatoes, drained
SAUCE:
1 tablespoon horseradish sauce
2 tablespoons soured cream

Place half the onion in a casserole dish. Sprinkle the inside of the mackerel with salt. Drain the gooseberries, reserving the syrup, and chop half of them. Mix with the breadcrumbs, allspice, orange rind, chopped tarragon, and pepper to taste; use to stuff the mackerel. Place in the casserole and cover with the remaining onion. Pour in the vinegar and 4 tablespoons of the gooseberry syrup.

Cook in a moderate oven, 180°C (350°F), Gas Mark 4, for 45 minutes, adding the potatoes after 15 minutes. Meanwhile, work the remaining gooseberries and syrup in a blender to make a purée. Mix with the horseradish, cream, and salt and pepper to taste to make the sauce.

Serve the mackerel hot with a mixed salad. Serve the sauce separately.

Serves 4

LEFT: *Cod with Mushrooms; Plaice with Spinach; Herrings in Oatmeal*
RIGHT: *Stuffed Mackerel with Gooseberry Sauce*

PILCHARD AND EGG SUPPER

2 × 227 g (8 oz) can pilchards in tomato sauce
2 hard-boiled eggs
2 celery sticks, chopped
125 g (4 oz) frozen peas
150 ml ($\frac{1}{4}$ pint) milk
25 g (1 oz) butter
3 tablespoons plain flour
pinch of sugar
salt and pepper
1 × 25 g (1 oz) packet potato crisps, crushed
chopped parsley to garnish

Drain the pilchards, reserving the juice. Arrange the pilchards in a shallow ovenproof dish. Cut the eggs into quarters and place in the dish. Scatter the celery and peas over the top.

Make the pilchard juice up to 300 ml ($\frac{1}{2}$ pint) with the milk.

Melt the butter in a saucepan and stir in the flour. Cook for 1 minute, then gradually blend in the liquid. Heat, stirring, until the sauce thickens. Add the sugar and salt and pepper to taste.

Pour the sauce over the fish, sprinkle with the crisps and cook in a preheated moderate oven, 180°C (350°F), Gas Mark 4, for 30 minutes.

Garnish with parsley. Serve immediately.

Serves 4

POTATO COD BAKE

625 g (1$\frac{1}{4}$ lb) cod fillet
1 small onion, finely chopped
6 black peppercorns
2 small dessert apples, peeled, cored and sliced
salt and pepper
$\frac{1}{2}$ teaspoon dried thyme
8 tablespoons dry cider
8–10 tablespoons milk
25 g (1 oz) butter
3 tablespoons plain flour

TOPPING:
2 × 85 g (3 oz) packet instant potato
600 ml (1 pint) boiling water
2 tablespoons milk
knob of butter
grated nutmeg

Place the cod, onion, peppercorns, apple, salt, thyme and cider in a buttered 1.75 litre (3 pint) ovenproof dish. Cover and cook in a preheated moderate oven, 160°C (325°F), Gas Mark 3, for 20 minutes.

Strain the fish liquor and make up to 300 ml ($\frac{1}{2}$ pint) with the milk. Melt the butter in a saucepan and stir in the flour. Cook for 1 minute, then gradually blend in the fish liquor. Heat, stirring until the sauce thickens. Add salt and pepper to taste.

Flake the fish and add to the sauce with the onion and apple. Heat through gently and transfer to the buttered ovenproof dish.

Make up the potato with the boiling water as directed on the packet. Beat in the milk and butter. Add nutmeg, salt and pepper to taste.

Spread the potato over the fish and mark a pattern on top with a fork. Place under a preheated medium grill for 2 to 3 minutes. Serve immediately.

Serves 4

HERBY COD CASSEROLE

500 g (1 lb) cod fillets
15 g ($\frac{1}{2}$ oz) butter
15 g ($\frac{1}{2}$ oz) plain flour
250 ml (8 fl oz) milk
$\frac{1}{4}$ teaspoon garlic salt
$\frac{1}{4}$ teaspoon dried thyme
$\frac{1}{4}$ teaspoon dried oregano
6 spring onions, finely chopped
salt and pepper
paprika

Arrange the cod fillets in a greased baking dish. Melt the butter in a saucepan. Add the flour and cook, stirring, for 1 minute. Gradually stir in the milk and bring to the boil. Simmer, stirring, until thickened. Stir in the garlic salt, herbs, spring onions and salt and pepper to taste. Pour over the fish and sprinkle with a little paprika.

Cook in a preheated moderate oven, 180°C (350°F), Gas Mark 4, for 30 minutes or until the fish is tender.

Serves 4

HERB FISH CAKES

750 g (1½ lb) potatoes, chopped
1 large onion, sliced
salt and pepper
2 tablespoons milk
25 g (1 oz) butter
500 g (1 lb) white fish fillet, skinned and chopped
2 tablespoons chopped parsley
1 teaspoon dried mixed herbs
2 eggs, separated
dry breadcrumbs for coating
oil for shallow-frying
parsley sprigs to garnish

Cook the potatoes and onion in boiling salted water until soft. Drain and mash, then beat in the milk.

Melt the butter in a saucepan, add the fish and fry for 10 to 15 minutes or until tender. Flake the fish and add to the potato. Stir in the herbs, egg yolks, and salt and pepper to taste. Mix well, then leave to cool.

On a floured surface, divide the mixture into 4 and shape each piece into a flat cake. Lightly beat the egg white. Dip the fish cakes into the egg white, then coat with breadcrumbs.

Heat the oil in a frying pan and fry the fish cakes until crisp and golden. Transfer to a warmed serving dish and garnish with parsley. Serve immediately.

Serves 4

PLAICE WITH BANANA AND NUTS

625 g (1¼ lb) plaice fillet
25 g (1 oz) butter
2 bananas, sliced
50 g (2 oz) peanuts
50 g (2 oz) Cheddar cheese, grated
parsley sprigs to garnish
SAUCE:
25 g (1 oz) butter
3 tablespoons plain flour
300 ml (½ pint) milk
3 tablespoons natural yogurt
salt and pepper

Place the fish in a greased shallow ovenproof dish. Dot with the butter and cook in a preheated moderate oven, 180°C (350°F), Gas Mark 4, for 10 minutes. Remove from the oven and arrange the banana and nuts over the fish.

To make the sauce, melt the butter in a pan and stir in the flour. Cook for 1 minute, then blend in the milk. Heat, stirring until the sauce thickens. Stir in the yogurt, with salt and pepper to taste.

Pour the sauce over the fish, sprinkle with the cheese and return to the oven for 15 minutes.

Garnish with parsley and serve.

Serves 4

LEFT: *Pilchard and Egg Supper*
RIGHT: *Mushroom-Stuffed Plaice*

MUSHROOM-STUFFED PLAICE

4 whole plaice, cleaned
1 tablespoon oil
1 onion, finely chopped
1 clove garlic, crushed
75 g (3 oz) fresh brown breadcrumbs
125 g (4 oz) mushrooms, finely chopped
1 tomato, skinned and chopped
1 teaspoon chopped marjoram
2 teaspoons chopped parsley
dash of Worcestershire sauce
watercress sprigs to garnish

Trim the fish by cutting the fins and tail with a sharp knife. With the white side uppermost, make an incision down the backbone of each fish. Working from each end of the cut in turn, on one half of the fish, cut about two-thirds of the way around to form a pocket. Repeat on the other half.

Heat the oil in a pan, add the onion, garlic and breadcrumbs and fry until the breadcrumbs are crisp. Stir in the remaining ingredients and sauté for 2 minutes. Divide the filling between the prepared pockets.

Place the fish in a buttered ovenproof dish and cover with foil. Cook in a preheated moderately hot oven, 200°C (400°F), Gas Mark 6, for 20 to 30 minutes.

Garnish with watercress. Serve with grilled tomatoes and mushrooms.

Serves 4 to 6

TUNA FISH CAKES

300 g (10 oz) potatoes, cooked
25 g (1 oz) butter or margarine
1 × 198 g (7 oz) and 1 × 99 g ($3\frac{1}{2}$ oz) can tuna, drained and flaked
2 tablespoons chopped parsley
salt and pepper
2 eggs, beaten
75 g (3 oz) dry breadcrumbs
oil for shallow frying
parlsey sprigs to garnish
lemon wedges to serve

Mash the potatoes with the butter or margarine, then mix in the tuna, parsley, salt and pepper to taste and half the beaten egg.

Chill the mixture for 20 minutes, then place on a floured surface and shape into a roll. Cut into 8 slices and shape each into a flat round, about 6 cm ($2\frac{1}{2}$ inches) in diameter. Dip into the remaining egg, then coat with breadcrumbs.

Heat the oil in a frying pan, add the fish cakes and fry for 2 to 3 minutes on each side or until golden brown and heated through. Garnish each fish cake with a parsley sprig. Serve with lemon wedges.

Serves 4

TUNA NOODLE CASSEROLE

500 g (1 lb) noodles
salt and pepper
1 × 298 g ($10\frac{1}{2}$ oz) can condensed cream of mushroom soup
2 tablespoons medium sherry
2 × 198 g (7 oz) cans tuna fish, drained and flaked
6 spring onions, finely chopped
4 hard-boiled eggs, sliced
25 g (1 oz) crisps, crushed
2 tablespoons grated Parmesan cheese

Cook the noodles in boiling salted water until tender. Drain well, then mix in the soup and sherry. Put about one-third of the noodle mixture in a greased casserole. Cover with half the tuna, spring onions and eggs, then season with salt and pepper to taste. Repeat the layers and top with the remaining noodle mixture.

Mix together the crisps and cheese and sprinkle over the top. Cook in a preheated moderate oven, 180°C (350°F), Gas Mark 4, for 25 to 30 minutes or until the top is golden brown.

Serves 4 to 6

GRILLED FISH CAKES

1 × 213 g ($7\frac{1}{2}$ oz) can pink or red salmon, drained
500 g (1 lb) potatoes, boiled
25 g (1 oz) margarine
1 tablespoon milk (optional)
1 heaped tablespoon chopped parsley
pepper to taste
finely grated rind of $\frac{1}{2}$ lemon
1 tablespoon oil
parsley sprigs to garnish

Place the salmon in a basin and mash with a fork, including the bones and skin.

Mash the potatoes with the margarine; add the milk if the mixture seems too dry. Add the salmon, parsley, pepper and lemon rind and mix well. Shape into small, flat cakes.

Brush the grill pan with oil and arrange the cakes on the base. Pour the oil into a saucer. Screw up a piece of kitchen paper, dip into the oil and use to dab the tops of the fish cakes. Cook under a preheated moderate grill for about 4 to 5 minutes on each side.

Garnish with parsley and serve with peas, a crisp green salad and wholewheat bread and butter.

Serves 4 to 6

LEFT: *Tuna Fish Cakes*
RIGHT: *Fish Pie; Smoked Haddock with Corn*

FISH PIE

500 g (1 lb) cod or haddock fillets
salt and pepper
1 tablespoon oil
50 g (2 oz) butter
1 large onion, chopped
1 × 397 g (14 oz) can tomatoes
1 clove garlic, crushed
125 g (4 oz) mushrooms, sliced
½ teaspoon dried thyme
1 teaspoon sugar
500 g (1 lb) potatoes, cooked
2 tablespoons milk
2 tablespoons grated Cheddar cheese

Place the fish in a saucepan with enough cold water to cover. Season to taste with salt and pepper. Bring to simmering point and simmer for 10 minutes.

Meanwhile, heat the oil and half the butter in a frying pan, add the onion and fry gently for 5 minutes or until softened. Stir in the tomatoes with their juice, garlic, mushrooms and thyme and cook for 5 minutes. Add the sugar, salt and pepper to taste.

Drain the fish, discard all skin and bones, then flake and add to the tomato mixture. Transfer to a 20 cm (8 inch) round deep pie dish.

Mash the potatoes with the remaining butter and the milk, and season well. Spread over the fish mixture and fork up. Sprinkle with the cheese and place in a preheated moderately hot oven, 200°C (400°F), Gas Mark 6, for about 20 minutes or until golden on top.

Serves 4

SMOKED HADDOCK WITH CORN

750 g (1½ lb) smoked haddock fillets
25 g (1 oz) butter
25 g (1 oz) plain flour
150 ml (¼ pint) milk
salt and pepper
1 × 326 g (11½ oz) can sweetcorn, drained
4 tablespoons soured cream
parsley sprig to garnish

Place the haddock in a large frying pan and add just enough boiling water to cover. Simmer, uncovered, for 5 minutes, skimming the surface occasionally. Remove the fish, reserving 150 ml (¼ pint) of the cooking liquor, cut into pieces and place in a casserole.

Melt the butter in a saucepan and stir in the flour. Cook, stirring, for 1 minute, then gradually add the milk and reserved cooking liquor. Bring to the boil, stirring constantly; season well with salt and pepper.

Stir in the sweetcorn and pour the sauce over the haddock. Cover and cook in a preheated moderate oven, 180°C (350°F), Gas Mark 4, for 20 minutes.

Just before serving, stir in the soured cream. Garnish with parsley and serve accompanied by boiled potatoes or crusty bread.

Serves 4

FISH CASSOULET

175 g (6 oz) dried haricot beans, soaked overnight
2 tablespoons olive oil
50 g (2 oz) bacon, diced
2 cloves garlic, chopped
1 medium onion, sliced
1 leek, sliced
125 g (4 oz) halibut, filleted and skinned
250 g (8 oz) coley, filleted and skinned
1 small mackerel, filleted and skinned
3 large tomatoes, skinned and chopped
salt and pepper
1 bay leaf
150 ml (¼ pint) dry white wine

Boil the beans in the water in which they have soaked for 1 to 1½ hours until tender. (Do not add salt as this tends to make them hard.) Drain and put to one side.

Heat the oil and fry the bacon, garlic, onion and leek for 5 to 8 minutes over moderate heat until soft.

Cut the fish into bite-sized pieces, discarding all the bones. Layer with the fried vegetables, bacon and chopped tomatoes in a large casserole dish, and season with salt and pepper. Add the bay leaf and pour on the white wine.

Cover and bake in a preheated moderate oven, 180°C (350°F), Gas Mark 4, for about 1 hour.

Serves 4

FISH IN SPICY YOGURT

1 kg (2 lb) haddock, filleted and skinned
2 tablespoons chopped coriander to garnish

MARINADE:

300 ml (½ pint) natural yogurt
4 whole cardamom pods
½ teaspoon whole fennel seeds
½ teaspoon whole cumin seeds
1 tablespoon ground coriander
2 teaspoons ground cumin
½ teaspoon ground turmeric
½ teaspoon ground ginger
½ teaspoon chilli powder
1 tablespoon olive oil

First prepare the marinade by combining all the ingredients. Then place the fish in it and marinate in the refrigerator for about 2 hours, turning occasionally.

Lift the fish out of the marinade and place in an ovenproof dish. Pour the marinade on top and bake in a preheated moderate oven, 180°C (350°F), Gas Mark 4, for about 30 minutes until the fish flakes easily.

Garnish with chopped coriander and serve with rice.

Serves 6

COD AND PEAR PIE WITH SULTANAS

275 g (9 oz) plain flour
pinch salt
140 g (4½ oz) butter
cold water to mix (about 9 teaspoons)

FILLING:

750 g (1½ lb) cod, filleted and skinned
salt and pepper
6 firm pears, peeled, cored and sliced
4 eggs, lightly beaten
grated rind of 1 lemon
juice of 1 lemon
50 g (2 oz) sultanas
150 ml (¼ pint) single cream

Sift the flour and a pinch of salt into a mixing basin. Using both hands, rub the butter into the flour between finger and thumb until the mixture resembles fine breadcrumbs. Sprinkle evenly with water and stir with a palette knife until the dough begins to stick together in large lumps. Turn onto a floured surface and knead lightly. Allow to 'rest' for at least 15 minutes.

Meanwhile, cover the cod in cold salted water and bring slowly up to simmering point. Poach gently for about 5 minutes until tender. Drain the fish, removing skin and bones, and flake.

Mix with the pears, three quarters of the beaten egg, lemon rind, lemon juice and sultanas and season with salt and pepper.

Roll out the pastry and use two-thirds of it to line a deep pie dish. Fill with the fish mixture and cover with a pastry lid. Cut a hole in the lid and glaze with the remaining beaten egg. Bake in a preheated moderately hot oven, 200°C (400°F), Gas Mark 6, for 35 to 40 minutes until golden brown.

When the pie is cooked, pour in the cream through the hole in the lid and shake gently to distribute it evenly.

Serve with julienne strips of carrot and courgette.

Serves 4

Cod and Pear Pie with Sultanas; Fish Cassoulet

EGGS FU-YUNG

3 dried Chinese mushrooms
3 spring onions
1 piece root ginger
2 tablespoons oil
1 clove garlic, crushed
25 g (1 oz) canned bamboo shoots, drained and diced
6 canned water chestnuts, drained and chopped
25 g (1 oz) frozen peeled prawns, thawed
1 × 177 g (6 oz) can crabmeat, drained
1 tablespoon dry sherry
salt
6 eggs, beaten
TO GARNISH:
radish flowers
cucumber twists

Soak the dried mushrooms in warm water for 15 minutes. Squeeze dry and discard the hard stalks, then chop the mushroom caps. Chop the spring onions and ginger finely.

Heat the oil in a wok or deep frying pan, add the spring onions, ginger and garlic and stir-fry for 1 minute. Add the mushrooms, bamboo shoots, and water chestnuts and cook for 30 seconds.

Stir in the prawns, crabmeat and sherry and season liberally with salt. Lower the heat and pour in the beaten eggs. Scramble until the mixture is just set.

Pile onto a warmed serving dish and serve immediately, garnished with radishes, cut into the shape of flowers, and cucumber twists.

Serves 4 to 6

Eggs Fu-Yung

SMOKED FISH FINGERS

350 g (12 oz) smoked fish fillet
1 bay leaf
250 g (8 oz) potatoes, peeled
salt and pepper
50 g (2 oz) butter
1 small onion, finely chopped
50 g (2 oz) plain flour
2 eggs, beaten
125 g (4 oz) fresh white breadcrumbs
oil for deep frying
1 lemon, quartered, to garnish
Rémoulade sauce (see page 152) to serve

Put the fish in a pan, cover with water, add the bay leaf and poach for 10 minutes. Skin the fish and remove any bones, then flake the flesh.

Boil the potatoes in salted water until tender. Drain well and mash with 25 g (1 oz) of the butter.

Melt the remaining butter in a pan and fry the onion until soft. Mix together the fish, potato, onion and salt and pepper to taste. Blend in half the beaten egg. Leave in a cool place for 15 to 20 minutes to firm up.

Shape the mixture into fingers, then coat in flour, beaten egg and breadcrumbs. Heat the oil to 190°C (375°F) and lower in half the fingers. Cook for 3 minutes or until golden, then drain on kitchen paper and keep warm while you cook the rest.

Serve garnished with lemon and hand the sauce round separately.

Serves 4

KIPPERS WITH MARMALADE

1 pair of kippers
15 g (½ oz) unsalted butter
TO SERVE:
orange wedges
1 slice buttered brown bread
1 tablespoon orange marmalade

Remove the head and trim the tail of the kippers with kitchen scissors. Line a grill pan with foil. Place the kippers on the foil, skin side uppermost, and cook under a preheated moderate grill for 1 minute. Turn the kippers over, dot with the butter and grill for a further 5 minutes, until sizzling.

Serve immediately, garnished with orange wedges and accompanied by the brown bread and marmalade.

Serves 1

NOTE: If you don't like the smell of cooking kippers, try this method: place them in a saucepan, cover with boiling water and put on the lid. Simmer for 5 minutes. Drain well.

MACKEREL IN HORSERADISH SAUCE

4 medium mackerel
2 teaspoons cornflour
3 tablespoons creamed horseradish
2 tablespoons lemon juice
4 tablespoons white wine
salt and pepper
cucumber slices to garnish (optional)

Cut the heads off the fish, then gut them and remove the backbones. Place the fish, skin side down, in a greased casserole.

Blend the cornflour into the horseradish, then gradually add the lemon juice and wine. Season with salt and pepper to taste and pour over the fish. Cover and cook in a preheated moderate oven, 160°C (325°F), Gas Mark 3, for 30 minutes, until tender.

Garnish with cucumber slices, if liked, before serving.

Serves 4

CHEESY COD

4 cod steaks
75 g (3 oz) Cheddar cheese, grated
1 teaspoon Worcestershire sauce
1 tablespoon milk
salt and pepper
parsley sprigs to garnish

Place the cod steaks on a greased grill pan and grill on one side for 4 to 5 minutes. Mix the remaining ingredients together, with salt and pepper to taste.

Turn the fish over and spread the uncooked side with the cheese mixture. Reduce the heat slightly and grill for about 5 minutes or until the fish is cooked and the topping golden and bubbling. Garnish with parsley.

Serves 4

Mackerel in Horseradish Sauce; Cheesy Cod

SMOKED MACKEREL KEDGEREE

3 hard-boiled eggs
250 g (8 oz) smoked mackerel fillet, flaked
175 g (6 oz) long-grain rice, cooked
40 g (1½ oz) butter
2 tablespoons single cream (optional)
1 tablespoon chopped parsley
1 tablespoon lemon juice
salt and pepper
TO GARNISH:
paprika
watercress sprigs

Separate one egg yolk from the white and keep on one side for garnish. Chop the white with the other eggs.

Combine the chopped eggs with the other ingredients in a large saucepan, adding salt and pepper to taste. Cover and heat gently for 3 to 4 minutes, shaking occasionally, until thoroughly heated. Transfer to a warmed serving dish.

Sieve the reserved yolk over the top and garnish with paprika and watercress. Serve hot.

Serves 4

SMOKED HADDOCK CRÊPES

125 g (4 oz) wholemeal flour
1 egg, beaten
300 ml (½ pint) milk
2–3 tablespoons oil
FILLING:
500 g (1 lb) smoked haddock fillets
300 ml (½ pint) milk
40 g (1½ oz) margarine
40 g (1½ oz) wholemeal flour
2 hard-boiled eggs, chopped
salt and pepper
25 g (1 oz) butter, melted
25 g (1 oz) grated Parmesan cheese

Sift the flour into a bowl and make a well in the centre. Add the egg, then gradually stir in half the milk and 1 tablespoon of oil. Beat thoroughly until smooth. Then add the remaining milk.

Heat a 15 cm (6 inch) omelette pan and add a few drops of oil. Pour in 1 tablespoon of the batter and tilt the pan to coat the bottom evenly. Cook until the underside is brown, then turn over and cook for a further 10 seconds. Turn onto a warmed plate.

Repeat with the remaining batter, making 12 pancakes. Stack, interleaved with greaseproof paper as they are cooked, keep warm.

Place the haddock in a pan, add the milk, cover and bring to the boil. Simmer for 5 minutes. Leave the fish to cool slightly in the pan, then lift out with a fish slice. Remove the skin and flake, discarding any bones. Strain the liquid and make up to 300 ml (½ pint) with extra milk if necessary; keep on one side.

Melt the margarine in a pan, remove from the heat and stir in the flour. Pour in the reserved liquid and stir until blended. Return to the heat and bring to the boil, stirring, until thickened. Add the eggs, fish, and salt and pepper to taste.

Place a spoonful of filling on each crêpe, roll up and place in an oiled shallow ovenproof dish. Brush with the melted butter and sprinkle with the Parmesan cheese. Cook in a preheated moderately hot oven, 190°C (375°F), Gas Mark 5, for 15 minutes until crisp. Serve immediately.

Serves 4 to 6

Smoked Haddock Crêpes

COD PROVENÇAL

1 tablespoon olive oil
1 onion, sliced
1 clove garlic, crushed
1 green pepper, cored, seeded and sliced
150 ml ($\frac{1}{4}$ pint) water
1 tablespoon tomato purée
3–4 tomatoes, skinned and quartered
750 g ($1\frac{1}{2}$ lb) cod fillet, cut into 4 pieces
salt and pepper
3–4 stuffed olives, sliced, to garnish

Heat the oil in a flameproof casserole. Add the onion and garlic and fry gently until transparent. Add the green pepper and continue cooking for 1 to 2 minutes. Stir in the water, tomato purée and tomatoes. Arrange the fish on top and season well with salt and pepper.

Cover and cook in a preheated moderate oven, 180°C (350°F), Gas Mark 4, for about 30 minutes or until the fish flakes easily with a fork.

Transfer to a warmed serving dish and garnish with sliced olives.

Serves 4

COD AND POTATO PIE

750 g ($1\frac{1}{2}$ lb) potatoes, grated
1 egg
4 tablespoons milk
250 g (8 oz) cod fillet, diced
50 g (2 oz) fresh breadcrumbs
1 onion, finely chopped
1 tomato, chopped
2 tablespoons chopped parsley
125 g (4 oz) Cheddar cheese, grated
salt and pepper
grated nutmeg
25 g (1 oz) butter
parsley sprigs to garnish

Cover the potatoes with cold water and leave to stand for 2 to 3 minutes; drain well.

Beat the egg and milk together in a bowl. Add the fish, breadcrumbs, onion, tomato, parsley, cheese, potato and salt, pepper and nutmeg to taste, mix well.

Place in a 1.2 litre (2 pint) casserole dish, dot with the butter. Cook in a preheated moderate oven, 160°C (325°F), Gas Mark 3, for 45 minutes to 1 hour, until the top is crisp and brown.

Serve immediately, garnished with parsley.

Serves 4

Cod and Potato Pie; Cod Provençal; Soused Mackerel

SOUSED MACKEREL

4 mackerel, cleaned and heads removed
1 teaspoon pickling spice
600 ml (1 pint) water
3 tablespoons vinegar
1 onion, chopped
1 red chilli pepper to garnish (optional)

Score the skin of the mackerel and put them in a large pan with the remaining ingredients.

Bring to the boil, then lower the heat and poach gently for 6 to 8 minutes.

Leave the mackerel in the cooking liquor until cold. Transfer to a serving dish and garnish with a chilli pepper if liked. Serve with wholemeal bread.

Serves 4

SALMON STEAKS WITH HERB BUTTER SAUCE

250 g (8 oz) carrots, cut into fine julienne strips
salt and pepper
75 g (3 oz) unsalted butter
1 tablespoon oil
6 × 175 g (6 oz) salmon steaks
350 g (12 oz) cucumber, peeled
150 ml (¼ pint) dry white wine
2 tablespoons chopped tarragon
2 tablespoons chopped chervil
1 tablespoon chopped chives

Cook the carrots in boiling salted water in a large pan for 1 minute; drain and leave on one side.

Melt 25 g (1 oz) of the butter and the oil in the same pan. Sprinkle the salmon steaks with salt and pepper to taste, add to the pan and fry for 5 to 7 minutes on each side. Transfer to a warmed serving dish and keep hot.

Cut the cucumber in half lengthways, remove the seeds and cut into 1 cm (½ inch) slices. Add to the pan with the carrots and wine, cover and cook for 4 to 5 minutes. Remove with a slotted spoon and arrange in a serving bowl, or around the fish; keep warm. Boil the liquor in the pan until it is reduced to 2 tablespoons.

Beat together the tarragon, chervil, chives and remaining butter in a basin. Beat in the reduced liquor until a smooth, thick herb sauce is obtained. Spoon onto the salmon and serve.

Serves 6

PICKLED HERRINGS

6 herrings, cleaned, backbone removed, then cut in half lengthways
2 small onions, sliced and separated into rings
2 dill cucumbers, sliced
dill leaves to garnish
MARINADE:
300 ml (½ pint) cider vinegar
300 ml (½ pint) dry cider
1 teaspoon soft brown sugar
2 bay leaves
4 cloves
6 black peppercorns
6 allspice berries
2 blades of mace
½ teaspoon sea salt
½ teaspoon chilli powder

Place the marinade ingredients in a saucepan, bring to the boil then simmer for 10 minutes.

Lay the herring fillets, flesh side uppermost, on a board. Divide the onion rings and cucumber slices between each fillet, laying along the fish. Roll up from head to tail and secure with a wooden cocktail stick.

Arrange the herring rolls in an ovenproof dish and pour over the marinade. Sprinkle with any remaining onion rings.

Cover with a lid or foil and cook in a preheated moderate oven, 180°C (350°F), Gas Mark 4, for 30 minutes.

Leave in the marinade until cool, then place in the refrigerator. Chill for 1 to 2 days before serving.

Garnish with dill leaves and serve with crusty bread and a green salad.

Serves 6

HERRINGS WITH APPLE AND HORSERADISH

4 small herrings, filleted
salt and pepper
2 tablespoons horseradish sauce
2 dessert apples, cored and grated
2 tablespoons cider
pinch of sugar
watercress to garnish

Place the herrings in a pan and add just enough water to cover. Add salt and pepper to taste. Bring to the boil, then lower the heat, cover and simmer for 10 to 15 minutes. Remove from the pan, drain and keep hot. Place the sauce in a pan with the apples and cider. Bring to the boil, then simmer for 3 minutes. Add sugar to taste.

Arrange the fish on a warmed serving plate and top with the sauce. Garnish with watercress.

Serves 4

LAYERED FISH CASSEROLE

50 g (2 oz) butter or margarine
4 rashers streaky bacon, derinded and chopped
2 onions, finely chopped
4 tomatoes, skinned and chopped
1 clove garlic, crushed
salt and pepper
1 tablespoon chopped parsley
4 haddock or cod fillets
1 tablespoon lemon juice
50 g (2 oz) fresh breadcrumbs
50 g (2 oz) Parmesan cheese, grated

Melt the butter in a frying pan. Add the bacon, onion, tomato and garlic, and fry until the onion is softened. Season to taste with salt and pepper, then place in a well-greased ovenproof dish and sprinkle with parsley. Arrange the fish on top and sprinkle with lemon juice.

Mix the breadcrumbs and cheese together and spoon evenly over the fish. Bake in a preheated moderate oven, 180°C (350°F), Gas Mark 4, for 30 minutes, until the fish is tender and the topping golden brown.

Serves 4

BAKED HALIBUT IN CIDER

1 onion, finely chopped
125 g (4 oz) mushrooms, chopped
4 halibut steaks
1 egg, beaten
3 tablespoons dry breadcrumbs
2 teaspoons lemon juice
salt and pepper
4 tablespoons cider
25 g (1 oz) butter
chopped parsley to garnish (optional)

Place the onion and mushrooms in an ovenproof dish.

Dip the fish steaks into the egg and coat with breadcrumbs. Arrange on top of the onion and mushrooms and sprinkle with the lemon juice, salt and pepper to taste. Spoon the cider over the fish.

Dot with butter and bake in a preheated moderate oven, 160°C (325°F), Gas Mark 3, for 40 minutes until tender. Garnish with parsley, if liked.

Serves 4

LEFT: *Salmon Steaks with Herb Butter Sauce*
RIGHT: *Layered Fish Casserole; Baked Halibut in Cider*

HERBED SMELTS WITH CUCUMBER SAUCE

4 tablespoons chopped parsley
2 tablespoons chopped chives
8 tablespoons plain flour
salt and pepper
6 tablespoons milk
750 g (1½ lb) smelts or sprats, cleaned
75 g (3 oz) butter
2 tablespoons vegetable oil
1 small cucumber, peeled, deseeded and cut into 1 cm (½ inch) lengths
300 ml (½ pint) dry white wine
2 × 142 ml (5 fl oz) cartons soured cream

Mix the parsley, chives and flour together on a flat plate and season. Pour the milk into a bowl. Turn each fish in the milk, then in the flour mixture until evenly coated.

Heat 50 g (2 oz) of the butter and the oil in a frying pan, add the fish a few at a time and fry for 1 minute on each side. Remove with a slotted spoon and drain on kitchen paper. Transer to a dish and keep warm.

To make the sauce, melt the remaining butter in a clean pan, add the cucumber sticks and fry for about 30 seconds. Add the wine with salt and pepper to taste and bring to the boil. Remove from the heat, then stir in the soured cream. Reheat the sauce but do not allow to boil. Pour the sauce over the fish and serve.

Serves 4

CURRIED SCALLOPS WITH SALSIFY

2 large carrots, peeled
175 g (6 oz) salsify, cut into 5 cm (2 inch) lengths
3 tablespoons plain flour
¾ teaspoon curry powder
salt and pepper
12 large scallops
4 tablespoons vegetable oil
300 ml (½ pint) medium white wine
2 tablespoons double cream

Cook the carrots and salsify together in boiling water until just tender. Drain and put to one side. Scoop the carrots into balls using a melon baller, or cut into small cubes.

Mix the flour and curry powder together with salt and pepper and use to coat the scallops; reserve any left-over flour. Heat the oil in a frying pan, add the scallops and fry for 1 minute on each side. Remove with a slotted spoon, transfer to a warmed serving dish and keep hot.

Mix any left-over flour to a smooth paste with a little of the wine. Add to the pan with the remaining wine. Stir to dissolve the juices and sediment in the pan, then bring to the boil. Simmer, stirring, until the sauce thickens a little. Add the carrots and salsify and heat through. Remove from the heat, stir in cream and pour over the scallops.

Serves 4

HALIBUT JULIENNE

6 halibut steaks
2 tablespoons sunflower oil
salt and pepper
2 carrots
1 leek
2 celery sticks
50 g (2 oz) butter
2 tablespoons lemon juice

Brush the halibut steaks on both sides with the oil and season well with salt and pepper. Place under a preheated moderate grill and cook for 5 to 6 minutes on each side, until tender. Transfer to a warmed serving dish and keep warm.

Shred the vegetables finely, preferably in a food processor with a grating disc or, even better, a julienne disc, keeping the vegetables horizontal to the disc.

Melt the butter in a pan, add the vegetables and fry gently until soft. Add the lemon juice and simmer for 2 minutes.

Pour over the fish to serve.

Serves 6

CITRUS SKATE WITH PEPPERS

4 × 250–300 g (8–10 oz) pieces of skate, skinned
300 ml (½ pint) medium white wine
150 ml (¼ pint) water
1 bay leaf
4 parsley stalks
salt and pepper
1 small yellow pepper, cored, seeded and cut into rings
1 small red pepper, cored, seeded and cut into rings
grated rind and juice of 1 orange
50 g (2 oz) butter
1 tablespoon chopped parsley to garnish

Put the skate into a pan with the wine, water, bay leaf, parsley stalks and salt and pepper to taste. Bring to the boil, then lower the heat and simmer gently for 15 minutes, until the fish is just cooked. Remove the skate from the liquid with a fish slice and place in a dish. Keep warm.

Discard the bay leaf and parsley stalks from the liquid in the pan. Add the pepper rings and strips of orange rind, bring to the boil and boil for 2 minutes. Remove the pepper and orange rind with a slotted spoon and sprinkle over the fish. Pour off two-thirds of the liquid in the pan; boil the remaining third rapidly until it is reduced to 1 tablespoon. Remove from the heat and stir in the orange juice.

Melt the butter in a separate pan and heat until it turns golden brown. Immediately add the orange juice mixture with salt and pepper to taste. Serve hot, garnished with parsley.

Serves 4

SKATE

Skate is a much underrated and little used fish, which is a pity because it is quite delicious. Some enthusiasts say its flavour is reminiscent of fresh crabmeat. It is available between September and April.

Only the wings are eaten and these can be served either whole or cut into strips before cooking. It is tough when very fresh and should be left for 1 to 2 days before eating. Wash under cold running water and pat dry with absorbent kitchen paper.

The classic way of serving skate is with black butter (see page 110), but a combination of orange juice with red and yellow peppers makes an interesting variation on the theme.

LEFT: *Halibut Julienne*
RIGHT: *Citrus Skate with Peppers; Herbed Smelts with Cucumber Sauce; Curried Scallops with Salsify*

SUPPER HERRINGS

4 herrings, filleted
1 tablespoon made English mustard
salt and pepper
1 large onion, sliced
1 large cooking apple, peeled, cored and sliced
½ teaspoon chopped sage
750 g (1½ lb) potatoes, thinly sliced
150 ml (¼ pint) boiling water
sage leaves to garnish

Spread the cut side of the herrings with the mustard, and sprinkle with salt and pepper. Roll them up.

Place a layer of onion in a buttered gratin dish. Cover with a layer of apple and place the herrings on top. Sprinkle with the sage. Cover with the remaining onion and apple and top with a layer of potato.

Pour in the boiling water, cover with foil and cook in a preheated moderately hot oven, 200°C (400°F), Gas Mark 6, for 45 to 50 minutes.

Garnish with sage and serve immediately.

Serves 4

BAKED MACKEREL IN CIDER

1 kg (2 lb) cooking apples, peeled, cored and thinly sliced
5 tablespoons dry cider
150 g (5 oz) natural yogurt
2 tablespoons course-grain mustard
salt and pepper
4 mackerel, filleted
TO GARNISH:
lemon slices
parsley sprigs

Spread the apples in a large buttered gratin dish.

Heat the cider gently and pour over the apples. Cover with foil and cook in a preheated moderately hot oven, 200°C (400°F), Gas Mark 6, for 15 minutes. Lower the temperature to 180°C (350°F), Gas Mark 4.

Meanwhile, mix the yogurt with the mustard, and salt and pepper to taste. Arrange the mackerel in the dish and pour over the yogurt mixture. Return to the oven and cook for 30 minutes.

Garnish with lemon slices and parsley to serve.

Serves 4

Supper Herrings; Baked Mackerel in Cider

MACARONI AND TUNA FISH LAYER

350 g (12 oz) short cut macaroni
salt and pepper
1 tablespoon oil
40 g (1½ oz) butter or margarine
1 large onion, sliced
1 clove garlic, crushed
125 g (4 oz) mushrooms, chopped
1 teaspoon dried marjoram or oregano
2 × 200 g (7 oz) cans tuna fish in brine, drained and roughly flaked
4–6 tablespoons natural yogurt or top of the milk
SAUCE:
50 g (2 oz) butter or margarine
3 tablespoons plain flour
600 ml (1 pint) milk or chicken or vegetable stock
1 teaspoon dry mustard
75 g (3 oz) mature Cheddar cheese, grated
3 tablespoons grated Parmesan cheese
2–3 tomatoes, skinned and sliced

Cook the macaroni in plenty of boiling salted water with the oil added for about 10 minutes or until barely tender. Drain, rinse under hot water and drain again thoroughly.

Meanwhile melt the butter in a pan and fry the onion and garlic gently until soft but not coloured. Add the mushrooms and continue frying for a few minutes. Stir in the herbs, tuna fish and yogurt or milk, and heat through until really hot. Season well.

Put half the macaroni into a greased ovenproof dish. Spoon the tuna fish mixture in an even layer over the macaroni and cover with the remaining macaroni.

Make the sauce. Melt the butter in a pan, stir in the flour and cook for 1 to 2 minutes. Gradually add the milk or stock and bring to the boil. Stir in the mustard and plenty of salt and pepper and simmer for 2 minutes.

Remove the sauce from the heat and stir in 50 g (2 oz) of the grated Cheddar cheese and 1 tablespoon of the Parmesan until melted, then pour over the macaroni.

Cover with sliced tomatoes, then sprinkle with the remaining Cheddar and Parmesan cheeses.

Cook in a preheated hot oven, 220°C (425°F), Gas Mark 7, for 25 to 30 minutes until golden brown and bubbling. Serve at once.

Serves 6

RIGHT: *Fish Faces*

FISH FACES

150 ml (¼ pint) milk
150 ml (¼ pint) water
250 g (8 oz) haddock fillet
salt and pepper
500 g (1 lb) potatoes, boiled and mashed
1 × 213 g (7½ oz) can pink salmon, drained and flaked
125 g (4 oz) tomatoes, skinned and chopped
4 tablespoons chopped parsley
2 tablespoons natural yogurt
75 g (3 oz) fresh wholewheat breadcrumbs
2 tablespoons grated cheese
25 g (1 oz) plain flour
1 egg, beaten
2 tablespoons oil
olive slices, tomato strips, and lemon slices to garnish

Bring the milk and water to the boil in a large pan, add the haddock and a little salt and pepper, and simmer for 10 minutes or until tender.

Remove any skin and bones from the haddock and flake the fish. Place in a bowl with the potato, salmon, tomato, half the parsley, yogurt, and salt and pepper to taste, and mix well. Divide the mixture into 8 and shape each piece into an oval.

Mix together the breadcrumbs, cheese and remaining parsley. Dip the fish cakes into the flour, then the beaten egg, and finally into the breadcrumb mixture to coat completely.

Heat the oil in a frying pan, add the fish cakes and fry for 3 minutes on each side, until golden. Transfer to a warmed serving plate and garnish each fish cake with an olive slice for an eye, a tomato strip for a mouth and lemon slices, quartered, for its tail.

Makes 8

HADDOCK QUENELLES

1 litre (1¾ pints) water
1 carrot, quartered
1 onion, quartered
1 bouquet garni
salt and white pepper
350 g (12 oz) haddock fillets, skinned
2 egg whites
142 ml (5 fl oz) double cream
TO SERVE:
Herb butter sauce (see page 146)
chopped chives

Place the water, carrot, onion, bouquet garni, and salt and pepper in a pan and simmer for 30 minutes.

Place the haddock in a food processor or electric blender with salt and pepper to taste, and chop finely. With the processor or blender running, gradually pour in the egg whites and cream until well blended and smooth. Shape the mixture into ovals, using 2 tablespoons, and place in a greased large shallow pan, leaving room for spreading.

Strain the hot vegetable stock over the quenelles. Cover and cook gently for about 10 minutes, until they are risen and firm. Drain thoroughly.

Pour over the herb butter sauce and sprinkle with chives to serve.
Serves 4

Haddock Quenelles

HALIBUT IN ORANGE HERB SAUCE

1 kg (2 lb) halibut, cut into 4 steaks
900 ml (1½ pints) cold Fish stock (see page 146)
1 small onion, finely chopped
15 g (½ oz) butter
2 teaspoons oil
175 ml (6 fl oz) frozen concentrated orange juice
2 teaspoons chopped tarragon
2 teaspoons chopped parsley
salt and pepper
2 teaspoons cornflour
1 tablespoon water
150 ml (¼ pint) soured cream
8 orange segments, cleaned of pith to garnish

Rinse the fish and dry it. Trim off any fins, then place in a lightly buttered flameproof dish. Pour over the fish stock, bring to the boil, reduce the heat immediately and poach for 10 minutes.

Remove the fish from the liquid onto a warm dish, remove skin and bones and keep hot. Strain off 150 ml (¼ pint) of the liquor and reserve.

Fry the onion gently in the butter and oil, stir in the orange juice, reserved fish liquor, herbs and salt and pepper to taste. Bring to the boil and simmer for 3 minutes.

Mix the cornflour with the water, stir into the sauce, bring slowly to the boil, stirring constantly.

Remove from the heat and stir in the soured cream. Taste and adjust the seasoning, then pour the sauce over the steaks and garnish with orange segments.
Serves 4

CHEVRON CODLING

1 tablespoon oil
1.2 kg (2½ lb) codling
1 red pepper, cored, seeded and sliced into thin rings
1 green pepper, cored, seeded and sliced into thin rings
2 large tomatoes, skinned and roughly chopped
50 g (2 oz) black olives
2 tablespoons tomato purée
3 tablespoons water
salt and pepper

Pour the oil into an ovenproof dish lined with a large sheet of foil. Turn the fish in the oil until evenly coated, then remove from the dish and set aside.

Put the peppers, tomatoes and olives in the dish with the tomato purée, water and salt and pepper to taste. Mix well, then replace the fish in the dish and fold over the foil loosely.

Bake in a preheated moderate oven, 180°C (350°F), Gas Mark 4, for 20 minutes. Uncover and carefully remove the top skin from the fish. Serve very hot.
Serves 4 to 6

HALIBUT CATALAN

6 tablespoons olive oil
juice of 1 lemon
salt and pepper
4 slices halibut fillet or halibut steaks
1 small onion, finely chopped
1 clove garlic, crushed with ½ teaspoon salt
1 tablespoon plain flour
250 g (8 oz) tomatoes, skinned, seeded and chopped
1 tablespoon tomato purée
300 ml (½ pint) dry white wine
TO GARNISH:
50 g (2 oz) finely chopped hazelnuts
2 tablespoons chopped parsley

Mix together 4 tablespoons of oil, the lemon juice, and salt and pepper to taste. Leave the halibut to soak in this marinade for 1 to 2 hours before cooking, basting and turning occasionally.

Heat the remaining oil in a deep flameproof casserole. Add the onion and garlic and fry gently until golden. Stir in the flour, tomatoes, tomato purée and white wine. Slowly bring to the boil, stirring constantly.

Add the marinated halibut, coating the fish with the sauce, and cover with a lid or foil. Transfer to a moderate oven, 180°C (350°F), Gas Mark 4, and bake for about 20 minutes or until the fish is tender and will flake easily with a fork.

Remove from the oven and top with the hazelnuts and parsley. Serve immediately with new potatoes.

Serves 4

TROUT WITH PRUNES

4 small trout, cleaned
200 g (7 oz) prunes, stoned
4 cloves garlic, crushed
4 tablespoons chopped parsley
200 ml (⅓ pint) olive oil
juice of 2 lemons
4 eggs, lightly beaten
salt and pepper

Stuff the trout with some of the prunes and place in an oiled flameproof oven dish. Scatter the remaining prunes round the fish and sprinkle with garlic and parsley. Add the oil, half the lemon juice and enough water just to cover. Bake in a preheated moderately hot oven, 200°C (400°F), Gas Mark 6, for 25 to 30 minutes until cooked.

Lift out the trout and prunes, arrange on a serving dish and keep warm. Stir the beaten eggs into 8 tablespoons of the juices from the dish, add the remaining lemon juice, and season with salt and pepper. Cook over low heat until the eggs are just set, a bit like scrambled egg. Spread the egg around the trout. Serve with courgettes and new potatoes.

Serves 4

Halibut Catalan; Trout with Prunes

MOROCCAN FISH

750 g (1½ lb) haddock, filleted and skinned
750 g (1½ lb) small turnips, finely sliced
8 fresh or dried dates, stoned and halved
MARINADE:
2 cloves garlic, crushed
1 small onion, finely sliced
1 teaspoon ground cumin
1 teaspoon ground coriander
1 teaspoon ground cinnamon
1 teaspoon ground paprika
½ teaspoon ground ginger
pinch of chilli pepper
salt and pepper
juice of 1 lemon
3 tablespoons olive oil
2–3 tablespoons chopped coriander to garnish (optional)

Mix all the ingredients for the marinade and marinate the fish in it for at least 1 hour in the refrigerator, turning the fish over once.

Place the turnips and dates in a casserole dish and pour over the marinade. Cut the fish into bite-sized pieces and place on top of the turnips and dates. Cook, covered, in a preheated moderate oven, 180°C (350°F), Gas Mark 4, for 45 minutes until the turnips are tender and the fish is just beginning to flake.

Serve hot, garnished with chopped coriander, if using.

Serves 4

FILLETING AND SKINNING FISH

To fillet a fish; place the fish on a board. Run a sharp knife along the centre bone. Scrape along the bones from the head towards the tail until the fillet is released. Repeat with the other side. Turn the fish over and remove the other 2 fillets in the same way. To skin a fish; place the fish fillet on a board, tail end towards you and flesh uppermost. Hold the tail firmly. Using a sharp filleting knife, keeping the blade as close to the skin as possible, work your way down the fillet.

To skin a whole small fish (so that it can be cooked on the bone); make a nick in the skin at the tail end, insert a finger and run it up the fish between the skin and the flesh. Ease the skin away from the flesh, pulling towards the head. Repeat the process on the other side. If the skin is too slippery to hold, dip your fingers in salt.

HERRING ROE FRITTERS

750 g (1½ lb) soft herring roes
olive oil for deep frying
salt
FRYING BATTER:
125 g (4 oz) plain flour
3 tablespoons olive oil
¾ glass warm water
salt
1 egg white, beaten
TO GARNISH:
chopped parsley
lemon wedges

First prepare the frying batter. Mix the flour and oil to a thick paste and gradually add the warm water. Then add a pinch of salt and stir well until the batter is smooth. Leave for at least 3 hours before use. Just before using, stir in the beaten egg white.

Dip the soft roes into the batter, and deep-fry in very hot olive oil. Drain on kitchen towels.

Continue in this way until all the herring roes have been used up. Pile up on a dish, sprinkle with salt and garnish with parsley and lemon.

Serve with a mixed salad.

Serves 4

MACKEREL WITH LEMON STUFFING

4 × 175 g (6 oz) mackerel, split and boned out
juice of ½ lemon
salt and pepper
1 bay leaf, crushed
STUFFING:
15 g (½ oz) butter
1 small onion, finely chopped
75 g (3 oz) fresh white breadcrumbs
finely grated rind and juice of 1 lemon
1 tablespoon freshly chopped parsley
1 small egg (size 4), beaten
TO GARNISH:
parsley sprigs
lemon slices

First prepare the stuffing. Melt the butter in a pan. Add the onion and fry gently for 5 minutes or until golden. Transfer to a mixing bowl and combine with the remaining stuffing ingredients.

Lay the mackerel flat on a board and sprinkle the flesh with lemon juice, and salt and pepper to taste. Spoon the prepared stuffing into the fish and reshape. Place in an ovenproof casserole, barely cover the bottom of the dish with water and add the bay leaf and more salt and pepper to taste.

Cover the casserole with a lid, or greased greaseproof paper or foil, and poach in a preheated warm oven, 160°C (325°F), Gas Mark 3, for 15 to 20 minutes or until the fish feels tender when pierced with a skewer.

Drain, garnish with parsley sprigs and lemon slices and serve at once.

Serves 4

Mackerel with Lemon Stuffing; Moroccan Fish

PASTA MEDITERRANEAN

1 tablespoon olive oil
2 cloves garlic, sliced
1 onion, sliced
1 × 539 g (1 lb 3 oz) can tomatoes
150 ml (¼ pint) dry white wine
1 teaspoon oregano
1 teaspoon basil
1 tablespoon tomato purée
salt and pepper
500 g (1 lb) long macaroni
2 teaspoons salt
2 tablespoons oil
175 g (6 oz) peeled prawns
125 g (4 oz) cooked shelled mussels
chopped parsley to garnish

Heat the oil in a pan, add the garlic and onion and cook for 5 minutes, without browning. Add the tomatoes with their juice, the wine, herbs, tomato purée, and salt and pepper to taste. Bring to the boil and cook, uncovered, for 20 to 25 minutes, until thickened.

Meanwhile, break the macaroni into 5 cm (2 inch) lengths. Place in a large pan of boiling water with the salt and oil and cook for 9 to 11 minutes, until just tender.

Add the prawns and mussels to the sauce and cook gently for 5 minutes.

Drain the pasta and arrange on a warmed serving dish. Spoon the sauce over, sprinkle with the parsley and serve immediately.

Serves 4

PACIFIC TUNA PIE

2 × 198 g (7 oz) cans tuna fish, drained and flaked
1 × 326 g (11½ oz) can sweetcorn, drained
1 × 113 g (4 oz) packet frozen peas
1 × 298 g (10½ oz) can condensed chicken soup
1 × 397 g (14 oz) can tomatoes, drained
75 g (3 oz) Cheddar cheese, grated
1 × 75 g (3 oz) packet potato crisps, crushed

Mix together the tuna, sweetcorn, peas and soup. Turn into a buttered casserole and cover with the tomatoes.

Mix together the cheese and crisps and sprinkle over the tomatoes. Cook in a preheated moderately hot oven, 190°C (375°F), Gas Mark 5, for 30 minutes, until the top is golden and bubbling.

Serve hot, with baked tomatoes if liked.

Serves 4

FISH AND POTATO PIE

350 g (12 oz) haddock or cod fillet
1 × 212 g (7½ oz) can button mushrooms, drained
1 × 227 g (8 oz) can tomatoes
125 g (4 oz) peeled prawns
1 × 300 ml (½ pint) packet onion sauce mix
200 ml (⅓ pint) milk
150 ml (¼ pint) white wine
1 × 70 g (2½ oz) packet instant mashed potato
6–7 tablespoons water
salt and pepper
25 g (1 oz) butter
TO GARNISH:
tomato slices
parsley sprigs

Cut the fish fillets into large pieces and place in a casserole. Cover with the mushrooms and tomatoes and pour over a little of the tomato juice. Sprinkle the prawns on top.

Make up the onion sauce as directed on the packet, using 150 ml (¼ pint) of the milk and the wine. Pour over the prawns.

Make up the potato as directed on the packet, using the remaining milk and the water. Add salt and pepper to taste. Spoon over the fish mixture to cover completely. Dot with the butter.

Bake in a preheated moderate oven, 180°C (350°F), Gas Mark 4, for 30 minutes, until the top is golden brown. Serve hot, garnished with tomato and parsley.

Serves 4

CRAB AND SPAGHETTI BAKE

175 g (6 oz) spaghetti
salt and pepper
25 g (1 oz) butter
1 large onion, chopped
1 medium red pepper, cored, seeded and diced
25 g (1 oz) plain flour
300 ml (½ pint) milk
150 ml (¼ pint) single cream
2 teaspoons French mustard
1 tablespoon Worcestershire sauce
250 g (8 oz) cooked fresh, or canned crabmeat, drained and flaked
4 hard-boiled eggs, sliced
125 g (4 oz) mature Cheddar cheese, grated

Break the spaghetti into short lengths and cook in boiling salted water until just tender. Meanwhile, melt the butter in a saucepan, add the onion and red pepper and sauté until softened. Stir in the flour and cook, stirring, for 1 minute, then gradually stir in the milk and cream. Bring to the boil and simmer, stirring, until thickened. Stir in the mustard, Worcestershire sauce, and salt and pepper to taste.

Drain the spaghetti and fold into the sauce. Spread half this mixture in a greased shallow casserole. Cover with the crabmeat, then the sliced eggs and top with the remaining spaghetti sauce. Sprinkle the cheese over the top. Cook in a preheated moderately hot oven, 190°C (375°F), Gas Mark 5, for 25 minutes or until heated through and bubbling.

Serves 4 to 6

COOKING PASTA

Pasta must be cooked in plenty of water. As a guide, allow at least 4 litres (7 pints) of water for every 500 g (1 lb) of pasta. Bring the water to the boil with 1 to 2 tablespoons of oil to prevent the pasta from sticking together, and 2 teaspoons of salt. Add the pasta, return to the boil and cook, uncovered, over a fairly high heat, stirring occasionally, until *al dente* – just tender but still firm to the bite. For fresh pasta, this will take 2 to 3 minutes; dried pasta 9 to 12 minutes. Do not simply follow manufacturers' instructions, but test frequently during cooking.

LEFT: *Pasta Mediterranean*
RIGHT: *Crab and Spaghetti Bake*

PRAWN PILAFF

50 g (2 oz) butter
1 small onion, finely chopped
1 clove garlic, crushed
250 g (8 oz) long-grain rice
200 ml ($\frac{1}{3}$ pint) dry white wine
2–3 strands of saffron
600 ml (1 pint) Fish stock (see page 146)
salt and pepper
4 tomatoes, skinned, seeded and chopped
1 tablespoon chopped basil
250 g (8 oz) peeled prawns
TO GARNISH:
basil leaves
few whole prawns (optional)

Melt the butter in a pan, add the onion and garlic and cook gently for 5 minutes. Add the rice and toss until coated in the butter. Add the wine and saffron and bring to the boil, stirring. Cook until most of the wine has evaporated, stirring constantly.

Stir in two-thirds of the stock and season with salt and pepper to taste. Bring to the boil, cover and simmer for 10 to 12 minutes until the rice is just tender, stirring occasionally; add more stock if required, to keep the rice slightly moist and ensure it does not burn. Stir in the tomatoes, basil and prawns and cook for 2 minutes.

Pile the pilaff into a warmed serving dish. Garnish with basil and whole prawns if using. Serve with grated Parmesan cheese.

Serves 6

Prawn Pilaff

SPICY PRAWNS

500 g (1 lb) peeled prawns
1 teaspoon ground coriander
1 heaped tablespoon chopped parsley
1 egg, beaten
40 g ($1\frac{1}{2}$ oz) fresh wholewheat breadcrumbs
3 tablespoons oil
2 onions, finely chopped
1 clove garlic, crushed
$\frac{1}{4}$ teaspoon chilli powder
$\frac{1}{2}$ teaspoon ground ginger
$\frac{1}{4}$ teaspoon ground bay leaves
150 ml ($\frac{1}{4}$ pint) hot water
juice of 1 lemon

Mince or chop the prawns finely, using a mincer or an electric food processor. Mix the prawn paste with the coriander and parsley, then shape into walnut-sized balls. Dip into the egg and coat with the breadcrumbs. Set aside.

Heat 2 tablespoons of the oil in a frying pan, add the prawn balls in batches and fry, turning frequently, until golden. Remove from the pan and keep warm. Heat the remaining oil, add the onions and fry until brown. Stir in the garlic, chilli, ginger and ground bay leaves and cook, stirring, for about 5 minutes.

Add the hot water and bring to the boil, then simmer for 8 to 10 minutes. Stir in the lemon juice.

Serve the sauce with the prawn balls. Accompany with rice and a green salad.

Serves 4 to 6

THE RAJAH'S FISH

750 g ($1\frac{1}{2}$ lb) white fish fillets
salt and pepper
juice of $\frac{1}{2}$ lemon
3 tablespoons sweet chutney
50 g (2 oz) stoned raisins, chopped
50 g (2 oz) blanched almonds, chopped
2 eggs, beaten
125 g (4 oz) fresh white breadcrumbs
oil for deep frying
Curried apricot mayonnaise (see page 152) to serve
TO GARNISH:
25 g (1 oz) browned, flaked almonds
rolled anchovy fillets

Rinse and dry the fillets of fish. Season with salt and pepper and sprinkle with lemon juice. Spread a little chutney on each fillet, cover with the raisins and almonds.

Roll up the fillets lengthways, secure with a wooden cocktail stick and dip each fillet in the egg, then coat thoroughly in the crumbs. Heat the oil to 190°C (375°F), then fry the fish until golden brown.

Drain on kitchen paper. Arrange on a serving dish and garnish with the almonds and anchovy fillets. Serve with curried apricot mayonnaise.

Serves 4

SMOKED HADDOCK ROULADE

50 g (2 oz) plain flour
4 large eggs (size 1), separated
2 tablespoons water
125 g (4 oz) Cheddar cheese, grated
4 tablespoons grated Parmesan cheese
salt and pepper
FILLING:
25 g (1 oz) butter
25 g (1 oz) plain flour
200 ml (7 fl oz) milk
250 g (8 oz) smoked haddock fillets, cooked, skinned and flaked
1 hard-boiled egg, chopped
1 tablespoon chopped parsley
TO GARNISH:
herb sprigs

Sift the flour into a bowl and beat in the egg yolks and water until smooth. Stir in the Cheddar cheese, half the Parmesan cheese, and salt and pepper to taste. Whisk the egg whites until stiff and carefully fold into the mixture.

Spread evenly into a lined and greased 30 × 20 cm (12 × 8 inch) Swiss roll tin and bake in a preheated moderately hot oven, 200°C (400°F), Gas Mark 6, for 12 to 15 minutes, until well risen and golden brown.

Meanwhile, melt the butter in a pan, add the flour and cook for 1 minute, stirring. Gradually stir in the milk and cook, stirring, for 1 minute. Season with salt and pepper to taste. Fold in the haddock, chopped egg and parsley.

Sprinkle the remaining Parmesan over a large piece of greaseproof paper. Turn the roulade onto this, removing the lining paper. Spread the filling over the surface and carefully roll up like a Swiss roll.

Serve immediately, while still hot, garnished with herbs.

Serves 6

Smoked Haddock Roulade

SKINNING AND DESEEDING TOMATOES

Many dishes call for skinned and seeded tomatoes. These are not nearly as difficult or as fiddly to prepare as you might think. You can quickly peel them in bulk by simply covering them with boiling water and leaving for 45 to 60 seconds. Then drain and slit the skins, which will now peel away easily.

Another method, which can sometimes be easier if you've got only the one tomato to peel, is to spear it with a fork and to turn it over in a gas flame on the hob until the skin puckers and blisters. Then allow to cool and gently peel away the skin.

To remove the seeds, cut the tomato in half and scoop out the seeds with a teaspoon.

KIPPERS IN LEMON DRESSING

1 large packet frozen kipper fillets, thawed and skinned
6 tablespoons olive oil
3 tablespoons lemon juice
freshly ground black pepper
TO GARNISH:
thinly sliced onion rings
lemon wedges

Cut the kipper fillets into thin slivers and place in a mixing bowl. Mix together the oil, lemon juice and plenty of black pepper and spoon over the kippers. Chill in the refrigerator, preferably overnight.

Arrange the kippers on a serving platter and spoon the dressing over. Top with onion rings and lemon wedges, and serve with thinly sliced brown bread and butter.

Serves 4

NOODLES WITH FISH SAUCE

10 anchovies
2–3 tablespoons milk
75 g (3 oz) butter
1 large onion, chopped
1–2 cloves garlic, very thinly sliced
150 ml ($\frac{1}{4}$ pint) dry white wine
250 ml (8 fl oz) Fish stock (see page 146)
175 g (6 oz) peeled prawns
salt and pepper
2–3 tablespoons chopped parsley
500 g (1 lb) fresh noodles
TO GARNISH:
anchovy fillets
whole prawns

Soak the anchovies in the milk for 30 minutes, drain, chop and set aside.

Melt 50 g (2 oz) of the butter in a pan, add the onion and cook until golden brown. Add the garlic and cook for 1 minute. Add the wine, bring to the boil and cook rapidly until reduced by half. Add the fish stock, anchovies, prawns, and salt and pepper to taste. Cook, uncovered, for 2 minutes. Remove from the heat and stir in the parsley

Cook the noodles until *al dente*. Drain thoroughly and turn into a warmed serving dish. Add the remaining butter and toss well.

Heat the sauce for 1 minute, pour over the noodles and toss well. Garnish with a lattice of anchovy fillets and whole prawns. Serve immediately with Parmesan cheese.
Serves 6

CRAB COBBLER

75 g (3 oz) butter
1 green pepper, cored, seeded and diced
1 medium onion, finely sliced
50 g (2 oz) plain flour
1 teaspoon dry mustard
250 ml (8 fl oz) milk
75 g (3 oz) Cheddar cheese, grated
250 g (8 oz) prepared crabmeat
350 g (12 oz) ripe tomatoes, skinned and diced
2 teaspoons Worcestershire sauce
salt and pepper
CHEESE SCONE TOPPING:
125 g (4 oz) plain flour
salt and pepper
2 teaspoons baking powder
50 g (2 oz) butter or shortening
25 g (1 oz) Cheddar cheese, grated
milk to mix

Melt the butter in a saucepan over a gentle heat and cook the green pepper and onion together for about 10 minutes, until tender.

Remove from the heat and blend in the flour, then the mustard and milk. Return to the heat and cook, stirring constantly, until the mixture is very thick. Add the cheese and reheat until melted. Stir in the crab, tomatoes, Worcestershire sauce and salt and pepper to taste. Turn the mixture into an ovenproof dish.

To make the topping, sift the flour, salt, pepper and baking powder into a bowl. Rub in the fat until the mixture resembles fine breadcrumbs. Stir in the cheese with a knife and mix to a stiff dough with a little milk. Mould the dough into small balls and place on top of the crabmeat mixture. Bake in a preheated hot oven, 220°C (425°F), Gas Mark 7, for 15 to 20 minutes. Serve with a green salad.
Serves 4

OILY FISH

The fat content of these fish, such as herring, mackerel, tuna, salmon, trout and sardines, is dispersed throughout the flesh and the amount varies according to type and time of year.

The herring, for example, spawns during spring and autumn, which means it uses up its fat and gets thin; so although the herring is available all year round, it's at its best in the summer. Ask at the fish counter about the best season for your particular favourite.

LEFT: *Noodles with Fish Sauce*
RIGHT: *Grilled Mackerel Japanese-Style; Breton Tuna*

GRILLED MACKEREL JAPANESE-STYLE

4 × 175 g (6 oz) mackerel fillets with skin on
salt
125 g (4 oz) mooli (white radish), finely grated
2 tablespoons soy sauce
lemon wedges to garnish (optional)

Cut the fillets of mackerel in half crossways and sprinkle lightly with salt. Leave for 5 minutes, then rinse in cold water and pat dry with kitchen towels. Sprinkle very lightly again with salt on both sides.

Cut a shallow cross in the skin of each fillet to prevent it from curling under the grill. Do not cut deeper than the skin.

Grill under a moderate heat for about 5 minutes on each side until golden. Arrange the fish on 4 serving plates, skin side uppermost.

Lightly squeeze out all the moisture from the grated mooli and divide between the 4 plates. Sprinkle the soy sauce over the mooli and garnish each plate with lemon wedges, if using.

Serves 4

BRETON TUNA

140 g (4½ oz) butter
2 large onions, chopped
1.5 kg (3 lb) tuna fish
salt and pepper
2–3 cloves garlic, chopped
4 tomatoes, quartered
500 ml (17 fl oz) dry white wine
1 sprig thyme
1 sprig parsley
1 bay leaf
1 small cauliflower
500 g (1 lb) small new potatoes (unpeeled)

TO GARNISH:
1½ tablespoons chopped parsley
1½ tablespoons chopped chives

Heat the butter in a large flameproof casserole dish and fry the onions over moderate heat for 5 minutes until soft and just beginning to brown. Add the tuna fish, season with salt and pepper and leave to brown gently, turning from time to time.

Add the garlic and tomatoes. Pour on the white wine, bring to the boil and add the herbs. Cover and simmer over low heat for 1 hour.

Lift out the tuna fish and keep warm. Divide the cauliflower into florets and add to the sauce, along with the new potatoes. Simmer gently for 20 to 30 minutes until tender.

Cut the fish into serving pieces and remove any skin and bones. Arrange on a serving dish, spoon on the sauce, cauliflower and potatoes and garnish with parsley and chives.

Serves 6

SEAFOOD NOODLES

4 fillets of sole, skinned, with bones
300 ml (½ pint) dry white wine
1 small onion, halved
½ teaspoon dried mixed herbs
50 g (2 oz) butter
1 clove garlic, crushed
2 shallots, chopped
6 large scallops
4 large tomatoes, skinned, seeded and chopped
1 teaspoon chopped basil
2 tablespoons chopped parsley
142 ml (5 fl oz) double cream
salt and pepper
500 g (1 lb) fresh egg noodles
250 g (8 oz) peeled prawns
whole prawns to garnish

Place the fish skin and bones in a pan with the wine, onion, and herbs. Simmer for 20 minutes. Cool and strain.

Melt half the butter in a pan, add the garlic and shallots and cook for 5 minutes. Cut the fish into 5 cm (2 inch) pieces and add to the pan with the fish stock. Bring to the boil, simmer for 2 minutes, remove the fish and set aside. Add the white part of the scallops and cook for 30 seconds, add the coral part and cook for just under 30 seconds; remove.

Boil the liquid until reduced to 2 tablespoons. Add the tomatoes and basil and cook for 10 minutes, stirring occasionally, until thickened. Stir in the parsley, cream, and salt and pepper to taste.

Cook the noodles until *al dente*. Drain and turn into a warmed serving dish. Add the remaining butter and toss well. Add the prawns and fish to the sauce, bring to the boil, then pour over the noodles. Serve garnished with prawns.

Serves 4

WHOLEWHEAT FISH BURGERS

250 g (8 oz) smoked haddock
500 g (1 lb) potatoes, boiled and mashed
1 spring onion, chopped
salt and pepper
25 g (1 oz) butter
2 eggs, beaten
50 g (2 oz) wholewheat flour
125 g (4 oz) fresh wholewheat breadcrumbs
2 tablespoons oil

Place the haddock on a plate over a pan of boiling water, cover and steam for 10 to 15 minutes, until the fish flakes easily from the skin. Remove the skin and any bones; flake the fish.

Mix together the potato, fish, spring onion, and salt and pepper to taste. Add the butter and a little of the egg to bind the mixture. Season the flour with salt and pepper.

Shape the mixture into 8 burgers and coat with the seasoned flour. Dip in the beaten egg and coat with the breadcrumbs. Heat the oil in a frying pan, add the fish burgers and fry for 2 to 3 minutes on each side, until crisp and golden. Serve hot.

Makes 8

COD IN THE HOLE

4 cod steaks
salt and pepper
1 tablespoon sunflower oil
lemon wedges to garnish
BATTER:
125 g (4 oz) plain flour
pinch of salt
1 egg
300 ml (½ pint) milk

Season the cod with salt and pepper.

Make the batter; sift the flour into a mixing bowl with a pinch of salt. Make a well in the centre and break in the egg. Add half the milk and gradually work in the flour, using a wooden spoon and beating the mixture until quite smooth. Gradually add the remaining milk and beat well until the surface is covered with little bubbles.

Heat the oil in a baking tin and pour in a thin layer of batter. Bake in a preheated hot oven, 220°C (425°F), Gas Mark 7, for 5 minutes. Then arrange the cod steaks on top, pour on the remaining batter and bake for 45 to 55 minutes, or until the batter is well risen, golden brown and crisp on top.

Garnish with lemon wedges and serve immediately with broccoli.

Serves 4

FISH GOULASH

3 tablespoons olive oil
2 onions, finely sliced
2 red peppers, cored, seeded and sliced
2 green peppers, cored, seeded and sliced
6 tomatoes, skinned, seeded and chopped
1 tablespoon tomato purée
1–2 teaspoons paprika
salt and pepper
1 kg (2 lb) cod, filleted and skinned
4 tablespoons natural yogurt

Heat the oil in a large casserole dish and fry the onions gently, over moderate heat, for 5 minutes until just beginning to soften. Add the peppers and cook for a further 5 minutes, stirring occasionally.

Add the tomatoes and tomato purée, and season with 1 teaspoon of paprika, salt and pepper. Cook, uncovered, over low heat for 30 minutes, stirring from time to time.

Meanwhile, cut the fish into generous bite-sized pieces. Add the fish to the casserole and cook for a further 20 minutes until the fish is cooked.

If the flavour of paprika is too weak for your liking, add another teaspoonful 10 minutes before the stew has finished cooking. Just before serving, spoon over the yogurt.

Serve with boiled rice and a green salad.

Serves 6

PLAICE AND BACON ROLLS

8 plaice fillets
8 rashers back bacon, rinded
freshly ground black pepper
juice of 1 lemon
marjoram sprigs to garnish

Place a fillet of plaice on each rasher of bacon, and season with black pepper and a squeeze of lemon juice.

Roll up the rashers of bacon and bake in a preheated, moderately hot oven, 190°C (375°F), Gas Mark 5, for 20 to 30 minutes.

Garnish with marjoram sprigs and serve immediately with baked potatoes and a mixture of chicory and red chicory.

Serves 4

LEFT: *Seafood Noodles*
RIGHT: *Fish Goulash; Plaice and Bacon Rolls*

ENTERTAINING

Entertaining can – and should be – fun, not hard work.

The key to success is forward planning. The best laid plans *do* produce the best meals. The successful hostess will prepare herself well in advance, paying careful attention to all the ingredients for a successful party – including the guests, food, wine and table setting. Then the party should go with a swing.

The first thing to do is to decide who you want to invite. A good mixture of guests is essential to the success of any party.

Then plan your menu. It's a good idea here to choose foods that are in season. This will not only help to keep the cost down but will also ensure that you will be able to obtain quality ingredients.

Unless you're really ambitious and you're one of the lucky few who seem to sail effortlessly through the most difficult of culinary operations, it's probably better to choose one spectacular course to impress your guests and to keep the other dishes simple.

Think about the visual impact of your menu: does it have a variety of colours, shapes and textures, as well – of course – as flavours? And don't underestimate the importance of the table setting, which can greatly enhance the appearance of the food. Cutlery and glasses should be sparkling, and flowers must be fresh.

Plan carefully and well in advance. Then you'll be able to relax and enjoy the party as much as your guests.

SCALLOPS WITH GARLIC AND PARSLEY

75 g (3 oz) butter
3 cloves garlic
12 fresh scallops, shelled, or frozen scallops, thawed
2 tablespoons chopped parsley
salt and pepper

Melt the butter in a pan, add the garlic and fry until browned; discard.

Add the coral and white scallop flesh to the pan and cook for 5 minutes. Sprinkle in the parsley, and salt and pepper to taste.

Pile into warmed individual serving dishes and serve immediately.

Serves 4

TROUT WITH ALMONDS

4 trout, cleaned, with heads and tails intact
salt and pepper
75 g (3 oz) butter
50 g (2 oz) flaked almonds
juice of 1 lemon
TO GARNISH *(optional)*:
parsley sprigs
lemon slices

Season the fish with salt and pepper. Melt the butter in a frying pan, add the trout and fry for 6 minutes on each side until golden and cooked through. Arrange on a warmed serving dish and keep hot.

Fry the almonds in the butter remaining in the pan until golden. Add the lemon juice and spoon over the fish. Garnish with parsley and lemon, if desired, and serve.

Serves 4

SWORDFISH PROVENÇAL

2 swordfish steaks
1 tablespoon sunflower oil
1 onion, sliced
750 g (1½ lb) tomatoes, sliced
250 g (8 oz) green beans, cut in half
125 g (4 oz) green olives, stoned
2 tablespoons capers
2 teaspoons chopped oregano

MARINADE:
150 ml (¼ pint) dry white wine
4 tablespoons lemon juice
1 small onion, sliced
1 bay leaf
2 thyme sprigs
2 parsley sprigs
2 rosemary sprigs
2 cloves garlic, crushed
salt and pepper

TO GARNISH:
basil sprigs

Cut the swordfish steaks in half, place in a shallow dish and add the marinade ingredients, with salt and pepper to taste. Chill for several hours.

Remove the fish with a slotted spoon; reserve the marinade. Heat the oil in a large pan, add the fish and fry for 5 minutes. Transfer to a casserole dish.

Add the onion, tomatoes, beans, olives, capers, oregano and reserved marinade to the pan and cook, stirring, for 5 minutes. Transfer to the casserole and season with salt and pepper to taste.

Cook in a preheated moderate oven, 180°C (350°F). Gas Mark 4, for 35 to 40 minutes.

Discard the bay leaf. Garnish with basil to serve.

Serves 4

BAKED TROUT

50 g (2 oz) butter
4 trout, cleaned
1 lemon, sliced
5 tablespoons dry white wine
1 teaspoon dried tarragon
salt and pepper
parsley sprigs to garnish

Line a baking dish with a large piece of foil, allowing sufficient to hang over the sides. Spread the butter over the foil. Lay the trout in the dish and arrange the lemon slices on top.

Mix together the wine, tarragon, and salt and pepper to taste and pour over the fish.

Fold the foil over the trout to make a parcel and fold the edges together to seal. Cook in a preheated moderate oven, 180°C (350°F), Gas Mark 4, for 30 minutes.

Transfer the trout to a warmed serving dish. Pour over the juices and garnish with parsley.

Serves 4

MACKEREL IN WHITE WINE

300 ml (½ pint) dry white wine
150 ml (¼ pint) water
1 onion, sliced
1 fennel sprig
strip of lemon rind
6–7 peppercorns
2 bay leaves
salt
2 large mackerel, boned
2 teaspoons French mustard
2 tablespoons chopped parsley
fennel leaves to garnish

Put the wine, water, onion, fennel, lemon rind, peppercorns, bay leaves and a pinch of salt in a pan. Bring to the boil and simmer for 10 minutes. Cool, then strain.

Poach the mackerel in this liquid for 10 to 15 minutes. Cool, then strain, reserving half the stock. Arrange the fish on a serving dish.

Mix the reserved stock with the mustard and spoon over the fish. Sprinkle with parsley. Chill before serving, garnished with fennel.

Serves 4

LEFT: *Scallops with Garlic and Parsley; Trout with Almonds*
ABOVE: *Swordfish Provençal*

GOUJONS OF SOLE

2 Dover sole, skinned and filleted
50 g (2 oz) hazelnuts, finely chopped
125 g (4 oz) fresh wholewheat breadcrumbs
25 g (1 oz) plain flour
salt and pepper
1–2 eggs, beaten
oil for deep-frying
Tartare sauce (see page 149) to serve
TO GARNISH:
parsley sprigs
orange segments

Cut the sole diagonally into strips about 2.5 cm (1 inch) wide.

Mix together the hazelnuts and breadcrumbs in a bowl.

Season the flour with salt and pepper and use to coat the fish. Dip into the beaten egg, then roll in the breadcrumb mixture to coat completely. Chill for about 30 minutes.

Deep-fry in hot oil, a few at a time, for 2 minutes, until crisp and golden. Drain on kitchen paper and place in a warmed serving dish.

Garnish with parsley sprigs and orange segments and serve immediately, accompanied by tartare sauce and a crisp green salad.

Serves 2 to 4

Goujons of Sole

SPINACH PANCAKES WITH CRAB

125 g (4 oz) wholewheat flour
½ teaspoon salt
1 egg, beaten
300 ml (½ pint) milk
125 g (4 oz) frozen chopped spinach, thawed
oil for shallow-frying
FILLING:
25 g (1 oz) butter
2 shallots, chopped
1 clove garlic, chopped
125 g (4 oz) mushrooms, sliced
25 g (1 oz) plain flour
300 ml (½ pint) milk
350 g (12 oz) crabmeat
4 tablespoons crème fraîche
4 tablespoons sherry
1 tablespoon grated Parmesan cheese
1 tablespoon chopped chervil
salt and pepper
TOPPING:
25 g (1 oz) butter, melted
1 tablespoon grated Parmesan cheese
TO GARNISH *(optional)*:
whole prawns
dill sprigs

To make the batter, place the flour and salt in a bowl, add the egg and half the milk and beat until smooth. Beat in the remaining milk, then stir in the spinach.

Heat a little oil in a 15–18 cm (6–7 inch) frying pan. Pour in about 1½ tablespoons of the batter and cook until the mixture has set and the edges are golden brown. Turn the pancake over and cook the other side. Repeat with the remaining batter, stacking the cooked pancakes on a plate, interleaved with greaseproof paper.

To make the filling, melt the butter in a pan, stir in the shallots, garlic and mushrooms and sauté until soft. Stir in the flour and cook for 1 minute.

Remove from the heat and stir in the remaining ingredients, seasoning with salt and pepper to taste.

Divide the filling between the pancakes, placing it down the middle, and roll up. Place in a shallow ovenproof dish, brush with the melted butter and sprinkle with the cheese.

Cook in a preheated moderately hot oven, 200°C (400°F), Gas Mark 6, for 10 to 15 minutes, until crisp.

Garnish with whole prawns and sprigs of dill, if using, and serve.

Serves 4

CARP

Carp is a round freshwater fish, at its best from November to January. Small carp may be grilled or fried, while larger fish are better stuffed and baked. Soaking the fish in salted water for 3 to 4 hours and rinsing well in vinegar and water before cooking counteracts the somewhat muddy flavour which this fish can sometimes have. Carp has a firm sweet flesh, and is a very rewarding fish for the adventurous cook.

RED MULLET NIÇOISE

150 ml (¼ pint) olive oil
2 small onions, chopped
1 clove garlic, chopped
25 g (1 oz) parsley, crushed
250 g (8 oz) tomatoes, skinned, seeded and chopped
1 teaspoon tomato purée
1 bouquet garni
salt and pepper
4 × 275 g (9 oz) red mullet, cleaned and scaled
16 black olives, stoned
4–5 tablespoons dry white wine

Heat 6 tablespoons of the olive oil over low heat and fry the onions gently for 5 to 10 minutes until soft and slightly brown. Add the garlic, parsley, tomatoes, tomato purée, bouquet garni, salt and pepper. Simmer for 15 minutes.

Meanwhile, fry the mullet gently in the remaining oil in a deep frying pan for 3 to 4 minutes on each side.

When the sauce is cooked, add the olives and wine, and pour over the mullet. Cover and cook for a further 10 minutes.

Transfer to a warmed serving dish and serve with new potatoes and courgettes.

Serves 4

SWEET AND SOUR CARP

If you do not have a fish kettle use the method for cooking Poached Salmon Trout (see page 118).

1 × 1.75 kg (4 lb) carp, cleaned and scaled
300 ml (½ pint) olive oil
2–3 onions, chopped
4 shallots, chopped
2 tablespoons plain flour
1 tablespoon sugar
1 tablespoon vinegar
salt and pepper
1 bouquet garni
50 g (2 oz) raisins
75 g (3 oz) flaked blanched almonds
1.5 litres (2¾ pints) Fish stock (see page 146)

Place the fish in a fish kettle.

Heat the oil in a large pan and gently fry the onions and shallots until they begin to soften. Stir in the flour, sugar, vinegar, salt and pepper, bouquet garni, raisins and almonds, and then pour on the fish stock. Bring to the boil and pour over the fish. The cooking stock should just cover the fish – if it doesn't, top up with boiling water. Simmer gently for about 10 minutes until cooked.

Lift out the fish, transfer to a heated dish and keep warm (if serving hot). Meanwhile, reduce the sauce by about half and check the seasoning. Serve either hot or cold.

Serves 6

Red Mullet Niçoise

SOLE PIE VERONIQUE

750 g (1½ lb) sole, filleted
600 ml (1 pint) milk
65 g (2½ oz) butter
175 g (6 oz) white grapes, peeled and deseeded
50 g (2 oz) plain flour
salt and pepper
150 ml (¼ pint) single cream
250 g (8 oz) frozen puff pastry
1 egg, beaten

Poach the fillets of sole in milk for 5 minutes until just tender, then drain and reserve the poaching liquid. Butter a deep pie dish and arrange the fish in the bottom. Scatter the grapes on top.

Melt the remaining butter. Take off the heat and stir in the flour. Gradually stir in the milk in which the fish was poached and bring to the boil, stirring continuously. Simmer gently over low heat. Season with salt and pepper, and stir in the cream. Pour the sauce over the fish and grapes.

Roll out the pie lid of puff pastry and cover the pie. Brush with beaten egg and bake in a preheated hot oven, 220°C (425°F), Gas Mark 7, for 20 minutes until the pastry has risen and is golden brown.

Serves 4

APRICOT-STUFFED TROUT

6 trout, cleaned
50 g (2 oz) butter
salt and pepper
300 ml (½ pint) dry white wine
parsley sprigs to garnish

APRICOT STUFFING:

125 g (4 oz) dried apricots, soaked overnight
125 g (4 oz) cooked long-grain rice
1 green pepper, finely chopped
40 g (1½ oz) butter, melted
salt and pepper
pinch of thyme
pinch of grated nutmeg

First prepare the stuffing. Drain the apricots, reserving the liquid. Chop the apricots and mix with the rice. Add the green pepper, butter, salt and pepper and pinches of thyme and nutmeg. Moisten with a little of the liquid reserved from the apricots.

Fill the fish with this stuffing. Butter an ovenproof dish and place the fish in it, season well with salt and pepper, and pour over the wine. Dot with butter, cover and poach in a preheated moderate oven, 180°C (350°F), gas Mark 4, for 25 to 30 minutes.

Transfer to a heated serving dish and garnish with parsley sprigs.

Serves 6

PRAWNS WITH ALMONDS

75 g (3 oz) blanched almonds
350 g (12 oz) peeled prawns
2 teaspoons cornflour
1 heaped teaspoon finely chopped fresh ginger
1 small clove garlic, crushed
2 tablespoons oil
1 celery stick, finely chopped
2 teaspoons soy sauce
2 teaspoons sherry
2 tablespoons water
pepper to taste
spring onions to garnish

Brush a frying pan with oil, add the almonds, then heat and toss until golden; be careful not to let them burn. Drain on kitchen paper.

Place the prawns in a basin with the cornflour, ginger and garlic and mix well.

Heat the oil in the pan, add the prawn mixture and celery and stir-fry for 2 to 3 minutes. Add the soy sauce, sherry, water and pepper and bring to the boil. Add the almonds and heat for 30 seconds, stirring.

Garnish with spring onions and serve hot with stir-fried mixed vegetables.

Serves 4

SKATE WITH BLACK BUTTER

This is the simplest way to cook skate and is delicious.

1–2 wings skate, weighing about 1 kg (2 lb) in all
Court-bouillon (see page 147)
1 tablespoon chopped parsley to garnish

BLACK BUTTER:

50 g (2 oz) butter
2 tablespoons wine vinegar
1 tablespoon capers
salt and pepper

Poach the skate in a shallow pan in the court-bouillon for 15 to 20 minutes or until just tender. Test with a fork: the flesh should flake easily.

Remove from the pan, drain and dry well on absorbent kitchen paper. Transfer to a hot serving dish and keep warm.

Melt the butter in a pan and cook until a rich brown. Stir in the vinegar and capers and boil to reduce slightly. Season to taste with salt and pepper.

Pour over the skate on the serving dish, sprinkle with parsley and serve immediately with boiled new potatoes.

Serves 4

Apricot-Stuffed Trout; Skate with Black Butter

Sea Bass Baked in Spinach

SEA BASS BAKED IN SPINACH

1 sea bass, weighing about 750 g ($1\frac{1}{2}$ lb), cleaned and gutted
250 g (8 oz) spinach
15 g ($\frac{1}{2}$ oz) butter, melted
2 shallots, chopped
150 ml ($\frac{1}{4}$ pint) dry white wine
3 orange slices, quartered, to garnish
STUFFING:
50 g (2 oz) fresh breadcrumbs
15 g ($\frac{1}{2}$ oz) butter, melted
2 tablespoons chopped chervil
1 tablespoon each chopped tarragon and basil
1 tablespoon lemon juice
salt and pepper

Mix the stuffing ingredients together, seasoning with salt and pepper to taste, and use to stuff the fish cavity.

Put the spinach in a colander in a bowl and pour over boiling water. Drain thoroughly.

Wrap the stuffed bass in the blanched spinach, leaving the head and tail exposed.

Pour the melted butter over the base of a gratin dish, sprinkle in the shallots and place the fish on top. Pour over the wine.

Cover with foil and cook in a preheated moderately hot oven, 200°C (400°F), Gas Mark 6, for 30 minutes.

Transfer to a warmed serving dish and garnish with quartered orange slices.

Serves 2

SWEET AND SOUR FISH

$\frac{1}{4}$ teaspoon ground ginger
2 teaspoons cornflour
500 g (1 lb) haddock or cod fillets, cut into pieces
1 tablespoon oil
SAUCE:
1 × 227 g (8 oz) can tomatoes, drained and chopped
1 tablespoon soy sauce
1 tablespoon tomato purée
2 teaspoons cornflour
5 tablespoons water
2 tablespoons sherry
1 teaspoon brown sugar
frisé to garnish

Mix the ginger and cornflour together and sprinkle over the fish. Heat the oil in a frying pan, add the fish and fry for 2 to 3 minutes, stirring. Remove from the pan with a slotted spoon and keep warm.

Wipe the pan clean with kitchen paper and lower the heat. Place the tomatoes and soy sauce in the pan. Combine the remaining sauce ingredients in a small basin, then pour into the pan and cook, stirring, until thickened. Place the fish on individual plates and spoon the sauce next to it.

Garnish with frisé and serve immediately with stir-fried mixed vegetables and rice.

Serves 4

MONKFISH PORTUGUAISE

750 g ($1\frac{1}{2}$ lb) monkfish
500 g (1 lb) tomatoes, skinned, seeded and chopped
2 onions, finely chopped
1 red pepper, cored, seeded and finely chopped
2 tablespoons olive oil
$\frac{1}{2}$ teaspoon chilli powder
1 teaspoon salt
TO GARNISH:
lemon slices
chopped parsley

Remove any bones from the monkfish, divide into 4 neat pieces and arrange in a greased ovenproof dish.

Cover with the tomatoes, onions and pepper. Add the oil, chilli powder and salt.

Cover and cook in a preheated moderately hot oven, 190°C (375°F), Gas Mark 5, for 20 minutes. Remove the lid for the last 5 minutes.

Garnish with lemon slices and parsley to serve.

Serves 4

FISH COUSCOUS

4 tablespoons olive oil
2 onions, roughly chopped
1 clove garlic, finely chopped
8 black peppercorns, crushed
$\frac{1}{2}$ teaspoon cumin
1.5 litres ($2\frac{1}{2}$ pints) water
3 tomatoes, skinned and roughly chopped
2 carrots, roughly chopped
2 turnips, roughly chopped
2 bay leaves
2 sprigs coriander
2 sprigs parsley
4 potatoes, thickly sliced
1.5 kg (3 lb) monkfish, skinned and cut into 6 thick slices
coriander sprigs to garnish
Harissa (see page 153) to serve
COUSCOUS:
500 g (1 lb) couscous
2 tablespoons olive oil

Heat the oil in a couscousier or large saucepan and gently fry the onion, garlic, peppercorns and cumin for 1 to 2 minutes. Add the water, tomatoes, carrots, turnips and herbs, and bring to the boil. Simmer for 20 minutes.

Meanwhile, place the couscous grains in a large bowl, cover with cold water and drain immediately. Stir quickly with a fork and allow to rest for 15 minutes until the grains begin to swell.

Add the potatoes and fish slices to the stew and bring back to simmering point.

Place the couscous grains in a muslin-lined steamer or in the top of the couscousier and place over the pan of vegetables. Steam the couscous, uncovered, for 30 minutes, by which time the fish and potatoes should be tender.

Remove the couscous from the steamer and stir in the olive oil.

To serve, pile the steamed couscous on a large warmed serving dish and serve the fish stew separately. Garnish with coriander sprigs. Pass round a small bowl of harissa.

Serves 6

COUSCOUS

Couscous refers both to the actual grains of semolina and to the cooked dish in which these are the main ingredient. It is the national dish of North Africa, and consists of a steaming mound of couscous with a meat or fish and vegetable stew on top. The traditional cooking pot for making couscous is a *couscousier*. This consists of a large deep stockpot, usually made of aluminium or stainless steel, with a perforated steamer and lid on top. The couscous grains are cooked in the steamer compartment, over the stew which cooks in the stockpot underneath.

Fish Couscous; Sweet and Sour Fish

ORANGE AND PEPPER STUFFED PLAICE

4 plaice fillets
salt and pepper
STUFFING:
1 green pepper, cored, seeded and chopped
50 g (2 oz) breadcrumbs
grated rind and juice of 1 orange
TO GARNISH:
green pepper rings
orange slices

Skin the plaice fillets and sprinkle with salt and pepper. Place on a flat surface.

Mix together the green pepper, breadcrumbs and half the orange rind. Add salt and pepper to taste and bind with a little orange juice. Divide the stuffing between the fillets, roll up and secure with cocktail sticks.

Place in a shallow ovenproof dish and sprinkle with the remaining orange rind, salt and pepper. Pour the remaining orange juice over the fish and cook in a preheated moderate oven, 180°C (350°F), Gas Mark 4, for 30 minutes or until the fish is tender. Remove the cocktail sticks.

Serve garnished with green pepper rings and orange slices.

Serves 4

BOUILLABAISSE WITH ROUILLE

1.2 litres (2 pints) white wine and water, mixed
2 fennel bulbs, quartered
2 bay leaves
2 leeks, chopped
rind of ½ orange
few thyme sprigs
3 onions, chopped
¼ teaspoon saffron
4 tablespoons olive oil
1 red pepper, halved, cored and seeded
salt and pepper
1.75 g (4 lb) assorted fish, cut into 5 cm (2 inch) chunks
pinch of chilli powder
150 ml (¼ pint) Mayonnaise (see page 152)
1 small cooked crab

Put all the ingredients, except the fish, chilli powder, mayonnaise and crab, in a large pan adding salt and pepper to taste. Bring to the boil and boil rapidly for 5 minutes.

Take out the red pepper and add all the fish. Boil rapidly for about 12 to 14 minutes, until the fish is tender but not broken. Discard the bay leaves, orange rind and thyme.

Meanwhile, pound the red pepper with a pinch each of salt and chilli powder until smooth. Fold into the mayonnaise to make the rouille.

Serve the bouillabaisse in individual bowls, dividing the crab between each. Top with rouille and accompany with French bread.

Serves 10

NOTE: Choose from halibut, turbot, eel, grey mullet, bass, hake or cod to make this hearty fish stew.

HADDOCK IN CIDER

750 g (1½ lb) haddock fillets, skinned and cut into chunks
2 eating apples, cored and sliced
2 celery sticks, chopped
1 teaspoon chopped sage
salt and pepper
300 ml (½ pint) dry cider
15 g (½ oz) butter
15 g (½ oz) plain flour
parsley sprigs to garnish

Put the fish in a greased flameproof casserole and cover with the apple slices and celery. Sprinkle with the sage and salt and pepper to taste, then pour in the cider.

Cover and cook in a preheated moderate oven, 180°C (350°F), Gas Mark 4, for 25 to 35 minutes or until the fish is tender.

Transfer the fish and apple slices to a warmed serving dish and keep hot.

Blend the butter with the flour to make a smooth paste. Add a little of the hot cooking liquid, then stir this into the remaining liquid in the casserole. Bring to the boil on top of the stove, stirring, and simmer until thickened, then pour over the fish. Garnish with parsley.

Serves 4

TURBOT AND PRAWN CREOLE

1 onion, chopped
1 green pepper, cored, seeded and chopped
1 × 397 g (14 oz) can tomatoes
½ teaspoon basil
½ teaspoon oregano
pinch of sugar
salt and pepper
250 g (8 oz) turbot, cut into cubes
250 g (8 oz) peeled prawns
2 teaspoons cornflour
2 tablespoons dry white wine
TO GARNISH:
whole prawns
chopped parsley

Place the onion, green pepper, tomatoes and their juice, basil, oregano and sugar in a pan. Add salt and pepper to taste. Bring to the boil, cover and simmer for 15 minutes.

Add the turbot and peeled prawns and simmer for a further 10 to 15 minutes. Blend the cornflour and wine until smooth, then stir into the sauce. Heat until the sauce thickens and continue cooking for 2 minutes.

Transfer to a hot serving dish and garnish with whole prawns and chopped parsley.

Serves 4

SMOKED HADDOCK WITH VEGETABLES

1 onion, finely chopped
1 celery stick, finely chopped
1 carrot, grated
2 tablespoons frozen peas
salt and pepper
500 g (1 lb) smoked haddock fillet
15 g (½ oz) butter
6 tablespoons tomato juice
parsley sprigs to garnish

Place the onion, celery, carrot and peas in a shallow ovenproof dish. Sprinkle with salt and pepper.

Cut the haddock into 4 portions and arrange on top of the vegetables. Dot with the butter and spoon the tomato juice over the fish.

Cover with foil and cook in a preheated moderately hot oven, 190°C (375°F), Gas Mark 5, for 30 minutes. Serve garnished with parsley.

Serves 4

LEFT: *Bouillabaise with Rouille*
RIGHT: *Turbot and Prawn Creole; Smoked Haddock with Vegetables*

SPAGHETTI WITH MUSSELS

1 kg (2 lb) fresh mussels, scrubbed clean and beards removed
4 tablespoons olive oil
75 g (3 oz) butter
2–3 cloves garlic, crushed
1 large onion, finely chopped
750 g (1½ lb) tomatoes, skinned, seeded and chopped
150 ml (¼ pint) dry white wine
1 teaspoon dried mixed herbs
salt and pepper
500 g (1 lb) fresh spaghetti
chopped parsley to garnish

Put the mussels in a large pan, cover with water, bring to the boil and cook for 5 to 6 minutes, until the shells have opened. Reserve 4 tablespoons of water. Drain the mussels, discarding any that have not opened.

Heat the oil and 25 g (1 oz) of the butter in a pan, add the garlic and onion and cook for 5 minutes, until pale golden. Add the tomatoes, wine, herbs, salt and pepper to taste, and the reserved cooking liquid. Bring to the boil and cook, uncovered, for 30 minutes, until thickened.

Meanwhile, cook the spaghetti until *al dente*. Drain thoroughly and turn into a warmed serving dish. Add the remaining butter and toss.

Add the mussels to the sauce and heat through. Pour over the pasta, sprinkle with parsley and serve.

Serves 4 to 6

FISH CASSEROLE

12 mussels, cleaned
salt and pepper
1 monkfish, cleaned and filleted
2 squid, cleaned and ink sac removed
2 tablespoons oil
2 onions, chopped
2 carrots, thinly sliced
6 celery sticks, sliced
2 cloves garlic, crushed
1 × 397 g (14 oz) can tomatoes
2 teaspoons sugar
2 tablespoons lemon juice
2 tablespoons lime juice
2 tablespoons chopped coriander
1 bouquet garni
150 ml (¼ pint) dry cider
few drops of Tabasco
4 scallops, cleaned and cut in half horizontally
6 small red mullet, scaled and cleaned
chopped coriander to garnish

Place the mussels in a pan of boiling salted water and cook for about 7 minutes, until they open; discard any that do not open.

Cut the monkfish into 2.5 cm (1 inch) chunks. Cut the squid into thin slices; leave the tentacles in small pieces.

Heat the oil in a large pan, add the onions, carrots, celery and garlic and sauté for 4 minutes. Add the remaining ingredients, except the fish, with salt and pepper to taste, and bring to the boil. Add all the fish except the mussels, cover and simmer for 15 to 20 minutes, until the fish is cooked. Discard the bouquet garni.

Stir in the mussels, and transfer to a warmed serving dish. Sprinkle with coriander and serve immediately.

Serves 6

MUSSELS AND SQUID

Mussels should be scrubbed clean and the hair-like beards removed before steaming to open them. Any mussels that don't open on cooking should be discarded.

To prepare squid, draw back the rim of the body pouch to locate the quill-shaped backbone and pull free to discard. Separate the body from the tentacles by pulling gently apart just below the eyes – the inedible head and ink sac will come away together. To skin the body, slip a finger under the skin and peel away gently.

LEFT: *Fish Casserole*
RIGHT: *Crispy Giant Prawns; Wok-Style Seafood*

CRISPY GIANT PRAWNS

125 g (4 oz) plain flour
pinch of salt
1 tablespoon oil
150 ml ($\frac{1}{4}$ pint) beer or lager
2 egg whites
1 tablespoon chopped parsley
16 giant Mediterranean prawns, shelled
oil for deep-frying
SAUCE:
8 tablespoons Mayonnaise (see page 152)
2 cloves garlic, crushed
2 tablespoons chopped thyme
1 teaspoon finely grated lemon rind
dash of Tabasco

Sift the flour and salt into a bowl, then gradually beat in the oil and beer. Whisk the egg whites until very stiff, then fold into the batter with the parsley. Drop in the prawns and coat well.

Heat the oil in a wok or deep-fryer to 190°C (375°F) and deep-fry the prawns in batches for 2 to 3 minutes, until golden brown and crisp. Drain on kitchen paper and keep hot while frying the remainder.

Mix all the sauce ingredients together, reserving a little of the lemon rind, and spoon into a bowl. Sprinkle the reserved lemon rind on top. Serve immediately, with the hot prawns.

Serves 4

WOK-STYLE SEAFOOD

1 fish carcass
300 ml ($\frac{1}{2}$ pint) dry white wine
1 bouquet garni
3 shallots, finely chopped
25 g (1 oz) butter
4 sole fillets, cut into small pieces
250 g (8 oz) haddock fillet, cut into small pieces
8 scallops, halved
350 g (12 oz) tomatoes, skinned, seeded and chopped
1 clove garlic, crushed
1 tablespoon chopped thyme
250 g (8 oz) peeled prawns
142 ml (5 fl oz) double cream
salt and pepper

Place the fish carcass, wine, bouquet garni and 1 shallot in a wok, bring to the boil, then cover and simmer for 15 minutes. Leave until cold, then strain. Wash the wok.

Melt the butter in the wok, add the remaining shallots and sauté for 2 to 3 minutes. Add the stock, chopped fish and scallops. Cook for 1 minute; remove with a slotted spoon.

Boil the stock rapidly for 8 to 10 minutes, until reduced to one-third. Stir in the tomatoes and garlic, lower the heat and cook for 5 to 7 minutes, stirring occasionally. Stir in the thyme and cook for 2 minutes, until thickened.

Return the fish to the pan, add the prawns and stir in the cream. Season with salt and pepper, and heat through gently. Serve immediately with rice or noodles.

Serves 4

POACHED SALMON TROUT

A method of cooking a salmon trout without a fish kettle.

1–2 tablespoons olive oil
1 salmon trout, weighing about 1 kg (2 lb), cleaned and gutted
1 bay leaf
1 lemon, sliced
1 teaspoon salt
12 black peppercorns
300 ml (½ pint) dry white wine
TO GARNISH:
½ × 25 g (1 oz) packet aspic powder
2 lemons, sliced
2 limes, sliced
small bunch of dill
bunch of watercress

Line a large roasting pan with foil and brush with oil. Place the fish on the foil, curving slightly. Place the bay leaf and lemon on the fish, then sprinkle with the salt and peppercorns. Pour over the wine. Bring the edges of foil together and seal to make a loose parcel.

Cook in a preheated cool oven, 150°C (300°F), Gas Mark 2, for 30 minutes. Leave to cool in the pan.

Unwrap the fish, carefully remove the skin, leaving some around the head and tail, and place on a dish.

Make up the aspic to 300 ml (½ pint) according to packet directions and coat the fish with a thin layer.

Cut most of the lemon and lime slices into quarters and arrange down the centre of the fish with the dill. Brush the lemon and lime slices with a little aspic jelly. Chill until set. Garnish with any remaining lemon and lime slices and watercress.

Serves 4

SEA BASS PROVENÇAL

1 × 1.25–1.5 kg (2½–3 lb) sea bass
1 glass olive oil
1 glass dry white wine
1 large bunch fennel, roughly chopped
2 cloves garlic, chopped
2 small onions, finely sliced
500 g (1 lb) potatoes, finely sliced
175 g (6 oz) mushrooms, sliced
salt and pepper
600 ml (1 pint) water
Aioli (see page 149) to serve

Place the fish in a large baking dish. Pour over the oil and wine, and cover with the fennel and garlic. Arrange the sliced onions, potatoes and mushrooms around the fish. Season with salt and pepper. Pour on the water and bake in a preheated moderately hot oven, 200°C (400°F), Gas Mark 6, for 1 hour.

Serve with a bowl of aioli and hunks of crusty bread.

Serves 4 to 6

MONKFISH AND SCALLOP CASSEROLE

40 g (1½ oz) butter
1 onion, sliced
1 celery stick, sliced
1 large carrot, diced
1–2 cloves garlic, crushed
500 g (1 lb) monkfish
350 g (12 oz) prepared scallops
1 × 425 g (15 oz) can tomatoes
1 tablespoon tomato purée
½ teaspoon Worcestershire sauce
1 tablespoon lemon juice
150 ml (¼ pint) dry white wine
salt and pepper
good pinch of ground coriander
1 bay leaf
1 tablespoon cornflour
bay leaves to garnish

Melt the butter in a flameproof casserole and fry the onion, celery, carrot and garlic gently until soft, stirring occasionally.

Skin the monkfish and cut it into 2 cm (¾ inch) cubes. Halve or quarter the scallops, depending on their size. Add the fish to the casserole and continue cooking for 2 to 3 minutes, stirring occasionally.

Add the can of tomatoes, tomato purée, Worcestershire sauce, lemon juice, wine, salt and pepper, coriander and the bay leaf and bring to the boil.

Cover the casserole tightly and cook in a preheated moderate oven, 160°C (325°F), Gas Mark 3, for 40 minutes.

Blend the cornflour with a little cold water, add it to the casserole, and bring back to the boil for 1 to 2 minutes. Taste and adjust the seasoning, discard the bay leaf. Garnish with bay leaves and serve with rice.

Serves 6

CITRUS HALIBUT STEAK

grated rind and juice of 1 orange, 1 lemon and 1 lime
2 halibut steaks, cut in half
TO GARNISH:
orange, lemon or lime slices

Place 1 tablespoon of each grated rind and all the fruit juices in an ovenproof dish. Add the fish and baste well. Cover and chill for 12 hours, turning the steaks over after 6 hours.

Cover the dish with foil and cook in a preheated moderate oven, 180°C (350°F), Gas Mark 4, for 20 minutes.

Garnish each portion with a slice of orange, lemon or lime, and serve with mangetout.

Serves 4

Monkfish and Scallop Casserole; Citrus Halibut Steak

SEAFOOD CHAUDRÉE

1 bottle dry white wine
4 cloves garlic, crushed
few parsley stalks
salt and white pepper
125 g (4 oz) long-grain rice
good pinch of powdered saffron
4 celery sticks, halved
250 g (8 oz) shelled broad beans
1 kg (2 lb) mixed white fish, cut into large pieces
250 g (8 oz) prawns in shells, tail shells removed
142 ml (5 fl oz) soured cream
1 tablespoon plain flour
chopped parsley to garnish

Put the wine, garlic, parsley stalks, and salt and pepper to taste in a large pan, cover and bring to the boil. Lower the heat and simmer, uncovered, for 15 minutes to reduce the wine.

Add the rice, saffron, celery and beans and cook, covered, for 15 to 20 minutes, adding all the fish after 5 minutes. Transfer the fish and vegetables to a warmed serving dish.

Mix the cream and flour together and add to the liquid remaining in the pan. Bring to the boil, stirring, until smooth.

Pour over the fish, sprinkle with parsley and serve with French bread.

Serves 4

NOTE: Use a selection of mixed white fish, such as coley, monkfish, bream and whiting.

DEVILLED CRAB

2 cooked crabs
142 ml (5 fl oz) double cream
1 teaspoon Dijon mustard
2 teaspoons anchovy essence
1 teaspoon Worcestershire sauce
½ teaspoon chilli powder
1 teaspoon lemon juice
2 tablespoons chopped parsley
1 teaspoon chopped marjoram
125 g (4 oz) tomatoes, skinned and chopped
2 tablespoons dry sherry
salt and pepper
2 tablespoons bread-crumbs, toasted
2 tablespoons grated Cheshire cheese
TO GARNISH:
lettuce leaves
watercress
cucumber slices

Place all the crabmeat in a large bowl. Stir in the cream, mustard, anchovy essence, Worcestershire sauce, chilli powder, lemon juice, parsley, marjoram, tomatoes, sherry, and salt and pepper to taste.

Brush the cleaned crab shells, inside and out, with oil. Divide the mixture between the shells; put any left-over mixture in a ramekin dish. Sprinkle with the breadcrumbs and cheese and cook in a preheated moderately hot oven, 200°C (400°F), Gas Mark 6, for 15 to 20 minutes, until golden brown.

To serve, place on a bed of lettuce and garnish with watercress and cucumber slices.

Serves 4

TO COOK A CRAB

Weigh the crab, if at all possible!

Have ready a large saucepan full of boiling salted water: use 175 g (6 oz) salt to 2–2.25 litres (3½–4 pints) water. Add 1 bay leaf, 5 peppercorns, 1 sliced onion and 2 sliced celery sticks.

Put the crab in the water, cover the pan and bring to simmering point. Cook, allowing 15 minutes for the first 500 g (1 lb) and 8 minutes for each additional 500 g (1 lb). Remove from the pan and leave until cool.

LEFT: *Devilled Crab*
RIGHT: *Dressed Crab*

DRESSED CRAB

1 medium cooked crab
salt and pepper
good pinch of chilli powder
1 teaspoon dry white wine or cider vinegar
1 teaspoon gin (optional)
1 tablespoon chopped parsley
TO GARNISH:
1 hard-boiled egg, chopped
2 tablespoons finely chopped parsley

Place the crab on its back. Using a twisting action, remove the legs and claws from the body and set aside.

To separate the body, have the tail flap towards you. Hold the shell firmly with your fingers and, using your thumbs, push the body upwards until it becomes loosened, then separate from the shell.

Remove and discard the intestines or stomach bag and the grey feathery gills known as 'dead man's fingers'.

Spoon out the brown meat from the shell and place in a dish.

Cut the body in half. Using a thin skewer, dig out the white meat from the crevices. This may take time and patience, but is well worth it. Place in a separate dish.

Carefully crack open the reserved claws and legs using the back of a wooden spoon or a rolling pin and remove all the white meat; don't hit too hard or you will break up the meat. Add to the other white meat.

Trim the crab shell by tapping gently with a spoon around the natural marked line on the shell. Clean the shell ready for serving.

Finely chop the white meat and season to taste with salt and pepper, chilli powder and the dry white wine or cider vinegar.

Mix the brown meat with salt and pepper to taste, the gin, if using, and the finely chopped parsley.

Place the brown crabmeat in the centre of the shell and the white crabmeat on either side. Garnish with rows of chopped hard-boiled egg yolk and white, and the finely chopped parsley, see picture right.

Serve with an avocado and lettuce salad and Mayonnaise (see page 152).

Serves 2 to 4

CORNISH EEL

25 g (1 oz) butter
1 onion, chopped
500–750 g (1–1½ lb) conger eel, cut into slices
15 g (½ oz) plain flour
450 ml (¾ pint) dry cider
1 cooking apple, peeled, cored and sliced
2 cloves
salt and pepper
TO GARNISH:
mint or parsley sprigs
lemon slices

Melt the butter in a flameproof casserole, add the onion and fry until softened.

Add the eel pieces and brown lightly. Stir in the flour and cook for 2 minutes, stirring, then gradually pour in the cider, stirring. Add the apple, cloves, and salt and pepper to taste and bring to the boil. Cook in a preheated moderate oven, 180°C (350°F), Gas Mark 4, for 1 hour.

Garnish with mint or parsley and lemon and serve immediately.

Serves 4

RED MULLET IN VINE LEAVES

6 vine leaves
2 × 250 g (8 oz) red mullet, scaled and washed
sunflower oil for brushing
STUFFING:
1 large tomato, chopped
2 anchovy fillets, chopped
2 tablespoons chopped parsley
1 tablespoon chopped basil
1 clove garlic, crushed
salt and pepper
TO GARNISH:
4 anchovies
2 black olives

Mix the stuffing ingredients together, seasoning with salt and pepper, and divide between 2 vine leaves, spreading over one side of each leaf.

Arrange the vine leaves overlapping into two groups of three, with a covered vine leaf forming the centre of each group. Place the mullet on top and wrap the vine leaves around.

Place in a roasting pan, brush with oil and cook in a preheated moderately hot oven, 200°C (400°F), Gas Mark 6, for 15 minutes.

Transfer to a warmed serving dish and top with the anchovies and olives.

Serves 2

AVOCADO-STUFFED RAINBOW TROUT

4 rainbow trout, cleaned and gutted
sunflower oil
STUFFING:
1 ripe avocado pear, peeled and chopped
1 teaspoon lemon juice
25 g (1 oz) pistachio nuts, finely chopped
1 tablespoon clear honey
1 tablespoon soy sauce
salt and pepper
TO GARNISH:
lime slices
coriander leaves

Mix all the stuffing ingredients together, adding salt and pepper to taste. Divide the stuffing between the trout, placing it in the cavity of each fish.

Place the trout in a roasting pan, brush with sunflower oil and cover with foil. Cook in a preheated moderate oven, 180°C (350°F), Gas Mark 4, for 20 minutes or until tender.

Transfer to a warmed serving dish. Garnish with lime and coriander and serve immediately.

Serves 4

Avocado-Stuffed Rainbow Trout

SALMON KOULIBIAC

625 g (1¼ lb) salmon, fresh or frozen and thawed
6 tablespoons milk
salt and pepper
125 g (4 oz) mushrooms, sliced
1 large onion, chopped
75 g (3 oz) brown rice, cooked
1 tablespoon chopped parsley
1 × 370 g (13 oz) packet frozen puff pastry, thawed
beaten egg to glaze
parsley sprigs to garnish

Put the salmon in a pan with the milk and salt and pepper to taste. Bring to the boil, cover and simmer for 5 minutes. Leave to cool in the pan. Drain, reserving the liquid.

Flake the fish, discarding the skin and bones. Combine the salmon with the mushrooms, onion, rice and parsley to make the filling.

Roll out the pastry to 37 × 33 cm (15 × 13 inches) and trim edges. Cut into 2 strips, one 15 cm (6 inches), and one 18 cm (7 inches) wide. Put the narrower strip on a baking sheet and cover, to within 1.5 cm (¾ inch) of the edges, with the filling. Dampen edges and cover with remaining pastry, sealing edges. Decorate with the pastry trimmings. Brush with egg and bake in a preheated moderately hot oven, 200°C (400°F), Gas Mark 6, for 30 minutes. Serve with Parsley sauce (see page 147) and garnish with parsley.

Serves 6

PRAWNS IN HERB BUTTER

1 kg (2 lb) unshelled raw prawns
salt and pepper
1.75 litres (3 pints) water
125 g (4 oz) butter
2 tablespoons chopped parsley
3 tablespoons chopped fresh herbs as available (preferably tarragon and basil)
juice of ½ lemon
chopped parsley to garnish

Cook the prawns in lightly salted boiling water for about 5 minutes or until pink. Drain and allow to cool slightly, then remove the shells.

Cream together the butter, parsley, herbs, salt and pepper to taste and the lemon juice. Spread half the herb butter over the bottom of a flameproof baking dish. Press the prawns into the butter, and cover with the remaining herb butter.

Cook in a preheated moderately hot oven, 200°C (400°F), Gas Mark 6, for 10 minutes. Pop the dish under a preheated grill and cook for a few more minutes or until the top browns. Garnish with parsley.

Serves 4

NOTE: If raw prawns are unobtainable, substitute 500 g (1 lb) frozen, shelled prawns. Do not precook; simply thaw before adding to the herb butter.

Salmon Koulibiac

OYSTERS À LA CRÈME

12 oysters
15 g (½ oz) butter
1 shallot, finely chopped
1 teaspoon chopped chervil
142 ml (5 fl oz) double cream
salt and pepper
25 g (1 oz) Gruyère cheese, grated
1 tablespoon dried breadcrumbs
TO GARNISH:
chervil sprigs
lemon wedges

Open the oysters (see page 125). Return the oysters to the deeper rounded shell and arrange on a baking sheet, keeping them level with foil.

Melt the butter in a small pan, add the shallot and sauté until soft. Stir in the chervil, cream, and salt and pepper to taste and gently bring to the boil. Remove from the heat and stir in the cheese.

Cover each oyster with the sauce and sprinkle with the breadcrumbs.

Place under a preheated moderate grill for 2 minutes, until golden brown. Garnish with chervil and lemon and serve immediately.

Serves 2 to 4

OYSTERS WITH SMOKED SALMON

12 oysters
75 g (3 oz) smoked salmon, chopped
½ × 397 g (14 oz) can artichoke hearts, drained and finely chopped
25 g (1 oz) Gruyère cheese, grated
2 tablespoons dried breadcrumbs
pepper
HERB BUTTER:
75 g (3 oz) butter, softened
1 tablespoon chopped chervil
1 tablespoon chopped tarragon
2 teaspoons lemon juice
TO GARNISH:
lime wedges
tarragon leaves

First make the herb butter by beating all the ingredients together in a small bowl.

Open the oysters (see page 125). Return the oysters to the deeper rounded shell.

Place a little chopped salmon and artichoke on each oyster and dot with the herb butter. Sprinkle with the cheese, breadcrumbs, and pepper to taste.

Place on a baking sheet, balancing the oyster shells with foil if necessary. Cook in a preheated moderately hot oven, 200°C (400°F), Gas Mark 6, for 15 minutes. Alternatively, place under a preheated moderate grill for 10 to 15 minutes, until golden.

Transfer to a warmed serving dish, garnish with lime wedges and tarragon leaves and serve with brown bread and butter.

Serves 2 to 4

JOHN DORY FILLETS

25 g (1 oz) plain flour
salt and pepper
6 John Dory fillets
175 g (6 oz) butter
350 g (12 oz) mushrooms, sliced
1 clove garlic, crushed
8 tablespoons double cream
1 teaspoon lemon juice
TO GARNISH:
parsley sprig
lemon wedges

Season the flour with salt and pepper and use to coat the fish.

Heat 125 g (4 oz) of the butter in a small pan until bubbling. Line a sieve with muslin and pour the butter through this into a frying pan. Add the fish and fry gently for 3 minutes on each side. Keep warm.

Melt the remaining butter in another pan, add the mushrooms and garlic, cover and simmer for 8 minutes. Stir in the cream, lemon juice, and salt and pepper to taste and heat gently.

Arrange the fish on a warmed serving dish and pour over the sauce. Garnish with parsley and lemon wedges to serve.

Serves 6

CURRIED PRAWN RING

350 g (12 oz) long-grain rice
salt
few saffron threads
1 tablespoon sunflower oil
1 tablespoon curry powder
8 spring onions, chopped
1 red pepper, cored, seeded and chopped
50 g (2 oz) pine nuts
75 g (3 oz) sultanas
250 g (8 oz) peeled prawns

DRESSING:
4 tablespoons olive oil
2 tablespoons white wine vinegar
1 teaspoon dry mustard
1 teaspoon sugar
2 tablespoons chopped coriander

TO GARNISH:
orange wedges
celery leaves

Cook the rice in boiling salted water, with the saffron added, for about 20 minutes, until the rice is tender and the liquid absorbed.

Meanwhile, place the dressing ingredients in a screw-top jar and shake well to blend.

Drain the rice, place in a bowl and stir in the dressing while still warm. Set aside to cool slightly.

Heat the oil in a pan, add the curry powder, spring onions, red pepper, pine nuts and sultanas and cook, stirring, for $1\frac{1}{2}$ minutes. Add to the rice and leave until completely cold.

Stir in the prawns, then spoon the mixture into a lightly oiled 1.5 litre ($2\frac{1}{2}$ pint) ring mould, pressing down well. Chill until required.

To serve, invert the ring onto a serving plate and garnish with orange wedges and celery leaves.

Serves 4 to 6

OPENING OYSTERS

To open oysters, use a special oyster knife, if possible, or a round short-bladed knife.

To protect your hand from the rough-edged shells, scrub them first and place a clean cloth in your palm. Holding the oyster over a bowl to catch the juice, insert the knife into the 'hinge' and twist between shells to prise them open.

Oysters are good on their own, *au naturel*. To ensure freshness, open them just before serving. To serve them *au naturel*, serve on the flat shell on a bed of crushed ice. Season lightly with black pepper and serve with lemon wedges, brown bread and butter.

LEFT: *Oysters à la Crème; Oysters with Smoked Salmon*
RIGHT: *Curried Prawn Ring; John Dory Fillets*

SOLE FILLETS WITH SOY AND GINGER

500–750 g (1–$1\frac{1}{2}$ lb) sole fillets, skinned skinned
2 egg whites
1 teaspoon cornflour
$\frac{1}{2}$ teaspoon sea salt
3 tablespoons grapeseed oil
1 × 5 cm (2 inch) piece fresh root ginger, grated
1 large clove garlic, finely chopped
3 tablespoons soy sauce
1 tablespoon dry sherry
3 tablespoons Fish stock (see page 146)
3 spring onions, cut into small pieces

Cut the sole into long thin strips. Beat the egg whites, cornflour and salt until frothy, then pour over the fish; mix well. Chill for 20 minutes.

Heat the oil in a wok or large frying pan. When nearly smoking, add the fish and stir-fry over a fairly high heat for 2 minutes. Remove from the pan with a slotted spoon. Discard all but 1 tablespoon of oil.

Add the ginger and chopped garlic and stir-fry for 1 minute, then pour in the soy sauce, sherry and fish stock. Bring to the boil quickly, then bubble for 2 minutes.

Return the fish to the pan and heat through for 1 minute, stirring constantly, then pile onto a warmed serving dish, sprinkling with the spring onion tops and serve at once, with boiled rice or baby corn-cobs.

Serves 6

SOLE VÉRONIQUE

750 g ($1\frac{1}{2}$ lb) sole or plaice fillets, skinned
2 shallots or small onions, chopped
1 sprig parsley
1 bay leaf
150 ml ($\frac{1}{4}$ pint) dry white wine
1 tablespoon lemon juice
salt and pepper
15 g ($\frac{1}{2}$ oz) butter
2 tablespoons plain flour
5 tablespoons milk (approximately)
1 tablespoon cream
175 g (6 oz) grapes, halved, deseeded and skinned

Fold the fillets in half and arrange in a buttered ovenproof dish. Sprinkle with the shallots or small onions, parsley, bay leaf, wine, lemon juice, and salt and pepper to taste. Add just enough water to cover the fish.

Cook in a preheated moderate oven, 180°C (350°F), Gas Mark 4, for 15 to 20 minutes until tender. Transfer the fillets to a warmed serving dish, using a slotted spoon. Keep warm. Strain the stock.

Melt the butter in a pan, stir in the flour and cook for 1 minute. Gradually stir in the stock and enough milk to make a smooth pouring sauce.

Adjust the seasoning and stir in the cream and grapes. Spoon over the fish and serve immediately.

Serves 4

BARBECUED SARDINES

16 fresh sardines, cleaned
Spicy gooseberry sauce (see page 148) to serve
MARINADE:
8 tablespoons lemon juice
2 tablespoons lime juice
3 cloves garlic, crushed
1 teaspoon paprika
1 teaspoon ground ginger
1 teaspoon ground cumin
1 teaspoon tomato purée
TO GARNISH:
lime slices
basil sprigs

Place the sardines in a flat dish. Mix the marinade ingredients together and pour over the fish. Leave to marinate in the refrigerator for 1 hour. Remove with a slotted spoon, reserving the marinade.

Line a grill pan with greased foil and place the sardines in the pan.

Cook under a preheated grill for 5 minutes on each side, basting with the marinade.

Garnish with lime and basil. Accompany with spicy gooseberry sauce.

Serves 6 to 8

Sole Fillets with Soy and Ginger

SCALLOPS PARISIENNE

250 g (8 oz) Jerusalem artichokes, sliced
250 g (8 oz) frozen, sliced green beans, thawed
1.2 litres (2 pints) boiling water
salt and pepper
25 g (1 oz) butter
1 tablespoon oil
1 small onion, chopped
12–16 frozen scallops, depending on size, thawed
2 tablespoons plain flour
1 teaspoon paprika
450 ml ($\frac{3}{4}$ pint) milk
TO GARNISH:
1 tablespoon chopped parsley
4 small tomatoes, halved

Put the Jerusalem artichokes and beans in a large pan, cover with the water, season with a pinch of salt, cover and bring back to the boil. Lower the heat and simmer for 15 minutes; drain.

Dry the pan, heat the butter and oil, add the onion and sauté for 3 to 4 minutes. Stir in the scallops and cook for 5 minutes. Add the flour and paprika and cook, stirring, for 1 minute. Gradually add the milk, stirring, to make a sauce.

Replace the vegetables and reheat for 3 to 4 minutes. Sprinkle with the parsley, garnish with the tomatoes and serve with hot buttered toast.
Serves 4

HONEY-GLAZED TROUT

15 g ($\frac{1}{2}$ oz) unsalted butter
2 tablespoons oil
25 g (1 oz) slivered almonds
2 shallots, chopped
4 celery sticks, sliced
salt and pepper
1 tablespoon plain flour
$1\frac{1}{2}$ teaspoons ground ginger
4 × 175 g (6 oz) trout, cleaned
2 tablespoons clear honey
6 tablespoons white wine
1 × 340 g (12 oz) can asparagus spears, drained

Melt the butter and oil in a large frying pan, add the almonds and fry until brown; remove with a slotted spoon. Add the shallots, celery, and salt and pepper to taste and fry gently for 5 minutes.

Season the flour with $\frac{1}{2}$ teaspoon of the ginger and use to coat the trout. Add to the pan and fry for 1 to 2 minutes on each side. Mix the remaining ginger with the honey and wine and pour over the trout. Add the asparagus.

Cover, lower the heat and cook for 5 minutes, until the fish is cooked, the asparagus is heated through and the liquid is a glaze.

Serve with a new potato salad.
Serves 4

Scallops Parisienne; Honey-Glazed Trout

LOBSTER WITH TOMATO SAUCE

2 × 500–750 g (1–1½ lb) cooked lobsters
25 g (1 oz) butter
1 tablespoon dry sherry
TOMATO SAUCE:
1 tablespoon sunflower oil
1 onion, finely chopped
1 carrot, finely chopped
2 cloves garlic, crushed
1 × 793 g (1 lb 12 oz) can tomatoes or
1 kg (2 lb) fresh tomatoes, skinned
1 teaspoon sugar
150 ml (¼ pint) dry red wine
salt and pepper
1 teaspoon chilli powder
TO GARNISH:
lime wedges
basil sprigs

First make the tomato sauce. Heat the oil in a pan, add the onion and carrot and fry until golden. Add the garlic, tomatoes with their juice, sugar, wine, and salt and pepper to taste. Bring to the boil, stirring with a wooden spoon to break up the tomatoes, then simmer for 20 to 30 minutes, until thickened.

Rub through a sieve, or work in an electric blender or food processor, and return to the pan. Stir in the chilli powder.

Extract the lobster meat and slice into pieces. Clean the shells and set aside.

Add the lobster meat to the warm tomato sauce and heat through. Stir in the butter and sherry. Return to the shells or place on a serving plate.

Garnish with lime wedges and basil to serve.

Serves 4 to 6

GREEK PRAWN CASSEROLE

300 ml (½ pint) water
juice of ½ lemon
1 kg (2 lb) unshelled raw prawns
3 tablespoons olive oil
1 onion, finely chopped
1 clove garlic, crushed
2 × 397 g (14 oz) cans tomatoes, drained and chopped
¾ teaspoon dried oregano
salt and pepper
75 g (3 oz) Feta cheese, crumbled

Bring the water and lemon juice to the boil in a saucepan. Add the raw prawns and simmer for 5 minutes or until pink in colour. Drain, reserving the liquid, cool slightly, then remove the shells. Boil the liquid until reduced to 150 ml (¼ pint).

Heat the oil in a flameproof casserole. Add the chopped onion and crushed garlic and fry until softened. Stir in the tomatoes, oregano, reserved prawn cooking liquid, and salt and pepper to taste. Simmer until the sauce is reduced and thickened.

Fold the cooked prawns into the sauce. Sprinkle the Feta cheese on top and cook in a preheated moderate oven, 180°C (350°F), Gas Mark 4, for 15 minutes.

Serves 4

COOKING AND PREPARING A LOBSTER

Have ready a large pan of boiling salted water: use about 175 g (6 oz) salt to 2 litres (3½ pints) water. Put the lobster in the water, cover the pan and return to simmering point. Cook, allowing 12 to 15 minutes for the first 500 g (1 lb) and 10 minutes for each additional 500 g (1 lb). Remove the cooked lobster from the pan and place it on its back. Remove the legs and claws with a firm twisting action and, using the back of a wooden spoon, crack them open and carefully extract the meat. Turn the lobster over and, using a sharp knife, draw it through the head from the shoulder up towards the eye. Now cut along the centre of the body to the tail, splitting the lobster into two halves. Discard the white gills, the dark intestinal vein which goes into the tail, and the small stomach sac which lies in the head. Don't discard the green creamy liver in the head, which is a delicacy and can be used to make lobster sauce; the red coral or roe in a female lobster can be used likewise. Finally, extract the white meat from the lobster and use as desired.

LOBSTER THERMIDOR

450 ml (¾ pint) milk
1 onion, cut into quarters
1 bay leaf
1 bouquet garni
150 ml (¼ pint) dry white wine
3 × 500–750 g (1–1½ lb) cooked lobsters
125 g (4 oz) unsalted butter
50 g (2 oz) plain flour
2 teaspoons Dijon mustard
2 large egg yolks (size 1)
142 ml (5 fl oz) single cream
2 teaspoons lemon juice
2 tablespoons finely chopped parsley
salt and pepper
TOPPING:
50 g (2 oz) fresh breadcrumbs
75 g (3 oz) Parmesan cheese, grated
TO GARNISH:
lemon or lime wedges
parsley sprigs

Pour the milk into a saucepan and add the onion, bay leaf and bouquet garni. Bring to the boil, then remove from the heat and leave to infuse for 30 minutes.

Place the wine in a small pan and boil for 3 minutes to reduce.

Prepare the lobsters as described on page 128. Cut the meat into 1 cm (½ inch) pieces and set aside. Sieve any coral and set aside. Clean the shells and set aside.

Melt half the butter in a frying pan, add the lobster meat and cook gently, stirring, for 2 minutes. Remove from the heat.

Melt the remaining butter in another pan, stir in the flour and cook for 1 minute. Remove from the heat.

Strain the infused milk, then gradually beat into the roux. Add the reduced wine, bring gently to the boil, then simmer for 4 minutes.

Leave to cool then stir in the mustard, egg yolks, coral if present, cream, lemon juice, parsley, and salt and pepper to taste. Spoon a little of this sauce into the bottom of each lobster shell.

Add the lobster meat to the remaining sauce and stir gently. Spoon into the shells and sprinkle with the breadcrumbs and cheese.

Place on a baking sheet and cook in a preheated moderately hot oven, 200°C (400°F), Gas Mark 6, for 7 to 10 minutes, until golden brown.

Garnish with lemon or lime wedges and parsley. Serve immediately.

Serves 6

LEFT: *Lobster with Tomato Sauce*
RIGHT: *Lobster Thermidor*

SEAFOOD CANNELLONI

SAUCE:
2 celery sticks, chopped
2 carrots, chopped
600 ml (1 pint) milk
1 onion, quartered
3 peppercorns
1 bay leaf
50 g (2 oz) butter
50 g (2 oz) plain flour
1 tablespoon chopped dill
2 tablespoons chopped parsley
salt and pepper
250 g (8 oz) Pasta dough (see page 132)
FILLING:
150 ml ($\frac{1}{4}$ pint) dry white wine
4 scallops, shelled and halved
15 g ($\frac{1}{2}$ oz) butter
2 spring onions, chopped
250 g (8 oz) peeled prawns
125 g (4 oz) matured Cheddar cheese, grated
4 tablespoons grated Parmesan cheese
1 tablespoon oil for cooking pasta
2 tablespoons dried breadcrumbs
TO GARNISH:
1 tablespoon finely chopped parsley
1 tablespoon finely chopped dill

First make the sauce. Put the celery and carrots in a pan with the milk, onion, peppercorns and bay leaf. Bring to the boil, remove from the heat and leave until cold. Strain and set aside the milk.

Melt the butter in a pan, stir in the flour and cook for 2 minutes, stirring. Gradually add the milk, stirring constantly. Bring to the boil and cook for 2 minutes, stirring. Stir in the herbs and salt to taste.

To make the filling, place the wine in a small pan and bring to the boil. Add the scallops and cook, uncovered, for about 2 minutes, until tender. Remove with a slotted spoon and set aside. Reserve the wine.

Melt the butter in a pan, add the spring onions and cook, without browning, for 1 minute. Add the reserved wine and boil for 1 to 2 minutes until reduced to about 2 tablespoons. Remove from the heat, stir in just over a quarter of the sauce and mix well. Add the prawns, scallops, salt, pepper and cheeses, heating if necessary to melt. Roll out and cook the pasta dough with the oil (see opposite).

Divide the filling between the pasta sheets and roll up from the shorter side. Arrange in a single layer, seam side down, in a lightly greased ovenproof dish. Spoon over the sauce and sprinkle with the breadcrumbs. Cook in a preheated moderately hot oven, 200°C (400°F), Gas Mark 6, for 15 to 20 minutes, until golden. Garnish with parsley and dill and serve immediately.
Serves 4

ROLLING AND COOKING THE PASTA DOUGH

Roll out the dough on a floured board. Flatten the dough with the rolling pin, giving it a quarter turn between each rolling, until it is 10–12 cm (4–5 inches) in diameter.

Hold down the near edge of the dough with one hand and place the rolling pin on the opposite edge. Curl the end of the dough around the rolling pin and push with the pin to stretch the dough. Continue rolling and stretching, giving the pin a quarter turn each time, until the dough has been stretched to a square measuring about 20–23 cm (8–9 inches) and the dough is paper thin.

Cut the pasta dough into 7.5 × 10 cm (3 × 4 inch) sheets and cook in boiling salted water, with the oil added, for 1 minute. Drain thoroughly and lay on clean dry tea-towels.

SOLE BONNE FEMME

75 g (3 oz) butter
150 g (5 oz) mushrooms, sliced
2 shallots or small onions, finely sliced
750 g ($1\frac{1}{2}$ lb) lemon sole, filleted and skinned
2 tablespoons chopped parsley
salt and pepper
120 ml (4 fl oz) dry white wine
2 tablespoons lemon juice
25 g (1 oz) flour
1 egg yolk
5 tablespoons double cream
chopped parsley to garnish

Melt 50 g (2 oz) of the butter over low heat and gently fry the mushrooms and shallots or onions for 5 minutes to soften.

Transfer to the bottom of an ovenproof dish and fold the sole fillets over and arrange on top of the mushrooms and shallots or onions. Sprinkle on the parsley and season with salt and pepper. Pour on the wine and lemon juice, cover and bake in a preheated moderate oven, 180°C (350°F), Gas Mark 4, for 20 minutes.

Lift out the fish, transfer to a warm serving dish and keep hot. Thicken the sauce by mixing together the remaining butter and an equal quantity of flour and then spooning into the sauce. Bring back to the boil.

Beat the egg yolk with cream. Remove the sauce from the heat and add the egg and cream *liaison*.

Pour the sauce over the sole and brown lightly under a hot grill. Garnish with parsley.
Serves 4

Sole Bonne Femme; Seafood Cannelloni

SALMON WITH FENNEL

4 × 175 g (6 oz) fresh salmon steaks
6 tablespoons dry white vermouth
4 tablespoons dry white wine
pinch of dried mixed herbs
50 g (2 oz) butter
2 teaspoons finely chopped shallots
1 fennel bulb, thinly sliced
3 small leeks, thinly sliced
6 tablespoons double cream
¼ teaspoon French mustard
salt and pepper
fennel tops to garnish

Place the salmon steaks in a flat-bottomed wok or large frying pan, pour over the vermouth and wine and add the herbs. Slowly bring to the boil, then cover and simmer very gently for 3 to 4 minutes.

Using a slotted spoon, transfer the salmon to a warmed plate, cover with foil and keep hot. Rub the liquor through a sieve and set aside.

Wash the wok or frying pan and return to the heat. Melt the butter, add the shallots, fennel and leeks and stir-fry for 4 to 5 minutes, without browning.

Add the fish liquor, increase the heat and boil rapidly until it has reduced by just under half. Stir in the cream and mustard and season with salt and pepper.

Spoon the sauce over the salmon and serve, garnished with fennel.

Serves 4

STUFFED PEPPERS

500 g (1 lb) cod fillets
300 ml (½ pint) boiling water
1 bouquet garni
½ onion
salt and pepper
1 tablespoon sunflower oil
1 onion, chopped
2 celery sticks, chopped
125 g (4 oz) brown rice
1 × 227 g (8 oz) can tomatoes
1 bay leaf
1 teaspoon chopped marjoram
150 ml (¼ pint) cold water
125 g (4 oz) peeled prawns
4 tablespoons frozen sweetcorn
4 green peppers
TO GARNISH:
marjoram sprigs
whole prawns in shell

Place the fish in a pan with the boiling water, bouquet garni, onion, and salt and pepper to taste. Cover and simmer for 10 to 15 minutes.

Remove with a slotted spoon. Remove any skin and bones and flake the fish into chunks. Set aside.

Heat the oil in a frying pan, add the chopped onion and celery and fry for 2 minutes. Add the rice and fry for a further 3 minutes.

Stir in the tomatoes, bay leaf, marjoram, and salt and pepper to taste. Pour in the cold water, bring to the boil, cover and simmer for 40 minutes, until the liquid is absorbed. Remove from the heat and stir in the fish, prawns and corn. Remove the top from each pepper and reserve. Core and deseed, and trim the base to level. Blanch in a pan of boiling water for 2 minutes, drain and plunge into cold water. Drain well.

Divide the fish mixture between the peppers. Arrange in an ovenproof dish and replace the tops. Cook in a preheated moderate oven, 180°C (350°F), Gas Mark 4, for 15 minutes. Garnish with marjoram and prawns.

Serves 4

PASTA DOUGH

250 g (8 oz) plain flour
good pinch of salt
2 large eggs (size 1)
1 teaspoon oil
3–4 tablespoons water

To make the pasta dough. Sift the flour and salt into a large bowl. Make a hollow in the centre and drop in the eggs and oil. Draw the flour into the centre, add 3 tablespoons of water and knead well; add another tablespoon of water if the mixture is too dry. Knead until smooth and very elastic; this is essential or the dough will not roll properly. Wrap in clingfilm and leave to rest for at least 15 minutes and not more than 2 hours.

Makes a 250 g (8 oz) quantity

CAPPELLETTI WITH SHRIMP SAUCE

1 small onion, halved
1 celery stick, roughly chopped
1 small carrot, roughly chopped
350 g (12 oz) sea bass or other white fish, skin removed
175 ml (6 fl oz) dry white wine
salt and pepper
2 egg yolks
20 g ($\frac{3}{4}$ oz) Parmesan cheese, grated
1 teaspoon chopped marjoram
pinch of grated nutmeg
250 g (8 oz) Pasta dough (see page 132)
25 g (1 oz) butter
SAUCE:
4 tablespoons olive oil
2 cloves garlic, crushed
8 tomatoes, skinned, seeded and chopped
4 tablespoons dry white wine
250 g (8 oz) peeled prawns, chopped
284 ml ($\frac{1}{2}$ pint) double cream
2 tablespoons chopped parsley
TO GARNISH:
parsley and marjoram sprigs

Put the onion, celery, carrot and fish in a frying pan, pour over the wine and season well with salt and pepper. Bring to the boil and simmer for 10 to 12 minutes, until the fish is tender. Drain and flake the fish into a bowl. Add the egg yolks, cheese, marjoram and nutmeg. Mix well and season with salt and pepper to taste.

Cut the pasta dough into 3.5 cm ($1\frac{1}{2}$ inch) squares. Place $\frac{1}{2}$ teaspoon of filling in the centre of each square and dampen the edges of the dough with water. With one corner facing you, fold into a triangle and seal the edges. Then take the left and right corners together to form a circle and pinch to seal. Place the cappelletti on a clean dry tea-towel and leave to dry for 1 hour.

Meanwhile, make the sauce. Put the oil and garlic in a pan and cook for 2 to 3 minutes, until the garlic is golden brown. Add the tomatoes and wine, bring to the boil and simmer, uncovered, for 15 to 20 minutes, until thickened. Stir in the prawns and season with salt and pepper to taste.

Add the cream and gradually bring to the boil, stirring constantly. Stir in the parsley and remove from the heat. Cook the cappelletti for 30 seconds to 1 minute, until *al dente.* Drain thoroughly and transfer to a warmed serving dish. Add the butter, toss well, then pour over the sauce. Garnish with parsley and marjoram and serve immediately.
Serves 4

LEFT: *Salmon with Fennel*
RIGHT: *Cappelletti with Shrimp Sauce*

PASTA WITH SQUID AND TOMATO

350 g (12 oz) prepared squid, cut into 5 mm (¼ inch) strips
150 ml (¼ pint) dry white wine
1 bouquet garni
6 tablespoons olive oil
1 large onion, chopped
750 g (1½ lb) tomatoes, skinned, seeded and chopped
2 tablespoons chopped basil
1 tablespoon chopped parsley
salt and pepper
1–2 cloves garlic, crushed
500 g (1 lb) fresh tagliatelle
25 g (1 oz) butter
parsley chopped to garnish

Place the squid in a pan with the wine and bouquet garni. Bring to the boil, cover and simmer for 2 minutes.

Using a slotted spoon, remove the squid and set aside. Discard the bouquet garni. Reserve the liquid.

Heat the oil in a pan, add the onion and cook for 5 minutes, without browning. Stir in the tomatoes, herbs, and salt and pepper to taste.

Strain the reserved liquid into the pan, bring to the boil, cover and simmer for 30 minutes. Add the garlic and boil, for about 5 minutes, until reduced and thickened.

Meanwhile, cook the tagliatelle until *al dente*. Drain thoroughly and turn into a warmed serving dish. Add the butter and toss well. Add the squid to the sauce, heat through, pour over the pasta and serve immediately, garnished with parsley.

Serves 4 to 6

SEA BASS WITH FENNEL

2 large fennel bulbs
6 tablespoons olive oil
8 tablespoons water
salt and pepper to taste
2 × 500 g (1 lb) sea bass, cleaned but with heads and tails left on
fresh fennel tops to garnish

Cut the fennel bulbs lengthways into 1 cm (½ inch) strips. Pour the oil into a wok or large frying pan, add the fennel and water and bring to the boil. Cover and simmer for 30 minutes, until the fennel is very tender, stirring occasionally. Uncover the pan, season with salt and pepper and boil until all the water has evaporated and the fennel is golden. Transfer to a plate and keep hot.

Season the fish with salt and pepper, add to the wok or large frying pan and baste with the hot oil. Cover and cook for 7 to 8 minutes. Turn the fish over, baste and then cook for 5 to 6 minutes.

Arrange the fish on a warmed dish, spoon the fennel and juices around and over the fish and serve garnished with fennel sprigs.

Serves 4

CASSEROLED SHELLFISH

750 g (1½ lb) potatoes
salt and pepper
40 g (1½ oz) butter
2 tablespoons plain flour
175 ml (6 fl oz) milk
175 ml (6 fl oz) dry white wine
250 g (8 oz) canned crabmeat, drained and flaked
350 g (12 oz) frozen shelled prawns, thawed
1 small onion, grated
3 tablespoons chopped parsley
75 g (3 oz) Cheddar cheese, grated

Parcook the potatoes in boiling salted water for 10 minutes. Drain and slice.

Melt 25 g (1 oz) of the butter in a saucepan. Add the flour and cook, stirring, for 1 minute. Gradually stir in the milk and wine and bring to the boil. Simmer, stirring, until thickened. Add salt and pepper to taste and fold in the crabmeat, prawns, onion, parsley and cheese.

Layer one third of the potato slices in a greased casserole. Cover with half the fish mixture. Repeat the layers, finishing with a layer of potato. Dot with the remaining butter.

Cook in a preheated moderate oven, 180°C (350°F), Gas Mark 4, for 45 minutes or until the potatoes are tender and the top is crisp.

Serves 4

Pasta with Squid and Tomato

HOT AND SOUR PRAWNS

125 g (4 oz) tamarind
300 ml (½ pint) hot water
2 teaspoons sugar (optional)
2 green chillies
25 g (1 oz) coriander, leaves and fine stalks
2 cloves garlic
1 onion, roughly chopped
2 tablespoons oil
1 teaspoon fennel seeds
1 teaspoon chilli powder
1 teaspoon salt
500 g (1 lb) large raw peeled prawns

Soak the tamarind in the water for 30 minutes, then squeeze the pulp and press through a strainer. Add the sugar if you don't like a sour curry.

Put the chillies, coriander, garlic and onion in an electric blender or food processor and work to a paste.

Heat the oil in a saucepan. Add the fennel seeds and fry for 30 seconds. Add the prepared spice paste, chilli powder and salt and fry gently for 5 minutes, stirring occasionally. Add the tamarind water, stir well, bring to the boil, then simmer for 5 minutes.

Add the prawns, cover and simmer for 10 minutes, or until cooked, stirring occasionally. Serve hot.

Serves 4

VINEGAR FISH

1 teaspoon turmeric
1 teaspoon salt
500 g (1 lb) haddock or cod steaks
3 tablespoons oil
2 onions, sliced
2–3 green chillies, thinly sliced
2 cloves garlic
2.5 cm (1 inch) piece ginger, cut in fine julienne strips
2 tablespoons white wine vinegar
4 tablespoons water
coriander leaves to garnish

Mix the turmeric and salt together on a plate. Coat the fish in the mixture, adding more turmeric and salt, if necessary.

Heat the oil in a frying pan, add the fish and fry gently on both sides for 1 to 2 minutes. Lift out the fish and set aside on a plate.

Add the onions, chillies, garlic and ginger and fry, stirring, until golden. Stir in the vinegar and water. Put in the fish, cover and cook gently for 5 to 6 minutes or until cooked through.

Transfer to a warmed serving dish and garnish with coriander to serve.

Serves 4

Hot and Sour Prawns; Vinegar Fish

SQUID WITH HERBS

1 kg (2 lb) prepared baby squid
4 tablespoons olive oil
3–4 cloves garlic, thickly sliced
salt and pepper
2 tablespoons chopped thyme
1 tablespoon chopped parsley
juice of ½ lemon
TO GARNISH:
lemon slices
tiny bunches of thyme

Cut the squid into slices and cut the tentacles in half if they are large. Heat the oil in a wok or deep frying pan, add the garlic and cook gently until browned, then discard. Season the squid with salt and pepper.

Increase the heat, add the squid to the wok and cook briskly for just under 1 minute. Sprinkle with the herbs and lemon juice. Serve immediately, garnished with lemon and thyme, and accompanied by crusty bread.

Serves 4

Squid with Herbs; Prawn and Squid Risotto

MEDITERRANEAN COD

4 tablespoons olive oil
2 onions, thinly sliced
1 clove garlic, finely chopped
1 green pepper, cored, seeded and sliced in rings
4 large tomatoes, skinned and sliced
2 teaspoons dried basil
salt and pepper
4 cod steaks
2 teaspoons lemon juice
12 black olives
6 tablespoons dry white wine

Heat the oil in a frying pan and fry the onions and garlic until softened. Add the green pepper rings and continue frying for 3 minutes. Remove from the heat and place half the mixture in a casserole.

Arrange half the tomato slices on top and sprinkle with half the basil and salt and pepper to taste. Place the cod steaks on top and sprinkle with the lemon juice. Add the rest of the tomato slices, basil, black olives and the onion and green pepper mixture. Pour in the wine.

Cover and cook in a preheated moderate oven, 180°C (350°F), Gas Mark 4, for about 45 minutes or until the fish is tender.

Serves 4

SPANISH HALIBUT IN SHERRY SAUCE

2 tablespoons olive oil
4 halibut steaks
salt and pepper
125 g (4 oz) flaked blanched almonds
6 tablespoons medium sherry
2 tablespoons coriander leaves

Lightly oil a large shallow ovenproof dish and place the fish steaks in it, preferably in a single layer. Season with salt and pepper, pour on the remaining oil and sprinkle with almonds. Add the sherry and bake in a preheated moderate oven, 180°C (350°F), Gas Mark 4, for 30 minutes, basting frequently.

About 10 minutes before the end of the cooking time, sprinkle with coriander leaves.

Serves 4

PRAWN AND SQUID RISOTTO

1 flat fish carcass, such as plaice
2 celery sticks, chopped
2 onions, sliced
2 carrots, sliced
1 bouquet garni
1.2 litres (2 pints) water
salt and pepper
75 g (3 oz) butter
2 tablespoons olive oil
3 cloves garlic, crushed
200 g (7 oz) Italian rice
good pinch each of ground cinnamon, nutmeg and cloves
250 g (8 oz) prepared squid, sliced
250 g (8 oz) peeled prawns
2 tablespoons chopped parsley
3 tablespoons grated Parmesan cheese

To make the fish stock, put the fish carcass, celery, onions, carrots, bouquet garni, water and seasonings in a pan, bring to the boil, then simmer for 30 minutes. Strain and set aside.

Heat 50 g (2 oz) of the butter in a wok or deep frying pan with the oil and fry the garlic for 1 minute. Add the rice and stir until golden.

Add 250 ml (8 fl oz) of the fish stock, cover and simmer for 10 minutes, or until all the liquid is absorbed. Add 600 ml (1 pint) fish stock, cover and simmer for 10 minutes.

Add the spices and squid and cook for 3 minutes. Stir in the prawns, parsley and cheese and cook for 2 minutes. Check the seasoning, dot with remaining butter and serve immediately.

Serves 4 to 6

Spanish Halibut in Sherry Sauce; Mediterranean Cod

PINK TROUT FILLETS IN ASPIC

4 small pink rainbow trout, filleted, or 8 fillets pink rainbow trout
900 ml (1½ pints) water
1 small onion, sliced
few parsley stalks
pared rind of ½ lemon
salt
½ level teaspoon black peppercorns
2 tablespoons lemon juice (optional)
150 ml (¼ pint) dry white wine
1 tablespoon powdered gelatine
1 egg white
2 egg shells, crushed
TO GARNISH:
fresh tarragon leaves
few black olives cut into small strips

If using whole fish, reserve the heads and bones and put them into a pan with the water, onion, parsley stalks, lemon rind, salt and peppercorns. Bring to the boil, then cover and simmer for 20 minutes. If you use fillets of fish make the stock as above but add 2 tablespoons of lemon juice instead of the fish heads and bones.

Strain the stock into a shallow ovenproof container, then add the fillets of trout, skin side downwards, in a single layer. Cover with foil and cook in a preheated moderate oven, 160°C (325°F), Gas Mark 3, for 5 minutes. Remove from the oven and leave undisturbed until cold.

Strain the liquor and boil until it has reduced to 350 ml (12 fl oz). Put the wine into a bowl or pan, sprinkle over the gelatine and heat gently to dissolve. Add to the fish stock with the egg white and crushed shells.

Bring to the boil, whisking all the time. Allow the foam to rise to the top of the pan, without further stirring, then remove and allow to subside. Bring to the boil again, and then pour through a scalded jelly bag. The aspic should come through clear. Cool, then chill until thickening up.

Meanwhile, carefully remove the skin from each trout fillet and place each fillet on an individual plate, or one large dish, if preferred.

Spoon or brush a thin layer of aspic over each fillet of fish. Garnish each with a pattern of tarragon leaves and strips of olive. Dip each into aspic before attaching to the fish. Add a little more aspic to give a second thin layer to the fish. Chill until set.
Serves 8

Salmon en Croûte; Brill with Avocado

SALMON EN CROÛTE

1 × 1.25 kg (2½ lb) salmon
salt and pepper
125 g (4 oz) butter, softened
1 × 10 cm (4 inches) piece ginger, grated
25 g (1 oz) sultanas
1 egg yolk, beaten
RICH SHORTCRUST PASTRY:
500 g (1 lb) plain flour
pinch of salt
300 g (10 oz) butter, cut into pieces
4 egg yolks
cold water to mix (about 4 tablespoons)

First prepare the pastry. Sift the flour into a large mixing bowl and add the salt. Rub the butter into the flour between finger and thumb until the mixture resembles fine breadcrumbs. Stir in the egg yolks and add a little water at a time, using a palette knife, to mix to a firm dough. Place on a floured surface and knead lightly. Allow to rest for at least 1 hour.

Ask at the fish counter for the salmon to be skinned and boned, giving you 2 thick fillets. Season these with salt and pepper. Cream the butter and mix in the ginger and sultanas. Sandwich half the flavoured butter between the 2 fillets of fish and spread the rest over the top.

Roll out the pastry and wrap the fish neatly in it. Brush with egg yolk and make a few vents in the top with the blade of a sharp knife to allow steam to escape. Bake in a preheated hot oven, 230°C (450°F), Gas Mark 8, for 30 to 35 minutes.

Serve with new potatoes, Hollandaise sauce (see page 148), baby carrots and broccoli florets.
Serves 8

BRILL WITH AVOCADO

1.25 kg (2½ lb) brill or lemon sole, filleted and skinned
200 ml (7 fl oz) dry vermouth
1 small onion, finely chopped
1 ripe avocado, finely sliced
1 tablespoon lemon juice
350 ml (14 fl oz) double cream
salt and pepper
1 avocado, chopped, to garnish

Fold both short sides of the fillets under each other to form a cushion, then place in a flameproof oven dish. Pour on the vermouth and scatter over the onion. Poach in a preheated moderate oven, 180°C (350°F), Gas Mark 4, for 15 minutes. Then transfer to a dish and keep warm.

Add the avocado, lemon juice and cream to the cooking juices, and simmer gently over low heat for 5 to 10 minutes until the sauce thickens to a coating consistency. Season with salt and pepper, and pour over the fish. Garnish with chopped avocado.
Serves 6

FISH WITH HORSERADISH CREAM

1 kg (2 lb) white fish cutlets such as cod or coley
300 ml ($\frac{1}{2}$ pint) Fish stock (see page 146)
1 tablespoon lemon juice
40 g ($1\frac{1}{2}$ oz) butter
40 g ($1\frac{1}{2}$ oz) plain flour
150 ml ($\frac{1}{4}$ pint) single cream
1 tablespoon horseradish sauce
salt and pepper
chopped chives to garnish

Arrange the fish in one layer in a baking dish. Pour over the stock and lemon juice and cook in a preheated moderately hot oven, 200°C (400°F), Gas Mark 6, for 15 to 20 minutes or until almost cooked.

Drain off the cooking liquid into a saucepan; keep the fish warm. Boil the liquid until it is reduced to 150 ml ($\frac{1}{4}$ pint).

Melt the butter in a clean saucepan. Add the flour and cook, stirring, for 2 minutes. Gradually stir in the reduced cooking liquid and bring to the boil, stirring.

Stir in the cream, horseradish sauce and salt and pepper to taste. Pour this sauce over the fish and return to the oven. Cook for a further 15 minutes. Serve garnished with chives.

Serves 4

PAELLA

Recipes for paella vary widely from region to region in Spain. Any kind of fish or shellfish can be used, depending on availability and the time of year.

2 tablespoons olive oil
1 large onion, finely chopped
1 clove garlic, crushed with $\frac{1}{2}$ teaspoon salt
125 g (4 oz) unsmoked bacon, derinded and diced
1 green or red pepper, cored, seeded and finely chopped
250 g (8 oz) long-grain rice
600 ml (1 pint) hot chicken stock
freshly ground black pepper
$\frac{1}{4}$ teaspoon powdered saffron
250 g (8 oz) white fish, filleted, skinned and diced
250 g (8 oz) cooked chicken meat, diced
125 g (4 oz) prawns, shelled
TO GARNISH:
1 unshelled King prawn, cooked
10 mussels, cooked
4 lemon wedges (optional)

Heat the oil in a deep flameproof casserole. Add the onion and garlic and fry gently for 5 minutes or until golden. Add the bacon and pepper and fry for a further 5 minutes.

Add the rice and cook, stirring for 1 to 2 minutes or until it is just beginning to change colour. Stir in the hot stock, add the black pepper and saffron and bring to the boil.

Add the white fish, cover and bake in a moderately hot oven, 190°C (375°F), Gas Mark 5, for 20 to 25 minutes or until the rice is tender and has absorbed most of the cooking liquid.

Add the chicken and prawns, cover and return to the oven for a further 10 minutes to heat through. Check the seasoning, then transfer to a hot serving platter and arrange the prawn and mussels on top. Garnish with lemon wedges if using.

Serves 4

LEFT: *Paella*
RIGHT: *Braised Cod in Black Bean Sauce*

BRAISED COD IN BLACK BEAN SAUCE

6 × 175–250 g (6–8 oz) cod steaks
2 tablespoons soy sauce
3 tablespoons dry sherry
2 tablespoons grapeseed oil
2 cloves garlic, crushed
1 × 5 cm (2 inch) piece fresh root ginger, chopped
3 tablespoons black bean sauce
3 spring onions, green tops only, finely shredded
$\frac{1}{4}$ teaspoon ground cinnamon
175 ml (6 fl oz) Fish stock (see page 146)
2 spring onions, to garnish

Rinse the cod steaks and pat dry. Put in a shallow dish and spoon over the soy sauce and sherry. Leave for 30 minutes at room temperature, turning them once.

Heat the oil in 1 or 2 frying pans. (The fish should lie in a single layer.) Add the garlic and ginger and stir-fry for about 30 seconds, then add the black bean sauce, spring onion tops and cinnamon and mix well.

Add the cod, with its marinade, to the pan and brown on both sides over a high heat for about 2 minutes.

Add the stock, turn the heat down slightly, bring the liquid to the boil, then simmer over the lowest possible heat for 15 to 20 minutes until the fish is just done. Add a little extra stock or water if it seems to be getting too dry. Remove the fish from the pan, place on a serving plate and spoon over the sauce.

Garnish with spring onion.

Serves 6

ORIENTAL-STYLE STEAMED BASS

1 kg (2 lb) bass, filleted and skinned
salt and pepper
1 tablespoon sesame oil
1 tablespoon soy sauce
1 × 7.5 cm (3 inches) piece ginger, grated
3 cloves garlic
3 spring onions, sliced lengthways
1 parsley sprig

SAUCE:
3 tablespoons sherry
3 tablespoons sunflower oil
$1\frac{1}{2}$ tablespoons sesame oil
$1\frac{1}{2}$ tablespoons soy sauce

TO GARNISH:
1 tablespoon chopped parsley
2 spring onions, sliced lengthways

Place the fish on a large piece of aluminium foil and season with salt and pepper. Sprinkle on the sesame oil and soy sauce, and add the ginger, garlic, spring onions and parsley. Wrap the fish securely so that no juice can leak out, and place in the top part of a steamer over boiling water. Cover and steam for 35 minutes.

Meanwhile, prepare the sauce. Place all the ingredients in a pan and heat over low heat until almost simmering.

When the fish is cooked, transfer the cooking juices into the sauce. Discard the garlic and spring onion and place the fish on a warmed serving dish.

Pour the sauce over the fish and garnish with chopped parsley and fresh spring onions. Serve with brown rice and mangetout.

Serves 4

TURBOT IN CHAMPAGNE

1 × 1 kg (2 lb) centre cut from a large turbot or 1 × 1.5 kg (3 lb) chicken turbot, cleaned
salt and pepper
400 ml (14 fl oz) dry champagne
300 ml (½ pint) Velouté sauce (see page 146)
50 g (2 oz) butter
TO GARNISH:
500 g (1 lb) creamed potato, piped into 4 halved, seeded tomatoes, and browned
chopped parsley

Rinse and dry the fish. Place it, white skin down, in a buttered baking tin, season with salt and pepper and pour over the champagne. Cover the tin with buttered greaseproof paper or foil and poach in a preheated moderately hot oven, 190°C (375°F), Gas Mark 5, for about 30 minutes. Carefully lift the fish into a hot serving dish, remove the black skin and keep the fish warm.

Place the tin over a brisk heat and reduce the liquor by half. Whisk in the velouté sauce, remove from the heat and flake in the butter.

Ladle enough of the sauce over the fish just to cover, then flash under a hot grill to glaze.

Garnish with the tomatoes and parsley and serve the remaining sauce separately.

Serves 4

TROUT EN GELÉE VERT

150 ml (¼ pint) dry white wine
300 ml (½ pint) water
1 tablespoon white wine vinegar
1 carrot, sliced
1 onion, stuck with cloves
1 bay leaf
2 marjoram sprigs
1 thyme sprig
2 parsley sprigs
12 peppercorns
½ teaspoon salt
2 strips of orange rind
4 × 175 g (6 oz) trout, cleaned and trimmed
3 tablespoons finely chopped parsley
TO GARNISH:
4 unpeeled orange slices
1 lettuce heart, quartered

Put all the ingredients, except the fish and chopped parsley, into a large pan. Cover and bring slowly to the boil, then simmer for 20 minutes. Allow to cool, then strain.

Lay the fish in a large sauté or frying pan and pour over the cold liquid. Bring carefully to the boil and immediately reduce the heat. Simmer the fish for 7 to 8 minutes.

Lift them onto a board, skin and remove the fillets. Arrange the fish on a serving dish.

Add the bones, heads, skin, etc. to the liquid in the pan and reduce by boiling rapidly until there is just enough liquid to cover the fish. Allow to cool, then chill for at least 1 hour.

Add the chopped parsley and pour over the trout. Garnish with twists of orange and lettuce. Serve mayonnaise (see page 152) separately.

Serves 4

MULLET AND BACON KEBABS

3 × 500 g (1 lb) grey mullet, cleaned, filleted and skinned
4 tablespoons olive oil
250 g (8 oz) streaky bacon rashers, rinded
2 tablespoons finely chopped sage leaves
1–2 cloves garlic, finely chopped
salt and pepper
sage leaves to garnish

Cut the mullet into large chunks, place in a bowl and pour on the olive oil.

Cut the bacon rashers into squares. Pound the sage with the garlic and a good pinch of salt in a mixing bowl.

Thread the fish, reserving the oil, and bacon on to 6 skewers, starting with bacon, using 2 squares every now and again if necessary between 2 cubes of mullet.

Rub a little of the sage and garlic mixture over the fish, then sprinkle with pepper. Dribble over the oil.

Cook under a preheated very hot grill for 7 to 12 minutes, turning every 2 minutes until the fish is done and the bacon crisp. Serve, garnished with sage leaves.

Serves 6

HERRING WITH BLACKBERRY SAUCE

6 medium herring, filleted
2 small onions, chopped
salt and pepper
15 cloves
3 bay leaves
1 thyme sprig
1 parsley sprig
juice of 2 lemons
450 ml (¾ pint) white wine vinegar
450 ml (¾ pint) water

BLACKBERRY SAUCE:
3 eating apples, peeled, cored and chopped
350 g (12 oz) blackberries
1½ tablespoon sugar
4 tablespoons red wine
1 teaspoon ground cinnamon
3 cloves

Place the fillets of herring in a large ovenproof dish and sprinkle with the onion, seasoning, herbs and lemon juice. Add the wine vinegar and water and bake in a preheated moderate oven, 180°C (350°F), Gas Mark 4, for about 25 minutes. Lift out the fish, transfer to a serving dish to keep warm, and prepare the sauce.

Place the apples, blackberries and sugar in a pan with a little water and bring to the boil. Add the wine and spices and 3 tablespoons of cooking liquid from the fish. Simmer gently for 5 minutes. Pour the sauce over the fish and serve with asparagus and broccoli florets.

Serves 6

COOKING FISH IN A MICROWAVE

This is now regarded by many people as one of the best ways of preparing fish, as it maintains its moisture, texture and appearance. A very rapid way of cooking, it also allows food to retain its maximum nutritional value and is a great boon to the modern health-conscious cook.

In terms of speed, the microwave can save up to 75% of the normal cooking time and up to 90% of fuel bills. Other benefits include safe and speedy thawing, as well as less washing up – since foods can be cooked and served in the same dish.

LEFT: *Turbot in Champagne*
RIGHT: *Mullet and Bacon Kebabs; Herring with Blackberry Sauce*

STOCKS, SAUCES, DRESSINGS AND BUTTERS

The basis for many dishes, especially soups, is a good home-made stock, and time taken to prepare a batch of fish stock will pay dividends in terms of flavour. Make up a large quantity and store it in small bags in the freezer for a few months so that it is to hand when needed. Stock cubes, although convenient, tend to be bland and salty.

The number of ways of preparing fish is equalled only by the number of different sauces that you can make to accompany it. Fish and shellfish have a delicate flavour, and this should not be overpowered by too rich, too heavy or too abundant a sauce.

Many of these sauces and butters are familiar accompaniments to fish, such as Hollandaise, Tartare and Parsley Sauce; others are less well known, such as Champagne Sauce, Tomato and Orange Sauce, and Pear Butter, and are worthy of closer acquaintance.

The choice of salad dressings is abundant. Choose from light clear Vinaigrette dressings of oil and vinegar spiked with lemon, garlic or herbs; from such variations on Mayonnaise as Tomato Mayonnaise and Rémoulade Sauce; or from exotic Chinese Soy Sauce Dressing.

It is important, however, to use dressings sparingly and never to drown a salad. Store dressings carefully in screw-topped jars or lidded containers in the refrigerator and ring the changes by varying your basic ingredients: oils can be olive, sunflower or walnut; vinegar can be wine, cider or tarragon; and flavourings can be garlic, herbs or lemon.

FISH STOCK

25 g (1 oz) butter
1 large onion, chopped
1 kg (2 lb) fish trimmings (bones, skin, heads, etc.)
1.2 litres (2 pints) water
1 bouquet garni
6 peppercorns
300 ml ($\frac{1}{2}$ pint) dry white wine
1 bay leaf
salt and pepper

Melt the butter in a pan, add the onion and cook until just beginning to colour. Remove from the heat and add the remaining ingredients, with salt and pepper to taste.

Return to the heat and bring to the boil. Simmer, uncovered, for 30 minutes, skimming the surface occasionally; do not boil or the flavour will be spoiled.

Cool slightly, then strain and check the seasoning. Store, covered, in the refrigerator for up to 2 days. Use as required.

Makes about 1.25 litres (2$\frac{1}{4}$ pints)

VELOUTÉ SAUCE

50 g (2 oz) butter
12 peppercorns
few parsley stalks
25 g (1 oz) mushrooms, sliced
50 g (2 oz) plain flour
600 ml (1 pint) Fish stock (see recipe left)
juice of $\frac{1}{2}$ lemon
salt and pepper
2 tablespoons double cream

Melt the butter in a pan, add the peppercorns, parsley stalks and mushrooms, and cook gently for 5 minutes. Stir in the flour and cook for another 2 minutes.

Remove from the heat and gradually stir in the stock. Return to the heat, then simmer gently for 10 minutes.

Strain the sauce, add the lemon juice, and salt and pepper to taste. Stir in the cream.

Serve with poached white or oily fish.

Makes 450 ml ($\frac{3}{4}$ pint)

Cold Curry Sauce; Herb Butter Sauce

COLD CURRY SAUCE

1 egg yolk
$\frac{1}{2}$ teaspoon turmeric
$\frac{1}{4}$ teaspoon ground cumin
$\frac{1}{4}$ teaspoon ground coriander
150 ml ($\frac{1}{4}$ pint) sunflower oil
1 tablespoon lemon juice
150 g (5.2 oz) natural yogurt
salt and pepper

Place the egg yolk and spices in a basin. Mix thoroughly, then slowly drip in the oil, stirring briskly with a wooden spoon the whole time or using a whisk, until the sauce is thick and smooth. Stir in the lemon juice and yogurt and season with salt and pepper to taste.

This light mayonnaise-type sauce is excellent served with salmon.

Makes 300 ml ($\frac{1}{2}$ pint)

HERB BUTTER SAUCE

142 ml (5 fl oz) double cream
75 g (3 oz) unsalted butter
juice of 1 lime or lemon
2–3 tarragon sprigs, chopped
2–3 chives, chopped
salt
paprika

Heat the cream almost to boiling point and pour into a bowl. Add the butter in pieces, stirring briskly with a wooden spoon or whisking in an electric blender, and gradually pour in the lime or lemon juice. Stir in the tarragon and chives and season with salt and paprika to taste.

Serve with plainly grilled white fish or shellfish.

Makes about 250 ml (8 fl oz)

COURT-BOUILLON

2 onions, sliced
3 carrots, sliced
2 celery sticks, sliced
2 lemon slices
25 g (1 oz) parsley
1 bay leaf
1 tablespoon salt
6 black peppercorns
15 g (½ oz) butter
600 ml (1 pint) dry white wine
1.2 litres (2 pints) water

Place all the ingredients in a pan, bring to the boil, then cover and simmer for 20 minutes. Allow to cool to blood heat before adding the fish.

Once the fish has been cooked, the stock can be strained and used as a basis for sauces for added flavour.

Makes 1.75 litres (3 pints)

WHITE SAUCE

25 g (1 oz) butter
25 g (1 oz) plain flour
300 ml (½ pint) milk
salt and pepper

Melt the butter in a pan, stir in the flour and cook, stirring, for 1 minute. Remove from the heat and gradually beat in the milk, and salt and pepper to taste. Return to the heat, bring to the boil and cook for 2 minutes, stirring constantly.

Serve with plaice, haddock or cod.

Makes 300 ml (½ pint)

VARIATIONS:

Parsley Sauce: Stir 50 g (2 oz) chopped parsley into the finished sauce.

Cheese Sauce: Stir 75 g (3 oz) grated Cheddar chese and 1 teaspoon dry mustard into the finished sauce.

Mushroom Sauce: Sauté 50 g (2 oz) sliced mushrooms in 15 g (½ oz) butter with 1 teaspoon lemon juice for 5 minutes. Stir into the finished sauce.

Onion Sauce: Sauté 1 finely chopped onion in the butter for 7 minutes, before stirring in the flour.

Prawn Sauce: Stir 75 g (3 oz) peeled prawns and ½ teaspoon chilli powder into the finished sauce.

White Sauce; Parsley Sauce; Cheese Sauce; Mushroom Sauce; Prawn Sauce

SPICY GOOSEBERRY SAUCE

500 g (1 lb) gooseberries
1 clove garlic, crushed
1 teaspoon salt
2 teaspoons dry mustard
150 ml (¼ pint) white wine vinegar
175 g (6 oz) demerara sugar
50 g (2 oz) sultanas
150 ml (¼ pint) water

Place all the ingredients in a saucepan, bring them to the boil, stirring, then simmer for 40 minutes, stirring occasionally. Cool slightly, then place in an electric blender or food processor and work until smooth; rub through a sieve to remove the pips.

Serve hot or cold. Delicious with baked herring and mackerel.

Makes 350 ml (12 fl oz)

HOLLANDAISE SAUCE

2 tablespoons white wine or tarragon vinegar
1 tablespoon water
2 egg yolks
175 g (6 oz) unsalted butter, cut into small pieces
salt and pepper

Place the wine or vinegar and water in a small pan, bring to the boil and reduce to about 1 tablespoon. Allow to cool slightly.

Put the egg yolks in a pudding basin and stir in the reduced liquid. Put over a bowl of hot water and heat gently, never allowing the water to go above simmering point and stirring continuously until the egg mixture begins to thicken.

Gradually whisk the butter into the sauce, adding a piece at a time. Season to taste with salt and pepper. The sauce should be barely thick enough to hold its shape.

Serve warm rather than hot with salmon and other fish dishes.

Makes 300 ml (½ pint)

MUSTARD SAUCE

1 egg yolk (size 1)
2 tablespoons Dijon mustard
½ teaspoon sugar
1 tablespoon vinegar
6 tablespoons oil
salt and pepper
1 tablespoon chopped dill

Beat the egg yolk with the mustard and sugar until smooth. Stir in the vinegar. Gradually beat in the oil and add salt and pepper to taste. Stir in the dill. Serve cold.

Makes 120 ml (4 fl oz)

FRESH HERB SAUCE

2 bunches of watercress
1 bunch of parsley
2 tarragon sprigs
4 chervil sprigs
2 tablespoons lemon juice
4 tablespoons oil
350 g (12 oz) fromage frais
salt and pepper

Finely chop the watercress and herbs and place in a bowl. Gradually stir in the lemon juice and oil, then the fromage frais. Season with salt and pepper to taste.

Serve warm, heated very gently, or cold, with scallops and trout fillets.

Makes 450 ml (¾ pint)

LEFT: *Mustard Sauce; Fresh Herb Sauce; Spicy Gooseberry Sauce*
RIGHT: *Tartare Sauce; Horseradish and Dill Sauce; Tomato Sauce*

HORSERADISH AND DILL SAUCE

2 tablespoons grated horseradish
2 tablespoons lemon juice
1 small dessert apple, peeled, cored and grated
142 ml (5 fl oz) soured cream
1 tablespoon chopped dill
salt and pepper

Stir the horseradish, lemon juice and apple into the soured cream.

Add the dill, and salt and pepper to taste.

Serve hot or cold. To serve hot, heat through very gently; do not allow to boil.

Makes 150 ml (¼ pint)

AÏOLI

3 cloves garlic, crushed
1 slice white bread, crusts removed, soaked in water and squeezed dry
1 egg yolk
150 ml (¼ pint) olive oil
1 tablespoon lemon juice
salt and pepper
1 tablespoon boiling water to finish

Put the garlic in a bowl with the bread and mash together until thoroughly combined. Beat in the egg yolk with a fork.

Add the oil, drop by drop at first, beating until the mixture begins to thicken. Then add the oil in a thin steady stream. When all the oil is incorporated, stir in the lemon juice and add salt and pepper to taste. Finish by stirring in the boiling water.

Makes 150 ml (¼ pint)

STOCKS AND SAUCES

A good fish stock is at the basis of many a successful fish dish. Once you have mastered your basic stock, you can then add herbs or other seasonings according to the character of the dish you are cooking. Stock can be made in advance and kept in the refrigerator or frozen in an ice-cube tray and stored in the freezer.

Many fish dishes are greatly enhanced by an accompanying sauce. This is unlikely to require a great deal of effort and what effort it does require will be more than fully repaid in terms of both flavour and appearance. Cold sauces can be prepared well ahead and stored in the refrigerator until required. A piece of buttered greaseproof paper will prevent the sauce from drying out or forming a skin or crust on top.

TOMATO SAUCE

1 tablespoon oil
50 g (2 oz) mushrooms, chopped
1 onion, chopped
1 clove garlic, crushed
1 × 397 g (14 oz) can chopped tomatoes
6 tablespoons red wine
1 teaspoon tomato purée
1 bay leaf
salt and pepper

Heat the oil in a pan, add the mushrooms and onion and sauté for 3 minutes, until softened.

Add the remaining ingredients, with salt and pepper to taste, bring to the boil, then simmer for 20 to 30 minutes, stirring occasionally, until the desired consistency. Remove the bay leaf.

Makes about 300 ml (½ pint)

TARTARE SAUCE

4 teaspoons capers
3 cocktail gherkins
few chives
150 ml (¼ pint) Mayonnaise (see page 152)
2 tablespoons yogurt

Chop the capers, gherkins and chives. Mix all the ingredients together. Serve cold.

Makes 200 ml (7 fl oz)

WHITE WINE SAUCE

300 ml (½ pint) dry white wine
1 shallot, chopped
1 bay leaf
25 g (1 oz) butter
25 g (1 oz) plain flour
150 ml (¼ pint) Fish stock (see page 146)
salt and pepper
100 ml (3½ fl oz) single cream

Reduce the wine by half by boiling briskly with the shallot and bay leaf.

Melt the butter in a small pan and add the flour. Cook for 2 to 3 minutes, then remove from the heat and gradually stir in the fish stock and strain in the wine. Return to the heat and slowly bring back to boiling point, stirring continuously. Simmer for 2 to 3 minutes.

Season to taste with salt and pepper and stir in the cream. Serve with sole and other fish dishes.

Makes 300 ml (½ pint)

BÉCHAMEL SAUCE

600 ml (1 pint) milk
2 slices onion
1 bay leaf
6 peppercorns
1 small carrot
1 parsley sprig
40 g (1½ oz) butter
40 g (1½ oz) plain flour
salt and white pepper

Put the milk in a saucepan and add the onion, bay leaf, peppercorns, carrot and parsley. Bring to the boil and remove from the heat at once. Cover and leave until cool to allow the flavours to infuse.

Melt the butter in a pan, stir in the flour and cook, stirring, for 2 minutes. Strain the milk and gradually add to the pan, stirring. Bring to the boil and cook for 2 minutes. Season to taste with salt and white pepper.

Makes a generous 600 ml (1 pint)

MORNAY SAUCE

50 g (2 oz) Gruyère cheese, grated
25 g (1 oz) Parmesan cheese, grated
300 ml (½ pint) hot Béchamel Sauce (see recipe above)
French mustard

Add the cheeses to the hot béchamel sauce and stir until melted; do not reheat. Stir in mustard to taste. Serve immediately.

Makes a generous 300 ml (½ pint)

TOMATO AND ORANGE SAUCE

2 tablespoons oil
1 bunch of spring onions, finely chopped
500 g (1 lb) tomatoes, skinned
juice of 1 orange
1 tablespoon lemon juice
2 tablespoons tomato purée
salt and pepper

Heat 1 tablespoon of the oil in a pan, add the spring onions and fry gently for 2 minutes. Drain well.

Purée the tomatoes in an electric blender or food processor and gradually add the onions, fruit juices, tomato purée and remaining oil while the machine is still running.

Transfer to a serving bowl and season with salt and pepper to taste. Chill well. Serve with fried fish.

Makes about 450 ml (¾ pint)

GOOSEBERRY SAUCE

500 g (1 lb) gooseberries
2 tablespoons water
25 g (1 oz) butter
1 tablespoon demerara sugar
1 egg
salt and white pepper

Place the gooseberries and water in a pan, bring to the boil, then simmer for 20 minutes. Stir in the butter and sugar.

Whisk the egg until pale and fluffy, using an electric blender or beater. Carefully pour the hot gooseberries onto the egg, while the motor is running, to form an emulsion. Season with salt and pepper. Serve hot or cold with mackerel or herring.

Makes 350 ml (12 fl oz)

LEFT: *White Wine Sauce; Béchamel Sauce; Mornay Sauce*
ABOVE: *Champagne Sauce; Tomato and Orange Sauce; Gooseberry Sauce*

CHAMPAGNE SAUCE

This delicious sauce is traditionally served with shellfish, such as lobster, scallops and crayfish.

25 g (1 oz) unsalted butter
3 shallots, finely chopped
300 ml (½ pint) champagne
284 ml (10 fl oz) single cream
salt and pepper
2 tablespoons finely chopped chervil (optional)
2 tablespoons finely chopped tarragon (optional)
50 g (2 oz) mushrooms, finely sliced (optional)

Melt the butter in a pan, stir in the shallots and fry for 5 minutes, until softened.

Pour in the champagne, bring to the boil, and boil gently for about 15 minutes, until reduced by half. Remove from the heat and cool slightly. Stir in the cream, add salt and pepper to taste, return to the heat and heat gently until thick enough to coat the back of a spoon. Stir in the herbs and mushrooms, if using. Serve hot, with shellfish or poached salmon.

Makes 350 ml (12 fl oz)

Niçoise Sauce; Mayonnaise

NIÇOISE SAUCE

1 tablespoon tomato purée
300 ml (½ pint) Mayonnaise (see next recipe)
1 green or red pepper, cored, seeded and chopped
1 teaspoon chopped fresh tarragon or pinch of dried tarragon
1 teaspoon chopped chives
1 clove garlic, crushed
salt and pepper

Put the tomato purée into a small bowl and stir in 1 tablespoon of the mayonnaise. Fold into the mayonnaise with the remaining ingredients. Add salt and pepper to taste.

Serve with fish and shellfish salads, grilled and fried white fish and deep-fried scampi.

Makes 300 ml (½ pint)

MAYONNAISE

2 egg yolks
2 teaspoons Dijon mustard
300 ml (½ pint) olive oil, or 150 ml (¼ pint) each olive and sunflower oil
1 tablespoon vinegar
salt and pepper

Beat the egg yolks and mustard in a bowl, and add the oil, drop by drop, beating constantly. As it starts to thicken, add the oil in a steady stream. Finally, stir in the vinegar, and salt and pepper to taste.

This can also be made in the food processor. Fit the plastic blade, place the egg yolks, mustard and 1 tablespoon oil in the processor bowl and process for 5 seconds. Dribble the remaining oil through the feed tube with the motor running. When all the oil has been amalgamated, turn off the motor. Add the vinegar, and salt and pepper to taste, and process again for 3 seconds.

Makes 300 ml (½ pint)

NOTE: All the ingredients must be at room temperature. If the mixture should curdle, switch off the machine and transfer the curdled mixture to a jug or basin. Put another egg yolk in the processor bowl and gradually pour in the curdled mixture, then the remaining oil.

VARIATIONS:

Mild Mayonnaise: Add 284 ml (½ pint) double cream, whipped, or 300 g (10.4 oz) natural yogurt to the prepared mayonnaise.

Garlic Mayonnaise: Add 2 cloves garlic to the processor bowl with the egg yolks, mustard and 1 tablespoon oil.

Tomato Mayonnaise: Add 2 tablespoons tomato purée to the prepared mayonnaise, stirring well to blend.

Lemon Mayonnaise: Replace vinegar with lemon juice.

Curry Mayonnaise: Add 1 teaspoon curry powder to the prepared mayonnaise.

Curried Apricot Mayonnaise: Replace the vinegar with lemon juice and add 1 teaspoon curry paste and 1 tablespoon good apricot jam to the prepared mayonnaise.

Spinach or Watercress Mayonnaise: Add 2 tablespoons spinach or watercress purée to the prepared mayonnaise.

Rémoulade Sauce: Fit the metal chopping blade. Place 1 tablespoon capers, 2 gherkins, 2 to 3 parsley sprigs and 1 anchovy fillet in the processor bowl and chop coarsely. Add to the prepared mayonnaise with 1 teaspoon Dijon mustard and stir well to blend.

Green Mayonnaise: Add 1 tablespoon each of chopped chives and parsley to the prepared mayonnaise.

VINAIGRETTE

175 ml (6 fl oz) olive oil
2 tablespoons cider vinegar
2 tablespoons lemon juice
1 teaspoon muscovado sugar
1 clove garlic, crushed
½ teaspoon mustard
2 tablespoons chopped mixed herbs (mint, parsley, chervil, chives and thyme)
salt and pepper

Put all the ingredients in a screw-topped jar, adding salt and pepper to taste. Shake well to blend before serving.
Makes 250 ml (8 fl oz)

HARISSA

75 g (3 oz) hot dried red chillies
6 cloves garlic, crushed
4 tablespoons coarse sea salt
6 tablespoons ground coriander
4 tablespoons ground cumin
9 tablespoons olive oil

Remove the stems and seeds from the hot chilli peppers and put in hot water to soften.

Meanwhile, pound the garlic in a mortar with half the salt until smooth. Remove and put to one side.

Add the drained red peppers to the mortar and pound to a smooth paste with the remaining salt. Add to the reserved garlic.

Combine the coriander and cumin in the mortar and add the garlic and hot red peppers. Add a little of the olive oil and pound until smooth. Continue this process, gradually adding all the olive oil, until the sauce is smooth and well blended.

Serve with Fish Couscous (see page 113), diluted with some of the cooking broth.
Makes 150 ml (¼ pint)

SOY SAUCE DRESSING

175 ml (6 fl oz) olive oil
4 tablespoons soy sauce
2 tablespoons lemon juice
1 clove garlic, crushed
1 cm (½ inch) piece root ginger, finely chopped
salt and pepper

Put all the ingredients in a screw-topped jar, adding salt and pepper to taste. Shake well to blend before serving.
Makes 300 ml (½ pint)

Harissa; Vinaigrette; Soy Sauce Dressing

French Dressing; Green Herb Dressing

FRENCH DRESSING

175 ml (6 fl oz) olive oil
4 tablespoons wine vinegar
1 teaspoon French mustard
1 clove garlic, crushed
1 teaspoon caster sugar
salt and pepper

Put all the ingredients in a screw-topped jar, adding salt and pepper to taste. Shake well to blend before serving.

Makes 250 ml (8 fl oz)

GREEN HERB DRESSING

25 g (1 oz) parsley
15 g (½ oz) mint
15 g (½ oz) chives
1 clove garlic, chopped
150 g (5 oz) natural yogurt
120 ml (4 fl oz) oil
juice of ½ lemon
salt and pepper

Remove the stalks from the parsley and mint. Place the leaves in an electric blender with the remaining ingredients, seasoning with ½ teaspoon salt and ¼ teaspoon pepper. Blend for 2 to 3 minutes. Refrigerate in an airtight container. Shake well to blend before serving.

Makes 300 ml (½ pint)

ROQUEFORT BUTTER

50 g (2 oz) butter
2 teaspoons chopped parsley
freshly ground black pepper
1 teaspoon wine vinegar
1 teaspoon made mustard
1 teaspoon anchovy essence
50 g (2 oz) Roquefort cheese

Cream all the ingredients together until well blended. Shape into a roll in greaseproof paper, then twist the ends tightly. Chill.

Serve slices as a garnish on grilled fish, or with hot French bread as an accompaniment.

WATERCRESS BUTTER

125 g (4 oz) butter
125 g (4 oz) watercress
few drops of anchovy essence
salt and pepper

Cream the butter well. Chop the watercress leaves and stems very finely, then work into the butter with the anchovy essence.

Add salt and pepper to taste. Press into a pot and chill.

This goes well with grilled or fried white or oily fish. Alternatively, spread on open or closed sandwiches made with creamed buckling, flaked cooked kipper or cold smoked trout.

HAZELNUT BUTTER

25 g (1 oz) ground hazelnuts
140 g (4½ oz) butter, softened

Place the hazelnuts in a dry saucepan and toast over moderate heat for about 5 minutes, shaking the pan continuously to stop them from burning. Allow to cool.

Beat the butter until creamy, then add the hazelnuts and incorporate well. Roll up into a fat sausage in greaseproof paper and keep in the refrigerator.

Serve with grilled fish. To use, simply cut off a generous slice and place on top of each portion of grilled fish.

ANCHOVY BUTTER

6 anchovy fillets
125 g (4 oz) unsalted butter, softened
1 teaspoon anchovy essence

Rinse the anchovies in cold water; dry thoroughly. Chop finely, then rub through a sieve. Beat into the butter with the anchovy essence.

Serve with grilled fish and herrings.

TARRAGON BUTTER

50 g (2 oz) tarragon
125 g (4 oz) unsalted butter, softened

Finely chop the tarragon and beat into the butter. Serve on top of a hot turbot steak.

PEAR BUTTER

1 × 213 g ($7\frac{1}{2}$ oz) can pear halves in natural juice, drained
125 g (4 oz) unsalted butter, softened
pepper

Place the pears in an electric blender or food processor and work until smooth. Beat in the butter and season with pepper to taste.

Serve on rye bread with smoked salmon.

MAÎTRE D'HÔTEL BUTTER

1 tablespoon finely chopped parsley
1 teaspoon grated lemon rind
1 tablespoon lemon juice
125 g (4 oz) unsalted butter, softened
salt and pepper

Beat all the ingredients together, seasoning with salt and pepper to taste.

Serve with grilled fish, such as skate wings.

VARIATION:
Chive Butter: Substitute 2 tablespoons chopped chives for the parsley.

Watercress Butter; Chive Butter; Hazelnut Butter; Tarragon Butter; Anchovy Butter; Roquefort Butter

INDEX

A

Aïoli 149
Almonds:
Prawns with 110
Trout with 106
Anchovies:
Anchoïde 35
Anchovy butter 155
Anchovy paste 42
Egg and anchovy pâté 39
Noodles with fish sauce 100
Salade Niçoise 55
Seafood ravioli 19
Tapenade 34
Apples:
Herring and apple pie 72
Herring and apple salad 63
Herrings with apple and horseradish 86
Whiting and apple soup 10
Apricot-stuffed trout 110
Artichokes:
Prawn and artichoke vol-au-vent 43
Asparagus and smoked salmon quiche 40
Aspic, Pink trout fillets in 138
Avocado:
Avocado-stuffed rainbow trout 122
Baked avocados with bacon and prawns 32
Brill with avocado 138
Chilled haddock and avocado soup 15
Prawn, avocado and pasta salad 62

B

Bacon:
Baked avocados with bacon and prawns 32
Grey mullet with sage and bacon 30
Mullet and bacon kebabs 142
Plaice and bacon rolls 103
Bananas:
Plaice with banana and nuts 77
Barbecued sardines 126
Bass *see* Sea bass
Bean sprouts:
Stir fried prawns with bean sprouts 46
Béchamel sauce 150
Beetroot sauce, Hake in 46
Bisque, Tuna and sweetcorn 10
Black bean sauce, Braised cod in 141
Black-eyed beans:
Tuna and bean salad 54
Blackberry sauce, Herring with 143
Bornholm kipper omelette 38
Bouillabaisse with rouille 114
Bourride 10
Bread:
Croûtons 12
Garlic bread 56
Breton tuna 101
Brill with avocado 138
Brioches, Smoked trout mousse in 48
Broccoli:
Mediterranean prawn and broccoli salad 58
Burgers, Wholewheat fish 102
Butter:
Anchovy 155
Hazelnut 154
Maître d'hôtel 155
Pear 155
Roquefort 154
Tarragon 155
Watercress 154
Buying fish 71

C

Canned fish 18
Cannelloni:
Mackerel and spinach 27
Seafood 130
Capers:
Tartare sauce 149
Cappelletti with shrimp sauce 133
Carp 108
Sweet and sour carp 109
Casseroles:
Casseroled shellfish 134
Fish 116
Fish cassoulet 80
Greek prawn 128
Herby cod 76
Layered fish 87
Monkfish and scallop 118
Tuna noodle 78
Caviar:
Eggs mimosa 18
Celeriac:
Smoked trout rémoulade 61
Ceviche 24
Ceviche of scallops with herbs 46
Champagne:
Champagne sauce 151
Russian salmon bubbly soup 10
Turbot in champagne 142
Cheese:
Cheddar cod 71
Cheese and shrimp soufflés 42
Cheese sauce 147
Cheesy cod 83
Cold monkfish with Roquefort yogurt 50
Mornay sauce 150
Prawn and cheese toasties 41
Roquefort butter 154
Chevron codling 92
Chicken and lobster salad 59
Chillies:
Chilli seafood pizza 66
Harissa 153
Choosing fish 33
Choux pastry:
Smoked mackerel gougère 45
Chowder, fish 15
Cider:
Baked halibut in 87
Baked mackerel in 90
Haddock in 114
Citrus halibut steak 118
Citrus skate with peppers 89
Cobbler, crab 100
Cockles in cream 28
Cod 33
Baked cod medley 70
Braised cod in black bean sauce 141
Cheddar cod 71
Cheesy cod 83
Chevron codling 92
Cod and pear pie with sultanas 80
Cod and potato pie 85
Cod in the hole 102
Cod Provencal 85
Cod salad with mint and cucumber 56
Cod with mushrooms 74
Fish pie 79
Herby cod casserole 76
Mediterranean cod 136
Mediterranean salad platter 54
Pitta parcels 69
Potato cod bake 76
Seafood pasta 42
Stuffed peppers 132
Cod roes:
Taramasalata 26
Coley 33
Coley stroganoff 49
Fish salad 62
Cornish eel 122
Coronation fish 63
Court-bouillon 147
Couscous, Fish 113
Crab 120
Casseroled shellfish 134
Crab and herb mousse 28
Crab and spaghetti bake 97
Crab cobbler 100
Cream of crab soup 8
Devilled crab 120
Dressed crab 121
Eggs fu-yung 82
Grilled crab 23
Spinach pancakes with 108
Cream of crab soup 8
Cream of whiting 14
Crêpes, Smoked haddock 84
Crispy giant prawns 117
Crispy tuna and egg 66
Croûtons 12
Cucumber:
Cod salad with mint and cucumber 56
Herbed smelts with cucumber sauce 88
Prawn-stuffed cucumbers 20
Curries:
Cold curry sauce 146
Coronation fish 63
Curried prawn ring 125
Curried scallops with salsify 88
Fish curry 70
Mussels in curry sauce 20

D

Danish salad 55
Dates:
Silvia's tuna and date salad 61
Devilled crab 120
Devilled sardines 28
Dill:
Horseradish and dill sauce 149
Scallops with dill 26
Dover sole *see* Sole
Dressed crab 121

Dressings:
French 154
Green herb 154
Soy sauce 153

E

Eels:
Cornish eel 122
see also Smoked eel
Eggs:
Bornholm kipper omelette 38
Crispy tuna and egg 66
Egg and anchovy pâté 39
Eggs Benedict with smoked mackerel pâté 43
Eggs fu-yung 82
Eggs mimosa 18
Haddock and egg mousse 18
Haddock and mushroom omelette 43
Normandy omelette 38
Omelette Arnold Bennett 38
Pilchard and egg supper 76
Smoked haddock soufflé omelette 44
Smoked salmon with spinach and egg 41
Tuna and oyster omelette 45

F

Fennel:
Salmon with fennel 132
Sea bass with fennel 134
Seafood and fennel salad 59
Filleting fish 94
Fish and potato pie 96
Fish cakes:
Grilled 78
Herb 77
Tuna 78
Fish casserole 116
Fish cassoulet 80
Fish chowder 15
Fish couscous 113
Fish curry 70
Fish faces 91
Fish fingers, smoked 82
Fish goulash 103
Fish in spicy yogurt 80
Fish lasagne 72
Fish pie 79
Fish salad 62
Fish soup with rouille 8
Fish stock 146
Fish with horseradish cream 140
Fisherman's pie 75
Flans, Individual fish 21
French dressing 154
Fritters, Herring roe 94
Fritto misto di mare 23

G

Garlic:
Garlic bread 56
Garnishes, soups 12
Sole fillets with soy and ginger 126
Gooseberries:
Gooseberry sauce 151
Spicy gooseberry sauce 148
Stuffed mackerel with gooseberry sauce 75
Gougère, Smoked mackerel 45
Goujons of sole 108
Goulash, fish 103
Grapefruit and prawn salad 60
Grapes:
Sole pie Véronique 110
Sole Véronique 126
Gratins:
Plaice au gratin 49
Smoked haddock au gratin 70
Gravad lax 35
Greek prawn casserole 128
Green herb dressing 154
Grey mullet:
Grey mullet with sage and bacon 30
Mullet and bacon kebabs 142

H

Haddock 33
Fish and potato pie 96
Fish curry 70
Fish faces 91
Fish in spicy yogurt 80
Fisherman's pie 75
Fresh haddock mousse 30
Haddock and leeks 27
Haddock and spinach layer 68
Haddock in cider 114
Haddock quenelles 92
Layered fish casserole 87
Moroccan fish 94
Sweet and sour fish 112
Vinegar fish 135
see also Smoked haddock
Hake in beetroot sauce 46
Halibut 33
Baked halibut in cider 87
Citrus halibut steak 118
Halibut Catalan 93
Halibut in orange herb sauce 92
Halibut julienne 88
Spanish halibut in sherry sauce 137
Ham and haddie 48
Haricot beans:
Fish cassoulet 80
Tuna and bean salad 54
Harissa 153
Hazelnut butter 154
Herb butter, Prawns in 123
Herb butter sauce 86, 146
Herb fish cakes 77
Herbed smelts with cucumber sauce 88
Herbs:
Fresh herb sauce 148
Green herb dressing 154
Herby cod casserole 76
Herring roes:
Herring roe fritters 94
Herring roe soufflés 44
Herring roes on toast 42
Herring roes Provençal 49
Herrings 33, 100
Herring and apple pie 72
Herring with blackberry sauce 143
Herrings in oatmeal 74
Herrings with apple and horseradish 86
Marinated herring and new potato salad 60
Sour cream herring salad 58
Supper herrings 90
see also Herring roes; Pickled herrings; Smoked herrings
Hollandiase sauce 148
Honey-glazed trout 127
Horseradish:
Fish with horseradish cream 140
Herrings with apple and horseradish 86
Horseradish and dill sauce 149
Mackerel in horseradish sauce 83
Hot and sour prawns 135
Huss in tomato sauce 46

I

Individual fish flans 21
Insalata di mare 21

J

John Dory fillets 124

K

Kebabs:
Mullet and bacon 142
Skewered monkfish 33
Kedgeree, Smoked mackerel 84
Kippers:
Bornholm kipper omelette 38
Hot kipper and mushroom salad 56
Kipper and tomato bake 72
Kipper toast 40
Kipper vol-au-vent 51
Kippers in lemon dressing 99
Kippers with marmalade 82

L

Lasagne, Fish 72
Layered fish casserole 87
Layered fish terrine 39
Leeks:
Haddock and leeks 27
Leeks and prawn salad 56
Lemon:
Kippers in lemon dressing 99
Mackerel with lemon stuffing 94
Trout and lemon mousse 32
Lobster 128
Lobster and chicken salad 59
Lobster thermidor 129
Lobster with tomato sauce 128

M

Macaroni:
Macaroni and tuna fish layer 91
Pasta Mediterranean 96
Seafood pasta 42
Mackerel 33, 100
Baked mackerel in cider 90
Grilled mackerel Japanese-style 101
Mackerel and peppercorn pâtés 25
Mackerel and spinach cannelloni 27
Mackerel in horseradish sauce 83

Mackerel in white wine 107
Mackerel parcels 68
Mackerel with lemon stuffing 94
Mackerel with mustard and oats 68
Marinated mackerel 67
Soused mackerel 85
Stuffed mackerel with gooseberry sauce 75
Maître d'hôtel butter 155
Marinated herring and new potato salad 60
Marinated mackerel 67
Marmalade, Kippers with 82
Mayonnaise 152
Coronation fish 63
Leek and prawn salad 56
Salmon mayonnaise with peaches 50
Skate with mayonnaise 30
Smoked trout rémoulade 61
Mediterranean cod 136
Mediterranean prawn and broccoli salad 58
Mediterranean ratatouille soup with shrimps 12
Mediterranean salad platter 54
Mélange of fish rillettes 30
Microwave ovens 143
Mint:
Cod salad with mint and cucumber 56
Monkfish:
Ceviche 24
Cold monkfish with Roquefort yogurt 50
Fish casserole 116
Fish soup with rouille 8
Monkfish and scallop casserole 118
Monkfish Portugaise 112
Salmon and monkfish mousselines 26
Skewered monkfish 33
Mornay sauce 150
Moroccan fish 94
Moules à la marinière 24
Mousses:
Crab and herb 28
Fresh haddock 30
Haddock and egg 18
Smoked eel 25
Smoked haddock 22
Smoked trout mousse in brioches 48
Smoked trout with Pernod 29
Trout and lemon 32
Mullet *see* Grey mullet; Red mullet
Mushrooms:
Cod with 74
Haddock and mushroom omelette 43
Hot kipper and mushroom salad 56
Mushroom sauce 147
Mushroom-stuffed plaice 77
Trout with mushrooms, cream and Pernod 51
Mussels 116
Fish casserole 116
Moules à la marinière 24
Mussel soup 13
Mussels in curry sauce 20
Normandy omelette 38
Pasta Mediterranean 96
Spaghetti with mussels 25, 116
Stuffed mussels 32
Mustard:
Mackerel with mustard and oats 68
Mustard sauce 148

N

Niçoise sauce 152
Noodles:
Noodles with fish sauce 100
Prawn and noodle soup 14
Seafood noodles 102
Tuna noodle casserole 78
Normandy omelette 38

O

Oats:
Herrings in oatmeal 74
Mackerel with mustard and oats 68
Oily fish 100
Olives:
Tapenade 34
Omelettes:
Bornholm kipper 38
Haddock and mushroom 43
Normandy 38
Omelette Arnold Bennett 38
Smoked haddock soufflé omelette 44
Tuna and oyster 45
Onion sauce 147
Orange:
Citrus halibut steak 118
Citrus skate with peppers 89
Halibut in orange herb sauce 92
Orange and pepper stuffed plaice 114
Tomato and orange sauce 150
Oriental-style steamed bass 141
Oysters:
Opening 125
Oyster soup with peanut butter 13
Oysters à la crème 124
Oysters with smoked salmon 124
Tuna and oyster omelette 45

P

Pacific tuna pie 96
Paella 140
Pancakes:
Smoked haddock crêpes 84
Smoked haddock pancakes 22
Spinach pancakes with crab 108
Parsley:
Maître d'hôtel butter 155
Parsley sauce 147
Pasta 97
Homemade 130, 132
Pasta Mediterranean 96
Pasta with squid and tomato 134
Prawn, avocado and pasta salad 62
Seafood pasta 42
Tuna pasta salad 62
Pâtés:
Egg and anchovy 39
Eggs Benedict with smoked mackerel pâté 43
Fresh salmon 35
Mackerel and peppercorn 25
Quick sardine 18
Peaches, Salmon mayonnaise with 50
Peanut butter:
Oyster soup with 13
Peanuts:
Plaice with banana and nuts 77
Pears:
Cod and pear pie with sultanas 80
Pear butter 155
Peppered mackerel soufflé 44
Peppers:
Bouillabaisse with rouille 114
Citrus skate with peppers 89
Fish goulash 103
Fish soup with rouille 8
Orange and pepper stuffed plaice 114
Stuffed peppers 132
Pernod:
Smoked trout mousse with Pernod 29
Trout with mushrooms, cream and Pernod 51
Pickled herrings 86
Danish salad 55
Herring and apple salad 63
Pies:
Cod and pear pie with sultanas 80
Cod and potato pie 85
Fish and potato pie 96
Fish pie 79
Fisherman's pie 75
Herring and apple pie 72
Pacific tuna pie 96
Salmon en croûte 138
Salmon koulibiac 123
Sole pie Véronique 110
Pilaff, Prawn 98
Pilchard and egg supper 76
Pink trout fillets in aspic 138
Pitta parcels 69
Pizza, Chilli seafood 66
Plaice 33
Individual fish flans 21
Layered fish terrine 39
Mushroom-stuffed plaice 77
Orange and pepper stuffed plaice 114
Plaice and bacon rolls 103
Plaice au gratin 49
Plaice with banana and nuts 77
Plaice with spinach 74
Portuguese sardine soup 9
Potatoes:
Cod and potato pie 85
Fish and potato pie 96
Fish faces 91
Fish pie 79
Grilled fish cakes 78
Herb fish cakes 77
Herring and apple pie 72
Marinated herring and new potato salad 60
Potato cod bake 76
Supper herrings 90

Tuna fish cakes 78
Tuna-stuffed potatoes 69
Wholewheat fish burgers 102
Prawns:
Baked avocados with bacon and prawns 32
Cappelletti with shrimp sauce 133
Casseroled shellfish 134
Crispy giant prawns 117
Curried prawn ring 125
Grapefruit and prawn salad 60
Greek prawn casserole 128
Hot and sour prawns 135
Individual fish flans 21
Leek and prawn salad 56
Mediterranean prawn and broccoli salad 58
Noodles with fish sauce 100
Pasta Mediterranean 96
Prawn and artichoke vol-au-vent 43
Prawn and cheese toasties 41
Prawn and noodle soup 14
Prawn and squid risotto 137
Prawn, avodaco and pasta salad 62
Prawn pilaff 98
Prawn sauce 147
Prawn-stuffed cucumbers 20
Prawns in herb butter 123
Prawns with almonds 110
Seafood cannelloni 130
Seafood noodles 102
Sesame prawn toasts 19
Spicy prawns 98
Stir fried prawns with bean sprouts 46
Turbot and prawn Creole 115
see also Shrimps
Profiteroles, Smoked salmon 29
Prunes, Trout with 93

Q

Quenelles, haddock 92
Quiche, Asparagus and smoked salmon 40
Quick sardine pâté 18

R

Rainbow trout *see* Trout
The Rajah's fish 98
Ratatouille soup with shrimps 12
Ravioli, seafood 19
Red mullet:
Red mullet in vine leaves 122
Red mullet Niçoise 109
Red snapper Creole 67
Rice:
Curried prawn ring 125
Paella 140
Prawn and squid risotto 137
Prawn pilaff 98
Seafood and fennel salad 59
Seafood risotto 24
Smoked mackerel kedgeree 84
Roes *see* Cod roes; Herring roes
Roquefort cheese:
Cold monkfish with Roquefort yogurt 50
Roquefort butter 154
Rouille:
Bouillabaisse with 114
Fish soup with 8
Roulade, Smoked haddock 99
Russian salmon bubbly soup 10

S

Sage:
Grey mullet with sage and bacon 30
Salads 53–63
Salade Niçoise 55
Salmon 100
Fish faces 91
Fresh salmon pâté 35
Gravad lax 35
Grilled fish cakes 78
Layered fish terrine 39
Russian salmon bubbly soup 10
Salmon and monkfish mousselines 26
Salmon en croûte 138
Salmon koulibiac 123
Salmon mayonnaise with peaches 50
Salmon steaks with herb butter sauce 86
Salmon with fennel 132
Scandinavian salmon soup 14
see also Smoked salmon
Salmon trout, Poached 118
Salsify, Curried scallops with 88
Sardines 100
Barbecued sardines 126
Devilled sardines 28
Portuguese sardine soup 9
Quick sardine pâté 18
Sardine and tomato salad 54
Sauces 149
Avocado 138
Béchamel 150
Beetroot 46
Blackberry 143
Champagne 151
Cheese 147
Cold curry 146
Cucumber 88
Curry 20
Fish (anchovy and prawn) 100
Fresh herb 148
Gooseberry 75, 151
Herb butter 86, 146
Hollandaise 148
Horseradish 83
Horseradish and dill 149
Mornay 150
Mushroom 147
Mustard 148
Niçoise 152
Onion 147
Orange herb 92
Parsley 147
Prawn 147
Sherry 137
Shrimp 133
Spicy gooseberry 148
Tartare 149
Tomato 46, 71, 128, 149
Tomato and orange 150
Velouté 146
White 147
White wine 150
Scallops:
Ceviche of scallops with herbs 46
Curried scallops with salsify 88
Monkfish and scallop casserole 118
Scallops Parisienne 127
Scallops with dill 26
Scallops with garlic and parsley 106
Seafood cannelloni 130
Scandinavian salmon soup 14
Sea bass:
Cappelletti with shrimp sauce 133
Oriental-style steamed bass 141
Sea bass baked in spinach 112
Sea bass Provençal 118
Sea bass with fennel 134
Whole fish with tomato sauce 71
Seafood and fennel salad 59
Seafood cannelloni 130
Seafood chaudrée 120
Seafood noodles 102
Seafood pasta 42
Seafood ravioli 19
Seafood risotto 24
Sesame prawn toasts 19
Sherry sauce, Spanish halibut in 137
Shrimps:
Cheese and shrimp soufflés 42
Mediterranean ratatouille soup with shrimps 12
see also Prawns
Silvia's tuna and date salad 61
Skate 89
Citrus skate with peppers 89
Skate with black butter 110
Skate with mayonnaise 30
Skewered monkfish 33
Skinning fish 94
Smelts:
Herbed smelts with cucumber sauce 88
Smoked eel mousse 25
Smoked fish 29
Smoked fish fingers 82
Smoked haddock:
Chilled haddock and avocado soup 15
Haddock and leeks 27
Fish lasagne 72
Fisherman's pie 75
Haddock and egg mousse 18
Haddock and mushroom omelette 43
Ham and haddie 48
Omelette Arnold Bennett 38
Seafood pasta 42
Smoked haddock au gratin 70
Smoked haddock crêpes 84
Smoked haddock mousse 22
Smoked haddock pancakes 22
Smoked haddock roulade 99
Smoked haddock soufflé omelette 44
Smoked haddock soup 8
Smoked haddock with corn 79
Smoked haddock with vegetables 115
Wholewheat fish burgers 102
Smoked mackerel:
Eggs Benedict with smoked mackerel pâté 43
Marinated mackerel 67
Peppered mackerel soufflé 44

Smoked mackerel gougère 45
Smoked mackerel kedgeree 84
Smoked mackerel pots 34
Smoked salmon:
Asparagus and smoked salmon quiche 40
Oysters with smoked salmon 124
Smoked salmon profiteroles 29
Smoked salmon with spinach and egg 41
Smoked trout:
Smoked trout mousse in brioches 48
Smoked trout mousse with Pernod 29
Smoked trout rémoulade 61
Trout and lemon mousse 32
Sole 33
Goujons of sole 108
Seafood noodles 102
Sole bonne femme 130
Sole fillets with soy and ginger 126
Sole pie Véronique 110
Sole Véronique 126
Wok-style seafood 117
Soufflés 45
Cheese and shrimp 42
Herring roe 44
Peppered mackerel 44
Soups 7–15
Sour cream herring salad 58
Soused mackerel 85
Soy sauce:
Sole fillets with soy and ginger 126
Soy sauce dressing 153
Spaghetti:
Crab and spaghetti bake 97
Spaghetti with mussels 25, 116
Spanish fish soup 9
Spanish halibut in sherry sauce 137
Spicy gooseberry sauce 148
Spicy prawns 98
Spinach:
Haddock and spinach layer 68
Layered fish terrine 39
Mackerel and spinach cannelloni 27
Plaice with spinach 74
Sea bass baked in spinach 112
Smoked salmon with spinach and egg 41
Spinach pancakes with crab 108
Squid 116
Fish casserole 116
Fritto misto di mare 23
Insalata di mare 21
Pasta with squid and tomato 134
Prawn and squid risotto 137
Squid with herbs 136
Starters 17–35
Stir fried prawns with bean sprouts 46
Stocks 149
Fish 146
Stuffed mussels 32
Supper herrings 90
Sweet and sour carp 109
Sweet and sour fish 112
Swordfish Provençal 107

T

Tapenade 34
Taramasalata 26
Tarragon butter 155
Tartare sauce 149
Terrines:
Layered fish 39
Three-fish 20
Tomato:
Huss in tomato sauce 46
Kipper and tomato bake 72
Lobster with tomato sauce 128
Pasta with squid and tomato 134
Sardine and tomato salad 54
Skinning and deseeding 99
Tomato and orange sauce 150
Tomato soup 149
Whole fish with tomato sauce 71
Trout 100
Apricot-stuffed trout 110
Avocado-stuffed rainbow trout 122
Baked trout 107
Honey-glazed trout 127
Pink trout fillets in aspic 138
Trout en gelée vert 142
Trout with almonds 106
Trout with mushrooms, cream and Pernod 51
Trout with prunes 93
see also Salmon trout; Smoked trout
Tuna 100
Breton tuna 101
Chilli seafood pizza 66
Crispy tuna and egg 66
Macaroni and tuna fish layer 91
Mediterranean salad platter 54
Pacific tuna pie 96
Salade Niçoise 55
Seafood ravioli 19
Silvia's tuna and date salad 61
Tapenade 34
Tuna and bean salad 54
Tuna and oyster omelette 45
Tuna and sweetcorn bisque 10
Tuna fish cakes 78
Tuna noodle casserole 78
Tuna pasta salad 62
Tuna-stuffed potatoes 69
Turbot 33
Turbot and prawn Creole 115
Turbot in champagne 142

V

Velouté sauce 146
Vinaigrette 153
Vine leaves, Red mullet in 122
Vinegar fish 135
Vol-au-vents:
Kipper 51
Prawn and artichoke 43

W

Watercress:
Fresh herb sauce 148
Watercress butter 154
White fish 33
White sauce 147
Whitebait, fried 27
Whiting 33
Cream of whiting 14
Fish soup with rouille 8
Whiting and apple soup 10
Whole fish with tomato sauce 71
Wholewheat fish burgers 102
Wine:
Mackerel in white wine 107
White wine sauce 150
Wok-style seafood 117

Y

Yogurt:
Cold monkfish with Roquefort yogurt 50
Fish in spicy yogurt 80

ACKNOWLEDGEMENTS

Editor: Nicola Hill

Art Direction: Alyson Kyles

Production Controller: Audrey Johnston

Designer: Sue Storey

The publishers would like to thank the following individuals who were involved in the preparation of material for this book:

Special Photography: Clive Streeter except pages 8, 13, 14, 18–25, 34, 38–40, 42, 44, 45, 51, 58, 60, 62, 66, 68, 70, 71, 74–76, 78, 79, 82–85, 87–89, 92, 96, 97–100, 102, 106, 114, 115, 117, 126, 127, 133, 135, 136, 142, 146 and 154

Photographic Stylists: Maria Kelly and Andrea Lambton

Food for photography prepared by Nichola Palmer pages 6, 9, 11, 12, 15, 16, 29, 31, 33, 36, 41, 47, 49, 50, 52, 57, 59, 61, 63, 67, 69, 73, 81, 93 and Allyson Birch pages 54, 55, 64, 86, 95, 101, 103, 105, 109, 111, 113, 119, 123, 131, 134, 137, 139, 140, 141, 143, 144, 150, 153 and 155